SWORD FIGHTING

Karyn Henley

Child Sensitive Communication, LLC

Sword Fighting (3rd Edition)

Exclusively administered by Child Sensitive Communication, LLC.

Child Sensitive Communication, LLC
PO Box 40269
Nashville, TN 37204-0269
1-615-383-8845, **www.karynhenley.com**

Edited by Betty Free
Layout by Kristi J. West

ISBN 0-9743197-3-2

Printed in the U.S.A.

Contents

Memorizing God's Word by Sword Fighting

Did you know that learning Scripture verses can be fun? It can be when you do it by playing a game. Did you know that learning Scripture verses can be useful, too? It can be when the verses you learn help you fight against temptations that you face every day.

What Is Sword Fighting?

Sword Fighting is a game in which you learn Scriptures that will help you fight temptations. When Jesus was tempted, he fought back by quoting Scriptures. With a little practice, you can do that too. The Sword Fighting game will help you practice fighting temptation. Sword Fighting can be played alone, with family, with a few friends, or even with a class full of friends!

How Do We Play Sword Fighting?

You will need a stack of 52 index cards, any color. That will give you one card for each week of the year. Every week you will read about a temptation to fight against. Write the temptation on a card. For example, for Week 29 you can write: "You are tempted to be afraid." Then you will learn an easy Scripture that will help you fight that week's temptation. For the temptation about fear, you will learn the Scripture, "In God I trust; I will not be afraid" (Psalm 56:11).

To play the game alone, stack the temptation cards face down or place them in a bag or bowl. Each week you will add a card to your collection. Mix the cards up, pick one card, and read the temptation. Then you can practice fighting that temptation by saying the Scripture you have learned or are learning for that temptation. This Scripture is your "sword" because the "sword of the Spirit ... is the word of God" (Ephesians 6:17). For example, you might draw the card that says, "You are tempted to be afraid." Then you will say, "I will not be afraid, because it is written, 'In God I trust; I will not be afraid,' Psalm 56:11." Then you are ready to draw another card.

To play the game with other people, stack the temptation cards face down or place them in a bag or bowl. Each week you will add a card to the collection. Mix the cards up. Then you pick one card and read the temptation aloud to someone else. This is the other person's challenge. That individual then says the Scripture he learned in order to fight that temptation. For example, you might read the card that says, "You are tempted to be afraid." The other person says, "I will not be afraid, because it is written, 'In God I trust, I will not be afraid.' Psalm 56:11." Then it is that person's turn to pick a temptation card and challenge you or someone else who is playing with you.

Another way to play the game is to play it as a card game. After you've learned eight Scriptures you can play the game with two people. If you know twelve Scriptures, you can play with three people. When you know sixteen Scriptures or more, you can play with four people. Mix the cards up and deal them. Give four cards to each person. Place the rest of the cards face down in the middle of the table. You can start by choosing a card from the hand of the person on your right. But don't look at the card. Instead, the person who was holding the card reads the temptation to you. Then you must say the Scripture that you learned to fight that temptation. If you can say the Scripture, you get the card and place it on the table in front of you. If you can't say the Scripture, the person on your left gets a chance to say it. If that person says it, he gets the card.

If no one remembers the Scripture, the one who was holding the card has a chance to say it, collect the card, and place it on the table in front of him. If he can't say the Scripture, he keeps the card in his hand.

Whenever a card goes from his hand, he chooses a new card from the center deck.

The play goes clockwise around the circle, so now it's the second person's turn to choose a card from the person at her right--this will be the person who just chose a card. The person who had the card reads it, and the second person says the Scripture. Play continues around the circle, with the person who says the Scripture collecting the card. When all the cards are out of the players' hands, the game is over. And, of course, the person who has collected the most cards wins!

WHEN CAN YOU USE SWORD FIGHTING?
You will enjoy using this book:

      ✓   For family devotionals
      ✓   For your private devotions
      ✓   For home-school Bible study
      ✓   For weekly Bible class

Unlocking the Doors to Long-term Memory

A NOTE TO PARENTS

We want our children to know and treasure God's Word. To achieve that, we ask them to memorize Scripture. But how can we help them with this task? How can we help them place Scripture into long-term memory instead of short-term memory? *Sword Fighting* helps children unlock the doors to long-term memory, if we use some important keys.

Key #1: Making it Meaningful

Children need to understand what they are memorizing and why they are memorizing it. *Sword Fighting* shows children how they can use the Scriptures they memorize to fight temptations that they face every day.

Sword Fighting is based on three key Scriptures:

Psalm 119:11
"I have hidden your word in my heart that I might
 not sin against you."
(God's word is memorized for the purpose of avoiding sin.)

Matthew 4:1-11
"It is written. . ."
(Jesus fought temptation by quoting Scripture.)

Ephesians 6:17
"Take. . .the sword of the Spirit which is the word of God."
(God's Word is meant to be used for the purpose of
  fighting the enemy.)

Key #2: Repeating It and Using It
Memorization is made easier by repetition. *Sword Fighting* is structured so that every Scripture learned is repeated often. Children have daily opportunity to sword-fight with the Scriptures they learn. In addition, each Scripture can be put into use as the children need it for fighting daily temptations.

Key #3: Making It Fun
It's always easier to learn when the learning methods are fun as well as challenging. *Sword Fighting* is played as a game in which children draw temptation cards and challenge each other to sword-fight with the Scriptures they have learned. There are also a variety of suggested activities each week which will help to support the theme of the week or the reading of the day.

Key #4: Make It Sensory
Some children learn best by touching and doing, some learn best by seeing, and some learn best by hearing. *Sword Fighting* incorporates all these approaches. Touching and doing: The children make paper swords on which they write the Scriptures. Seeing: They hang these swords up where they can see the Scriptures as well as the sword. Hearing: Finally they speak and hear the Scripture as they sword-fight against the temptations on the temptation cards.

Key #5: Focusing On It
Sword Fighting makes it easy for the child to focus on the Scripture for each week. There is a Bible reading for each day. Some of the Bible readings are about Bible characters are tempted to abandon the character trait or goal that is the focus for the week. Other Bible readings are teachings from Jesus or from letters, psalms, or proverbs that deal with the theme of the week. After each day's reading there are thought questions that focus the children's

attention on the theme, on the verse they are learning, and on how the theme applies to their life.

Excerpts of the recommended readings are taken from the **Day By Day Kid's Bible**. This children's Bible is paraphrased at a second-grade reading level and told in the order in which the events happened. Although an excerpt is provided, a page reference is given so that you can read the entire story if you wish. The **Day By Day Kid's Bible** was chosen because it is easy to read and understand, and it contains all the books of the Bible. However, the memory verses come from traditional translations. If you prefer different versions for the readings or for the memory work, feel free to use the version of your choice.

Using *Sword Fighting* in the Classroom

A NOTE TO TEACHERS

Sword Fighting is easily adapted for use in the classroom. It provides 52 weeks of scripture learning. Simply follow the lesson plan below for each week.

Theme of the Week: *(Title of the Lesson)*

Each student will need a three-ring binder and a Bible for the year. Encourage the students to bring their binders and Bibles to every class.

Scripture to Memorize: *(found at the top of each lesson in the book)*

Introductory Activity:
As soon as the children begin arriving, give them a piece of paper with the three holes punched down one side. Ask them to design a sword on the paper. You may bring pictures of different kinds of swords, if you wish, so they can see different ways to design the sword blades and hilts. Ask them to write the memory scripture on this page. This page then goes into their binder. Add a new one each week.

Large Group Discussion:
• Pray
• Ask someone to read the scripture passage listed under "Day 1" in the book.
• Ask discussion questions of your choice from "Day 1," "Day 2," and/or "Day 3."
• Ask the students to repeat the memory verse after you.

Review:
Gather as a large group again, and play the *Sword Fighting* game as described in the second paragraph on page x in the book. Encourage the children to say the Scripture several times each day this week.
• Say the verse together several times.
• Ask for individual students to volunteer to say it by themselves.

Groups:
Divide into two or three groups (depending on the number of students).
• Group 1: Do the reading, discussion, activity, and **practice** listed under "Day 4."

• Group 2: Do the reading, discussion, activity, and **practice** listed under "Day 5."

• Group 3: Do the reading, discussion, activity, and **practice** listed under "Day 6."

Students can change groups twice if your time allows, so they can do each activity. If you need an extra activity or group, use the suggestions in "Day 7."

Fighting Temptation

Your sword of the Spirit for this week is:

I have hidden your word in my heart that I might not sin against you. PSALM 119:11

With the above sword you can fight back when you face this temptation:

You are tempted to stop learning Scriptures.

DAY 1

READ

Matthew 4:1-11 ("Trying to Make Jesus Do Wrong," page 513 in the *Day By Day Kid's Bible*)

"Get away from me, Satan!" said Jesus. "God's Word says to worship only the Lord your God. Serve only him."

THINK AND TALK

To *tempt* means "to draw people toward sin by causing them to hope or believe that they will get something good or pleasant out of it." Look at each temptation Satan tried with Jesus. Did Satan lie, or did he say something true? If Satan said what was true, why would it have been wrong for Jesus to do it?

Do you think this was the only time when Jesus was tempted, or do you think there were other times? Do you think Jesus may have been tempted to refuse to die on the cross for us? If so, why?

How did Jesus fight temptation? Why do you think he quoted God's Word, the Scriptures? If Jesus came to show us how to

1

live, what does this reading tell you about how we should fight temptation?

PRACTICE
Read the verse on page 1. Then try to say it without looking. Try to repeat it several times without looking. Cut a sword shape from paper or cardboard and write the verse on it. You'll want to hang it up in your house where it will remind you of why you are hiding God's Word in your heart.

DAY 2

READ
Genesis 4:1-7 ("The First Children," page 6 in the *Day By Day Kid's Bible*)
[God told Cain,] "Sin wants to catch you. But you must not let it get to you."

THINK AND TALK
Is temptation sin? If not, what is the difference between temptation and sin?

PRACTICE
Challenge a friend or family member (or yourself!) to a "sword fight." One person says, "What will you do if you are tempted to stop learning Scriptures?" The other person answers, "I will not stop learning Scriptures, because it is written, 'I have hidden your word in my heart that I might not sin against you.'"

DAY 3

READ
1 Corinthians 10:1-13 ("A Way to Say No," page 683 in the *Day By Day Kid's Bible*)
God won't let a sin come to your mind unless he knows you can say no to it. Let's say a sin comes to your mind. Then God gives you a way to say no. That way, you can win over sin.

THINK AND TALK

What temptations are hard for you to resist? If something is easy to resist, it's not much of a temptation. Do you think it was easy for Jesus to resist temptation? Why or why not?

PRACTICE

Challenge each other to sword-fight with your sword for this week. Write on an index card: "You are tempted to stop learning Scriptures." Take turns reading this temptation to each other. This is "challenging" the other person. The person who is "challenged" uses his sword for this week, saying the verse.

DAY 4 ✓

READ

James 1:1-15 ("Like a Sea Wave," page 762 in the *Day By Day Kid's Bible*)

What if a sin comes to your mind? Then we shouldn't say, "God is trying to make me sin." Nothing sinful can make God want to sin... People sin when sin looks good to them. Sin leads them on. First they think about it. Then they sin. Sin grows. It ends up in death.

THINK AND TALK

Where do temptations come from? How can you avoid being tempted as you make choices about where to go, what to watch and hear, and which friends to choose? Be specific.

PRACTICE

Challenge someone to a sword-fight with your sword for this week. Ask each other what you would do if you were tempted to stop learning Scriptures.

TRY THIS

Line up dominoes, standing them close together, one behind the other. Tap the first one to see all of them tumble. Sin affects all of our life, just like the first domino affects the others. What are some of the effects of sin?

DAY 5

READ

Hebrews 2:14-18 ("Jesus' Brothers and Sisters," page 780 in the *Day By Day Kid's Bible*)

Jesus had to become human like us. That's so he could understand us. Now he can tell God what it's like to be human. It hurt Jesus to have sins come to his mind. He had to say no to sin. Sins come to our minds too. But Jesus knows what that's like, so he can help us.

THINK AND TALK

To *tempt* also means "to test." In what ways did temptations test Jesus? What did Jesus show about himself when he resisted temptation? In what ways do temptations test us? What kinds of "tests" have you been going through lately?

PRACTICE

Challenge someone to a sword-fight with your sword for this week.

TRY THIS

Bake biscuits. Mix one cup flour, one-half teaspoon salt, one-fourth teaspoon baking soda, one and one-half teaspoon baking powder, and two tablespoons shortening. Slowly stir in one-half cup buttermilk. Drop tablespoonsful of this batter onto a greased pan. Bake for 10 to 12 minutes at 450 degrees. Think about how Jesus was tempted to turn stones into bread.

DAY 6

READ

1 Timothy 6:6-10 ("Loving Money," page 753 in the *Day By Day Kid's Bible*)

People who want to get rich have problems. It's like getting into a trap. They get pulled into doing wrong things... You are a man of God. Run away from all these sinful things. Go for what's right. Go for what's godly.

THINK AND TALK

Tell of a time when you or someone you know was tempted. What happened? How is temptation like a trap? What does it mean to "run away from" these things?

PRACTICE

Challenge someone to a sword-fight with your sword for this week.

TRY THIS

Turn a box upside down and cut two or three arched doors in one side. Make one door just large enough for a Ping-Pong ball (or other small ball you have chosen) to roll through. Make the next door a bit larger, and make the third door the largest. Now set the box on the floor some distance away from you and try to roll the ball through the smallest door. Give yourself more points for rolling the ball through the small door and fewer points for rolling it through the larger door. When the ball is in the box, it's trapped. What makes temptation a trap for us?

DAY 7

READ

Ephesians 6:10-18 ("Putting on God's Armor," page 744 in the *Day By Day Kid's Bible*)

We don't fight people. We fight rulers, kings, and powers of this dark world. We fight bad, sinful spirits in places around the heavens. So put on God's whole armor... Hold faith like a shield in front of you... Your sword will be the Spirit's sword, God's Word.

THINK AND TALK

How can we use the word of God like a sword? How did Jesus use God's Word like a sword? How can faith be like a shield?

PRACTICE

Challenge someone to a sword-fight with your sword for this week.

TRY THIS

Cut a shield shape out of poster board or cardboard. Cover it with aluminum foil and decorate it by coloring, painting, or gluing on construction-paper symbols related to our Christian faith. A cross stands for Jesus. A sun means light. A lion means courage. A crown means authority. A dove represents the Holy Spirit. An olive leaf means peace. What symbol would you choose to represent yourself? If God's Word is our sword of the Spirit, what is our shield? (See Ephesians 6:16.)

Having
Self-Control

Your sword of the Spirit for the week is:

Be self-controlled. 1 PETER 1:3

With the above sword you can fight back when you face this temptation:

You are tempted to lose your self-control.

DAY 1

READ

1 Samuel 24 ("A Chance to Kill the King," page 150 in the *Day By Day Kid's Bible*)

Saul started chasing David again...Saul had to go to the bathroom. So he went inside a cave. It was the same cave where David and his men were hiding. They were at the back of the cave. David's men said, "God is giving your enemy to you today!" ...[David said,] "He is the king God chose." So David wouldn't let his men hurt Saul.

THINK AND TALK

Self-control is making yourself do what you know you should do, and keeping yourself from doing what you know you shouldn't do. King Saul's plan was to kill David. What do you think David might have been thinking when he saw Saul so close to him? What did David's men tempt him to do? Did David choose to use self-control or not? What happened because of the choice David made? Tell about a time when you didn't do something wrong that you were tempted to do.

7

PRACTICE

Read the verse. Try to repeat it several times without looking. Cut a sword shape from paper or cardboard and write the verse on it. You'll want to hang it up in your house where it will remind you of the Spirit's sword from 1 Peter 1:13. You can use it to fight against the temptation to lose your self-control.

DAY 2

READ

Genesis 42 ("Visitors from Canaan," page 37 in the *Day By Day Kid's Bible*)
It wasn't long before Joseph's brothers got to Egypt. They went to see the man in charge. He was the one who sold the wheat. He was Joseph. Joseph's brothers bowed to him. Joseph knew who they were right away. But he acted as if he didn't know them.

THINK AND TALK

Joseph's brothers had been very mean to him. They had made fun of him, and they had sold him to slave traders. Joseph probably thought he'd never see any of his family again. But here were his brothers bowing to him, not knowing who he was. What could Joseph have been tempted to do? Did Joseph choose to control himself or not? What happened because of the choice Joseph made? Joseph kept his identity a secret for a long time. It takes self-control to keep a secret when you really want to tell it. Tell about a time when it was hard for you to keep a secret.

PRACTICE

Challenge a friend or family member (or yourself!) to a sword fight. One person says, "What will you do if you are tempted to lose self-control?" The other person says, "I will control myself, because it is written, 'Be self-controlled.'"

DAY 3

READ

Exodus 32:1-20 ("The Gold Calf," page 70 in the *Day By Day Kid's Bible*)

Moses went back down the mountain...Joshua was with Moses...They got closer to the camp. Then they saw the gold idol...Moses got very angry. He threw down the stone charts. They broke into pieces at the bottom of the mountain.

THINK AND TALK
Sometimes we lose our self-control when we get angry, and we do things we hadn't planned. Did Moses choose to control himself or not? What happened because of the choice he made? Is it always easy to have self-control? When is it hardest for you to control yourself? Some people count to ten when they get angry so that they will remember to calm down and control themselves. What are some other things you could do to help yourself stay in control?

PRACTICE
Challenge someone to a sword-fight with your sword for this week. Write on an index card: "You are tempted to lose self-control." Place it in a bowl with the temptation card from last week. The first person draws a card and challenges the second person with that temptation. The second person repeats the sword of the Spirit that he can use to fight the temptation. Then it's his turn to draw a card and challenge the first person.

DAY 4

READ
Daniel 1 ("The King's Food," page 395 in the *Day By Day Kid's Bible*)
The king gave [the young men] food and wine from his table. He wanted them to study for three years. Then they could be his helpers...But Daniel chose not to eat the king's food. He chose not to drink the king's wine. He wanted to keep himself right and good.

THINK AND TALK
What was Daniel tempted to do? Did Daniel choose to have self-control or not? What happened because of his choice? Many people have a hard time controlling themselves when it comes to eating—what to eat, when to eat, and how much to eat. Why? What is your favorite food? Tell about a time when you had to use

self-control with food. What can happen if you don't use self-control when you eat?

PRACTICE
You and another person can challenge each other to practice fighting temptation. Do this by taking turns drawing the temptation cards from a bowl. Ask each other what you would do if you were tempted in that way, and answer by saying the appropriate verse.

TRY THIS
Cut small bites of different kinds of foods that have different flavors, such as dill or sweet pickles, apples, cheese, grapes, peanuts, etc. Ask a friend to close his eyes and hold his nose while you put one bite at a time into his mouth. As he tastes each bite, let him guess what food it is. What does self-control have to do with eating?

DAY 5
READ
John 18:1-11 ("Judas and the Guards," page 615 in the *Day By Day Kid's Bible*)
Judas walked up to Jesus to kiss him. Jesus said, "Judas! Are you going to turn against me by kissing me?"... Then the guards took hold of Jesus... Peter had a sword. He pulled it out. He swung it at Malchus, the high priest's servant. Peter cut off the servant's right ear... "Put your sword back," said Jesus... Then Jesus touched Malchus's ear. Malchus was well again.

THINK AND TALK
Peter was tempted to hit the servant with his sword. Did Peter choose to use self-control or not? What happened because of the choice he made? Why does God want us to control ourselves?

PRACTICE
Challenge someone to practice fighting temptation. You can take turns drawing the temptation cards from the bowl. Ask each other what you would do if you were tempted in that way.

TRY THIS

You will need several friends or family members to play this. Whisper a very short story or a phrase in one person's ear. It could be something like, "Polly put the kettle on and told Jack to climb the hill. But Jill told Old King Cole who frightened the mouse under her chair. So the mouse ran up the clock. The clock struck one and frightened the cow who jumped over the moon." The person who hears the story or phrase must tell the next person. That person tells the next person, and so on, until everyone has heard the "secret." The last person to hear it must tell it aloud to everyone else. Was it the same as what you first whispered? Why would a person need self-control in order to keep a secret?

DAY 6

READ

Proverbs 25:28 and 29:11 ("Self-Control and Pride," page 240 in the *Day By Day Kid's Bible*)

Someone who can't control himself is like a city with broken-down walls. A fool shows all his anger. But a wise person controls himself.

THINK AND TALK

Long ago, cities were built with walls around them for protection. Why is someone who can't control himself like a city with broken-down walls? Why is a person who controls himself wise? When is it hardest for you to control yourself? When you are tempted to lose self-control, what can you do?

PRACTICE

Challenge someone to practice fighting temptation. You can take turns drawing the temptation cards from the bowl. Ask each other what you would do if you were tempted in that way.

TRY THIS

In a sandbox, a box of dirt, or a dirt area of your yard, dig a river bed. Line it with plastic from a trash bag weighted down with rocks. Fill the river bed with water. Try to build a dam across the river, using sticks or mud or whatever you can invent. How does a dam control water? How do we control ourselves? What does it feel like to lose control?

DAY 7

READ

Numbers 20 ("Finding More Water," page 83 in the *Day By Day Kid's Bible*)

God told Moses, "Get your walking stick... Talk to the rock. Water will flow out of it. Then the people can drink." . .Moses said, "Listen! Do we have to get water from this rock for you?" Then Moses hit the rock two times with the walking stick. Water flowed out... But God had said just to talk to the rock.

THINK AND TALK

The people had been complaining to Moses, and he was angry at them. He was tempted to hit the rock instead of talk to it. Did Moses choose to control himself and do what he knew he should do? What happened because of the choice Moses made? How do you feel when you're not controlling yourself? How does it feel when other people are not controlling themselves? Why does God want us to control ourselves?

PRACTICE

Challenge someone to practice fighting temptation. You can take turns drawing the temptation cards from the bowl. Ask each other what you would do if you were tempted in that way.

TRY THIS

Make a walking stick from a thin tree branch or from a dowel. The walking stick should be taller than your waist, but no taller than your shoulder. If you have chosen a tree branch for your walking stick, peel the bark off. You can also sand it if you wish. If you are using a dowel, you may want to stain it or use a permanent marker to decorate it. Why do you think Moses hit the rock with his walking stick?

Showing Confidence

Your sword of the Spirit for this week is:

My help comes from the Lord, the Maker of heaven and earth. PSALM 121:2

With the above sword you can fight back when you face this temptation:

You are tempted to feel sorry for yourself.

DAY 1

READ

Exodus 4:1-17 ("The Snake," page 50 in the *Day By Day Kid's Bible*)

Moses said, "I've never been good at talking to people... I'm too slow." "Who gave people their mouths," asked God. "Who makes people able to hear or see? Don't I do that? So go. I'll help you talk. I'll teach you what to say." "Please, God," said Moses. "Send somebody else."

THINK AND TALK

Confidence is being sure. It's trusting. Moses was not confident. He knew he was not good at talking. So he felt sorry for himself. But he forgot one thing: It's God who makes us able to do what he asks us to do. Moses could be sure that he could do what God wanted, because he could trust God. He could be confident that he would have God's help. Have you ever been tempted to say, "I can't do it"? Have you ever been tempted to feel sorry for yourself? How can you be confident?

13

PRACTICE

Read the verse. Try to repeat it several times without looking. Cut a sword shape from paper or cardboard. Write the verse on it. You'll want to hang it up in your house where it will remind you of the Spirit's sword from Psalm 121:2. You can use to fight against the temptation to feel sorry for yourself.

DAY 2

READ

1 Kings 19:1-18 ("Afraid in the Desert," page 283 in the *Day By Day Kid's Bible*)

Elijah got scared. He ran away... Then God spoke. "Why are you here, Elijah?" "I've worked hard for you, God," said Elijah. "But your people have turned away from you. They broke your altars. They killed your prophets. I'm the only prophet left. Now they're trying to kill me."... "Go back," said God..."I have saved 7,000 people for myself in Israel. They do not worship Baal or follow him."

THINK AND TALK

Did Elijah choose to have confidence in God or to feel sorry for himself? Why do you think Elijah thought he was the only one left who followed God? Why is it important to be confident? What happens when people feel sorry for themselves?

PRACTICE

Challenge a friend or family member (or yourself) to a sword fight. One person says, "What will you do if you are tempted to feel sorry for yourself?" The other person answers, "I will not feel sorry for myself, because it is written, 'My help comes from the Lord, the Maker of heaven and earth.'"

DAY 3

READ

Jeremiah 1:4-10 ("I'm Like a Child," page 380 in the *Day By Day Kid's Bible*)

"I chose you before you were born," said God. "I chose you to be a prophet. I chose you to tell my words to the nations." "Lord God," said. "I'm not good at talking to people. I'm like a child." "Don't say that you're like a child," said God. "You have to go where I tell you to go... I will take care of you."

THINK AND TALK
What were Jeremiah's choices? What did he choose to do? Why could Jeremiah be confident? Why did God want Jeremiah to be confident? When is it hardest for you to be confident? Why can you be confident?

PRACTICE
Challenge someone to a sword-fight with your sword for this week. Write on an index card: "You are tempted to feel sorry for yourself." Add this temptation card to the other cards you've collected. Place these in a bowl. The first person draws a card and challenges the other person with that temptation. The second person repeats the sword of the Spirit that he can use to fight the temptation. Then it's his turn to draw a card and challenge the first person.

DAY 4

READ
Judges 16:23-30 ("Samson's Secret," page 119 in the *Day By Day Kid's Bible*)
Samson prayed, "God, remember me. Make me strong one more time... " Samson reached out to the posts... Then Samson pushed as hard as he could. The building fell down on everyone.

THINK AND TALK
Why might Samson have been tempted to feel sorry for himself? What did he choose to do? Do you think he felt confident in his own strength or in God's strength? What did Samson do at the end of his life that showed he had confidence in God? Tell about a time when you felt sorry for yourself. Tell about a time when you felt confident.

PRACTICE
You and another person can challenge each other to practice

fighting temptation. Do this by taking turns drawing the temptation cards from a bowl. Ask each other what you would do if you were tempted in that way, and answer by saying the appropriate verse.

TRY THIS
Build a tower using paper cups turned upside down, or cardboard tubes from toilet paper. Stand some distance away from this building and go "bowling" by rolling a ball and trying to knock the building down. Try different sizes of balls. Which ball do you feel most confident with?

DAY 5

READ
Genesis 16 ("Sarai Tries to Get a Son," page 12 in the *Day By Day Kid's Bible*)
Sarai was mean to Hagar. So Hagar ran away. God's angel found Hagar. She was out in the desert by a road... "Where did you come from, Hagar?" asked the angel. "Where are you going?" "I'm running away from Sarai," said Hagar. The angel said, "Go back to her. Keep being her servant. You will have children... God has heard how sad you are." [Hagar said,] "Now I have seen 'The God Who Sees Me.'" Hagar went back to Sarai.

THINK AND TALK
Why was Hagar tempted to feel sorry for herself at first? What did she choose to do? Have you ever felt sorry for yourself because someone treated you badly? What did you do? How did Hagar get the confidence to go back to Sarai? Where does God want our confidence to come from? What are some things you can do to help yourself feel confident?

PRACTICE
Challenge someone to practice fighting temptation. You can take turns drawing the temptation cards from the bowl. Ask each other what you would do if you were tempted in that way.

TRY THIS

In the middle of a piece of paper, draw a triangle with its point at the top. Draw a circle on top of the point. The circle is the head of an angel and the triangle is his body. Pour a bit of water-based, washable paint onto a plate and press your right hand onto it. Then press your hand onto the paper to the left of the triangle to make a wing. Do the same with your left hand, pressing it onto the right side of the triangle to make the other wing. How did an angel give Hagar confidence?

DAY 6

READ

Judges 6:11-23 ("God Chooses Gideon," page 107 in the *Day By Day Kid's Bible*)

"Go," said God [to Gideon]…"You are strong. Save your people from the people of Midian. I'm sending you." "How can I save them?" asked Gideon. "My family is not strong. And everyone in my family is more important than I am." "I'll be with you," said God. "You'll win"

THINK AND TALK

When God first talked to Gideon, Gideon was tempted not to feel confident. Why? Read the rest of Gideon's story. Did Gideon choose to feel sorry for himself, or did he choose to be confident? How could Gideon be confident? What would you suggest to a friend who was not confident?

PRACTICE

Challenge someone to practice fighting temptation. You can take turns drawing the temptation cards from the bowl. Ask each other what you would do if you were tempted in that way.

TRY THIS

Do this with a partner. Stand back to back, with a string taped to the floor three feet in front of each of you. Without turning around, each person should try to push the other one across the string in front of that person. Whose strength never fails?

DAY 7

READ
Numbers 13 - 14:9 ("A Look into the New Land," page 79 in the *Day By Day Kid's Bible*)
Moses chose 12 leaders. Moses told them, "Go into the hill country... Find out if the people are strong or not." ... After 40 days the 12 men came back to Moses... Caleb ... said, "We should go into the land. We should take it. I'm sure we can do it." "We can't fight those people," said the other men. "They are stronger than we are. Those people are very big. We felt like grasshoppers next to them."

THINK AND TALK
The 12 leaders were tempted to feel sorry for themselves. Why? How many of them chose to be confident? Why were they confident? How many chose not to be confident? What happened because of their choice?

PRACTICE
Challenge someone to practice fighting temptation. You can take turns drawing the temptation cards from the bowl. Ask each other what you would do if you were tempted in that way.

TRY THIS
Make a dill pickle "grasshopper." Place a dill-pickle spear on a plate, soft side down. Ask an adult to supervise or help as you cut a one-inch slit down the back at one end to spread apart for wings. Use two toothpicks to attach a green olive at the other end with the red pimento as the nose. The toothpicks stick out the top of the olive to make antennae. If you want to make legs, use more toothpicks. If you want eyes, use two whole cloves. How can you be confident when you face a problem that makes you feel as small as a grasshopper?

Listening

Your sword of the Spirit for this week is:

Be quick to listen and slow to speak. JAMES 1:19

With the above sword you can fight back when you face this temptation:

You are tempted not to listen.

DAY 1

READ

John 10:1-16 ("The Shepherd's Voice," page 576 in the *Day By Day Kid's Bible*)

"The sheep listen for the shepherd's voice," said Jesus. "He calls his sheep by their names... The sheep follow the shepherd... They know his voice. They'll never follow a stranger. In fact, they run from strangers. They don't know the stranger's voice... I am the Good Shepherd," said Jesus. "I know my people. They are my sheep."

THINK AND TALK

Listening means paying attention. It means more than hearing because when you're listening, you are thinking about what you're hearing. What are some things you like to listen to? What are some things you don't like to listen to? Is there ever a time when it's best *not* to listen? When? Are you ever tempted not to listen when you should?

PRACTICE

Read the verse. Try to repeat it several times without looking. Cut a sword shape from paper or cardboard and write the verse on it. You'll want to hang it up in your house where it will remind

19

you of the Spirit's sword from James 1:19. You can use it to fight against the temptation to ignore something you should listen to.

DAY 2

READ
Luke 10:38-42 ("All This Work," page 579 in the *Day By Day Kid's Bible*)
Martha had a sister named Mary. She sat down at Jesus' feet. She listened to what he said. But Martha was thinking. She thought about all the things she had to do... "Lord," she said... "Tell Mary to help me." "Martha, Martha," said Jesus. "You're upset. You're worried about so many things. There is only one thing that's important right now. That's what Mary chose to do."

THINK AND TALK
What do you think James meant when he wrote, "Be quick to listen [and] slow to speak?" What or who does God want you to listen to? What happens when we don't listen? Why was Martha tempted not to listen like Mary did? What did Martha choose to do? How can you listen to Jesus?

PRACTICE
Challenge a friend or family member (or yourself) to a sword fight. One person says, "What will you do if you are tempted not to listen?" The other person answers, "I will listen, because it is written, 'Be quick to listen and slow to speak.'"

DAY 3

READ
1 Samuel 3 ("A Voice at Night," page 124 in the *Day By Day Kid's Bible*)
Eli told Samuel to say these words if God called again. "I'm your servant. I'm listening, God." So Samuel went back to bed. Then God came and stood there. He called, "Samuel! Samuel!" "I'm your servant," said Samuel. "And I'm listening."

THINK AND TALK
What choices did Samuel have? What did Samuel choose to do? Why is it so important to listen to what God has to say? How do we find out what God has to say? Who else is it important to listen to? When is it the hardest for you to listen?

PRACTICE
Challenge someone to sword-fight with your sword for this week. Write on an index card: "You are tempted not to listen." Add this temptation card to the other cards you've collected. Place them in a bowl. The first person draws a card and challenges the other person with that temptation. The second person repeats the sword of the Spirit that she can use to fight the temptation. Then it's her turn to draw a card and challenge the first person.

DAY 4

READ
Matthew 7:24-27 ("Good Fruit and Bad Fruit," page 536 in the *Day By Day Kid's Bible*)
"Some people hear me and obey," said Jesus. "They are like the wise man. He built his house on a rock... Some people hear me, but they don't obey," said Jesus. "They are like the foolish man. He built his house on sand."

THINK AND TALK
Is there a difference between *hearing* and *listening*? If so, what's the difference? In Jesus' story, both the wise and foolish men heard. What made one wise and one foolish? Have you ever heard someone's advice, but you didn't listen to it? Tell about a time when you listened, and you are glad you did. Or tell about a time when you didn't listen and how you wish you had.

PRACTICE
You and another person can challenge each other to practice fighting temptation. Do this by taking turns drawing the temptation cards from a bowl. Ask each other what you would do if you were tempted in that way.

TRY THIS

Build a landscape of sand or dirt outdoors. Build a second landscape of rocks. Pour water from a garden hose over each landscape. What happens to each one? Which one erodes? Why do you think Jesus used these to represent the wise and foolish men?

DAY 5

READ

Acts 23:12-24 ("The Secret Plan," page 722 in the *Day By Day Kid's Bible*)

The Jews got together. There were more than 40 of them. They made a promise to each other. They wouldn't eat or drink anything until they killed Paul... Now, Paul had a sister, and she had a son. Her son heard about the Jews' plan. He told Paul about it.

THINK AND TALK

God allowed Paul's sister's son to hear something very important. Why? What are some things that God wants you to hear? What are some things that God does not want you to hear? How do you know what to listen to and what *not* to listen to?

PRACTICE

Challenge someone to practice fighting temptation. You can take turns drawing the temptation cards from a bowl. Ask each other what you would do if you were tempted in that way.

TRY THIS

Use an audiocassette tape recorder to record sounds that most people hear every day, such as a dog barking, a door slamming, a piano being played, water dripping, a phone ringing, a computer keyboard being typed on, etc. Play this for younger children and see if they can identify the sounds. If you choose sounds that would be harder to identify, play them for your friends or parents. When is listening most important?

DAY 6

READ

Proverbs 1 ("Listen and Learn," page 230 in the *Day By Day Kid's Bible*)

These sayings will teach people the wise way to think. They'll help you do what's right and fair... They'll help young people know and choose what's good. So if you're wise, listen and learn even more. Treat God as the most important one. That gets you started to know what's right. The person who hates what's wise is a fool.

THINK AND TALK

Solomon wrote many of his wise sayings to his sons. Why did he want his sons to listen to him? Why do your parents want you to listen to them? Tell about someone you know who is a good listener. How can you tell that this person is a good listener? What can you do to help yourself be a good listener?

PRACTICE

Challenge someone to practice fighting temptation. You can take turns drawing the temptation cards from a bowl. Ask each other what you would do if you were tempted in that way.

TRY THIS

Draw several faces on paper, but do not draw ears, eyes, nose or mouths. Cut ears, eyes, noses, and mouths out of different magazine pictures. Glue them onto the faces you have drawn. Draw hair and any other features you want to add. Are all people wise? How can listening make people wise?

DAY 7

READ

Matthew 17:1-13 ("As White As Light," page 564 in the *Day By Day Kid's Bible*)

Jesus took Peter, James and John...up on a high mountain...Jesus' face started shining...Then a bright cloud came down around them. A voice came from the cloud. It said, "This is my Son. He is the Son I love. I'm happy with him. Listen to him."

THINK AND TALK

Sometimes it's hard to listen because we are *distracted*. That means other things take our attention away from what we are supposed to be doing. What are some things that could distract you (take your attention away) from something important you should listen to? What can help you keep your attention on what you need to listen to?

PRACTICE

Challenge someone to practice fighting temptation. You can take turns drawing the temptation cards from a bowl. Ask each other what you would do if you were tempted in that way.

TRY THIS

Make "cloud cake" by slicing a loaf of pound cake. To serve it, put one slice on each plate. With a butter knife, spread caramel sauce over each slice. Then place a cloud-like heap of whipped topping over the sauce. The reading says, "a bright cloud came down around them." Why do you think the cloud was bright?

Being Hopeful

Your sword of the Spirit for this week is:

May the God of hope fill you with all joy and peace as you trust in him, so that you may overflow with hope by the power of the Holy Spirit.

ROMANS 15:13

With the above sword you can fight back when you face this temptation:

You are tempted to feel hopeless.

DAY 1

READ

1 Samuel 1:1-20 ("A Sad Prayer and a Happy Answer," page 121 in the *Day By Day Kid's Bible*)

Hannah...cried to God. She asked God for a baby boy... Eli thought Hannah was drunk... "I'm not drunk, sir," said Hannah. "Don't think I'm sinning. I'm just very sad. I was praying to God." "Then you can go home feeling better," said Eli. "I pray that God will give you what you asked for." So Hannah went and ate. She didn't look sad anymore.

THINK AND TALK

Hope is knowing that no matter what problems we may have, there is someone here to take care of us: God. At first, Hannah did not have much hope. She didn't eat. She cried. Have you ever known someone who felt hopeless? What did the person do? Have you ever been tempted to feel hopeless? After Eli talked to Hannah, how did she feel? How do you know?

PRACTICE
Read the verse. Try to repeat it several times without looking. Cut a sword shape from paper or cardboard and write the verse on it. You'll want to hang it up in your house where it will remind you of the Spirit's sword from Romans 15:13. You can use it to fight against the temptation to feel hopeless.

DAY 2

READ
Luke 2:22-40 ("No More Waiting," page 507 in the *Day By Day Kid's Bible*)
Simeon had been waiting for someone special. This person would save God's people. The Holy Spirit had told Simeon he would see this special person... the Promised One. The Spirit told Simeon to go to the worship house. That's when Joseph and Mary brought Jesus there. Simeon held baby Jesus and praised God. "God, you promised this," he said. "Now you are letting me die in peace. I have seen the one who will save."

THINK AND TALK
Hoping and waiting go together because you don't hope for something you already have. Simeon expected to see God's Son, and he finally saw what he had hoped for. What happens when we put our hope in the world—in things and in people? What happens when we put our hope in God and his will? Why does God want us to be full of hope? What happens when we are not full of hope?

PRACTICE
Challenge a friend or family member (or yourself) to a sword fight. One person says, "What will you do if you are tempted to feel hopeless?" The other person answers, "I will not feel hopeless, because it is written, 'May the God of hope fill you with all joy and peace as you trust in him, so that you may overflow with hope by the power of the Holy Spirit.'"

DAY 3

READ

Genesis 40 ("Two Strange Dreams" and "The King's Dreams," pages 35 and 36 in the *Day By Day Kid's Bible*)

[Joseph told the waiter,] "Three days will pass. Then the king will let you out of jail... Please tell him about me. See if you can get me out of jail, too." ... But the waiter didn't tell the king about Joseph. He forgot... Two years passed... Then the waiter remembered Joseph.

THINK AND TALK

Why might Joseph have been tempted to feel hopeless? Why could he feel hopeful? Even though Joseph had hope that God would get him out of jail, did it work out when and how Joseph thought it would? When is it hardest for you to feel hopeful?

PRACTICE

Challenge someone to a sword-fight with your sword for this week. Write on an index card: "You are tempted to feel hopeless." Place this card in the bowl with your other cards. The first person draws a card and challenges the second person with that temptation. The second person repeats the sword of the Spirit he can use to fight it. Then it's his turn to draw a card and challenge the first person.

DAY 4

READ

Luke 8:40-56 ("The Sick Little Girl," page 551 in the *Day By Day Kid's Bible*)

A leader from the town's worship house... bowed down in front of Jesus. "My little girl is sick," he said. "She is going to die. Please come with me. Touch my little girl so she will live." So Jesus went... A woman was in the crowd. She had been sick for 12 years... So she pushed her way through the crowd. She crept up right behind Jesus. "I just need to touch his clothes!" she thought. "Then I'll be well." So she touched Jesus' coat.

THINK AND TALK

Two people in this story were tempted to feel hopeless. Who were they? Why might they have felt hopeless? What did they choose to believe that gave them hope? Tell about a time when you were hopeless or hopeful. What happened?

PRACTICE
You and another person can challenge each other to practice fighting temptation. Do this by taking turns drawing the temptation cards from a bowl. Ask each other what you would do if you were tempted in that way.

TRY THIS
Collect some small household items like a comb, gift-wrap bow, sunglasses, screwdriver, birthday candle, and so on. But don't get anything sharp. Put these items inside a pillowcase. Let different people reach into the bag and, without looking, feel an item and guess what it is. Then let the person take it out to see what the item really is. You can make it easy for young children by choosing simple thing they know about. You can make it harder for friends your age or for adults by choosing things they might not recognize, or things that are a lot alike in shape and size. How do you think Jesus' hem felt?

DAY 5

READ
Acts 1:1-5 ("Going into the Clouds," page 630 in the *Day By Day Kid's Bible*)
"I'll send you the gift my Father has promised," said Jesus. "But stay in Jerusalem for a while. Stay there until the Father gives you power."... Then Jesus went up off the ground. His friends watched until a cloud hid him... Suddenly, they saw two men standing by them. The men were dressed all in white. "Men from Galilee!" said the two men… "Jesus has gone up into heaven. He will come back the same way you saw him go."

THINK AND TALK
Jesus' friends had two things to be hopeful about. What were they? (Hint: Why did they need to wait in Jerusalem? And what did the two men tell them?) Do these two things make us hopeful

28

even now? Explain. When you are tempted to feel hopeless, what are some things you can do to help yourself be hopeful?

PRACTICE
Challenge someone to practice fighting temptation. You can take turns drawing the temptation cards from a bowl. Ask each other what you would do if you were tempted in that way.

TRY THIS
Cut clouds of different shapes and sizes out of paper. An encyclopedia or a book on weather will show the shapes and names of different kinds of clouds. Punch a hole in the top of each cloud and tie strings of different lengths to the clouds. Tie the tops of the strings to a clothes hanger and hang this mobile up in your room to remind you that Jesus is coming back.

DAY 6

READ
John 2:1-12 ("A Wedding Party," page 515 in the *Day By Day Kid's Bible*)
Jesus' mother went to him. "They're out of wine!" she said... Jesus' mother talked to the servants. "Do whatever he asks you to do," she told them.

THINK AND TALK
Jesus' mother and the people giving the party could have been tempted to be hopeless. Why? Why could Jesus' mother be hopeful? Who is it that you can put your hope in? Who would it be wise *not* to put your hope in? Why? What are some of your hopes?

PRACTICE
Challenge someone to practice fighting temptation. You can take turns drawing the temptation cards from a bowl. Ask each other what you would do if you were tempted in that way.

TRY THIS
Make a grape-juice slush by freezing grape juice in an ice tray.
When the juice is frozen, place the juice cubes into cups. Stir and
chop them until they're slushy. How does the juice remind you of
the wedding party Jesus went to?

DAY 7

READ
Jeremiah 29:1-14 ("A Letter to Babylon," page 400 in the *Day By
Day Kid's Bible*)
"I'll come back for you in 70 years... I plan to bring good things to
you," says God. "I plan to give you hope. I plan good things for the
days that are coming. Then you'll pray to me, and I will listen to
you. You'll look for me. You'll find me when you look with all your
heart."

THINK AND TALK
God's people had been taken away from their own land. They had
been taken to Babylon. Why might they have been tempted to feel
hopeless? Why could they be hopeful instead? What reasons do
you have for being hopeful about the days that are coming? What
would you suggest to a friend who felt hopeless?

PRACTICE
Challenge someone to practice fighting temptation. You can take
turns drawing the temptation cards from a bowl. Ask each other
what you would do if you were tempted in that way.

TRY THIS
Fill a cup with water. Choose a friend to guess how many pennies
can be placed into the cup of water before the cup overflows. You
can guess too. Hold your head at a place where you can look
straight across the rim of the cup and not see the water. Watch
carefully as you slip the pennies into the cup, one at a time. Before
the cup overflows, you will see the surface of the water mound up
above the top of the cup. The water is held in by its surface
tension. Will one more coin make it overflow? What does the
verse for this week mean when it says "you may overflow with
hope"?

Showing Humility

Your sword of the Spirit for this week is:

By the grace of God, I am what I am.
1 CORINTHIANS 15:10

With the above sword you can fight back when you face this temptation:

You are tempted to be haughty or prideful.

DAY 1

READ
Genesis 11:1-9 ("The Tower," page 8 in the *Day By Day Kid's Bible*)

"Let's make some bricks," said the people. "Let's stick them together with tar. Let's build a city and a tower. We will build the tower as high as the sky. Then everyone will know who we are."

THINK AND TALK
Humility is knowing that you are not the best or most important person. It is knowing that God has made you who you are and given you what you have. So you aren't haughty, boastful, arrogant, or prideful. What is it about the tower of Babel that makes us think that the people who built it may not have been humble? Are you tempted to be prideful when you have done something great? What can you remember that will help you stay humble?

PRACTICE

Read the verse. Try to repeat it several times without looking. Cut a sword shape from paper or cardboard and write the verse on it. You'll want to hang it up in your house where it will remind you of the Spirit's sword from 1 Corinthians 15:10. You can use it to fight against the temptation to be prideful.

DAY 2

READ

John 3:22-36 ("The Groom," page 517 in the *Day By Day Kid's Bible*)

John's followers went to John. "Remember the man you told us about? He is the man who was at the Jordan River. He is dipping people in water too. Now everybody is going to him." "A person has only what God gives him," said John... "Jesus has to become more and more important. I have to become less and less important."

THINK AND TALK

People had heard of John before they heard of Jesus. John had been teaching and baptizing people first. Then Jesus came along. Why might John have been tempted to be prideful? What did John choose to do? What happened because of his choice? Why does God want us to be humble? What happens when we are not humble?

PRACTICE

Challenge a friend or family member (or yourself) to a sword fight. One person says, "What will you do if you are tempted to feel prideful?" The other person answers, "I will not be prideful, because it is written, 'By the grace of God, I am what I am.'"

DAY 3

READ Acts 12:20 - 25.

("The Angel in the Jail," page 649 in the *Day By Day Kid's Bible*)

Herod put on his kingly clothes. He sat on his throne. Then he talked to all the people who came. They shouted, "His voice is the voice of a god!" Herod let them praise him. He didn't give praise to God. So at once, an angel from God made him sick. Then worms began to eat him up, and he died.

THINK AND TALK
Herod was tempted to be prideful. What did he choose to do? What happened because of his choice? What makes it hard for people to resist the temptation to be prideful? When is it hardest for you to resist the temptation to be prideful?

PRACTICE
Challenge someone to a sword-fight with your sword for this week. Write on an index card: "You are tempted to be prideful." Place this card in the bowl with your other cards. The first person draws a card and challenges the second person with that temptation. The second person repeats the sword of the Spirit he can use to fight it. Then it's his turn to draw a card and challenge the first person.

DAY 4

READ
Acts 14:8-20 ("People Who Wanted to Worship Paul," page 654 in the *Day By Day Kid's Bible*)
Paul looked right at the man. Paul knew the man believed he could get well. So Paul said, "Stand up on your feet!" The man jumped up. He started walking! The crowd saw this. They shouted, "The gods are here!... The people wanted to offer worship gifts to Paul and Barnabas... "What are you doing?" they asked. "We are just people like you... Worship the living God."

THINK AND TALK
What happened that might have tempted Paul and Barnabas to be prideful? Did they choose to be humble or prideful? What happened because of their choice? What do you think might have happened if they had chosen differently? Tell about a time when you were tempted to be prideful. What did you do?

PRACTICE
You and another person can challenge each other to practice

fighting temptation. Do this by taking turns drawing temptation cards from a bowl. Ask each other person what you would do if you were tempted in that way, and answer by saying the appropriate verse.

TRY THIS
Make a photo frame. On top of the plastic lid from a large margarine tub, and toward one side, draw a rectangle, one inch wide from side to side and about three inches long from top to bottom. Cut along all the sides of the rectangle *except* the top. Fold the rectangle gently out, using the top side as the fold. The lid is the photo frame and the rectangle is the stand that it leans back on. On the other side of this same lid, glue a photograph of yourself. You can put decorations around the photo. Perhaps you want to glue sequins or glitter onto the frame, place stickers on it, or color designs on it using permanent markers. What does this week's verse tell you about why you are *you*?

DAY 5

READ
Daniel 4 ("The King Who Lived with Wild Animals," page 434 in the *Day By Day Kid's Bible*)
I was walking on my palace roof. I said, "This is the great Babylon that I built. I built it by my strong power. It shows how great I am!" ... Right away, it happened. I was sent away from my people. I ate grass like a cow. Dew from the sky made my body wet. My hair grew out like eagle feathers. My nails grew out like bird claws. After seven years, I, Nebuchadnezzar, looked up to heaven. My right mind came back to me. Then I praised the Most High God who lives forever. I treated him as the most important one.

THINK AND TALK
What did King Nebuchadnezzar do that showed he was full of pride? When did he choose to be humble? How did he show his humility? What are some things you can do to help you remember to be humble instead of prideful?

PRACTICE
Challenge someone to practice fighting temptation. You can take turns drawing the temptation cards from a bowl. Ask each other

what you would do if you were tempted in that way, and answer by saying the appropriate verse.

TRY THIS
In your kitchen, go on a hunt to find all the things that are made from grains (grasses). Besides bread, look for pastas, flours, cereals, oats, and so on. If you want to explore further, look in an encyclopedia or other resource book to find out what these grasses look like as they are growing. Draw a picture of each grain at the top of a piece of paper. List some things that are made from each grain underneath its picture. What kinds of grasses do you think Nebuchadnezzar ate?

DAY 6

READ
Luke 18:9-14 ("The Proud Prayer," page 587 in the *Day By Day Kid's Bible*)
The leader stood up tall. He prayed about himself. "God, thank you that I'm not like other men. I'm not a robber. I don't sin... " The tax man stood a little way off. He wouldn't even look up... "God be kind to me," he said. "I'm a sinful person." "God forgave the tax man," said Jesus... "Some people think they're great. God will make those people feel like they're not important... "

THINK AND TALK
Which man fell for the temptation to be prideful? How do you know? Which man was humble? How do you know? In your life every day, how can you tell humble people from prideful people? Tell about someone you know who is humble. How does that person talk and act that shows you he or she is humble?

PRACTICE
Challenge someone to practice fighting temptation. You can take turns drawing the temptation cards from a bowl. Ask each other what you would do if you were tempted in that way.

TRY THIS
Make foot puppets. You can use your own feet or do this with a

friend. Take off shoes and socks. Draw a face on the bottom of one foot. The toes will form the top of the head. The heel will be the chin. Make the mouth a straight line instead of a smile or frown. To make a nose, stick one side of a plain adhesive bandage in between the eyes of your foot face. The pad of the bandage becomes the main part of the nose. Let it bend out, away from your foot. Then stick the second side of the bandage to your foot so that the pad "nose" points out. By holding your foot straight up, you can make this puppet look proud. By curling your foot a bit, the puppet bows down like a humble person.

DAY 7

READ

Proverbs 11:2; 12:9; 13:10; 16:5; 16:18; 21:4, 24; 27:21.
("Self-Control and Pride," page 240 in the *Day By Day Kid's Bible*)
People get proud. They think they're the best. Then others treat them like they're not important. But people become wise when they make others feel important... Thinking you're the best comes before you get into trouble.

THINK AND TALK

How do people become proud? Have you ever thought you were the best, and then something happened to prove that you were wrong? Who is the greatest? Why? What would you suggest to a friend who is being tempted to be prideful?

PRACTICE

Challenge someone to practice fighting temptation. You can take turns drawing the temptation cards from a bowl. Ask each other what you would do if you were tempted in that way.

TRY THIS

Get some craft sticks. (Popsicle sticks sold in packages at craft stores or in craft departments of discount stores.) Using the craft sticks and glue, build a tower of any design you wish. Try building it as high as you can. Why do we think that the people who built the Tower of Babel were proud? (See Day 1.)

BEING THANKFUL

Your sword of the Spirit for this week is:

No matter what happens, always be thankful.
1 THESSALONIANS 5:18

With the above sword you can fight back when you face this temptation:

You are tempted to be ungrateful.

DAY 1

READ
Luke 17:11-19 ("Ten Men and One Thank-You," page 577 in the *Day By Day Kid's Bible*)
Jesus saw ten sick men... They called out loudly, "Jesus! Master! Feel sorry for us!" "Go to the priests," said Jesus. "Let them look at your skin." ... While they were walking, they looked at their skin. Their skin was well! One of the men ran back to Jesus... He thanked Jesus... "Weren't there ten men who got well?" asked Jesus. "Where are the nine other men?. . "

THINK AND TALK
What choices did the ten men have when they saw they were well? What did they choose to do? Why do you think that only one man went back to thank Jesus? When a person is not thankful, we say they are ungrateful. Have you ever done something for someone, but they didn't thank you? How did you feel? How do you feel when someone thanks you?

PRACTICE

Read the verse. Try to repeat it several times without looking. Cut a sword shape from paper or cardboard. Write the verse on it. You'll want to hang it up in your house where it will remind you of the Spirit's sword from 1 Thessalonians 5:18. You can use it to fight against the temptation to be ungrateful.

DAY 2

READ

1 Chronicles 16 ("The Ark Comes Back," page 162 in the *Day By Day Kid's Bible*)

David and the leaders went to get the Ark... They all brought the Ark into the city. There was shouting. There was music... Then David talked to the priests who led the music. He told them to thank God with this song. "Give thanks to God... Sing praise to him. Tell about the wonderful things he has done... " All the people said, "Yes!"

THINK AND TALK

What choices did David have? What did David choose to do? David was thankful that God let him bring the Ark back to Jerusalem. How did David show his thanks? What are some ways you can show your thanks to God and others? Why does God want us to have a thankful heart? What happens when we are not thankful?

PRACTICE

Challenge a friend or family member (or yourself) to a sword fight. One person says, "What will you do if you are tempted to be ungrateful?" The other person answers, "I will not be ungrateful, because it is written, 'No matter what happens, always be thankful.'"

DAY 3

READ

Nehemiah 12:27-43 ("Singers on the Wall," page 499 in the *Day By Day Kid's Bible*)

Now the day came to give the city wall of Jerusalem to God. It was time to say that God was in charge of it. It belonged to him. So people from the family group of Levi came to help. They led songs to give thanks to God... Two groups of singers gave thanks. Then they went to the worship house.

THINK AND TALK
Why did the people give thanks for a wall? Do you think any of the people might have been tempted to be ungrateful for the wall? If so, why? When it is the hardest for you to be thankful?

PRACTICE
Challenge someone to a sword-fight with your sword for this week. Write on an index card: "You are tempted to be ungrateful." Add this temptation card to the other cards you've collected. Place them in a bowl. The first person draws a card and challenges the other person with that temptation. The second person repeats the sword of the Spirit that he can use to fight the temptation. Then it's his turn to draw a card and challenge the first person.

DAY 4

READ
Matthew 26:17-30 ("The Room Upstairs," page 608 in the *Day By Day Kid's Bible*)
Jesus held up a cup of wine. He thanked God. "Take this," he said to his friends. "Share it with each other." ...Then Jesus picked up the flat bread. He thanked God. He broke some off to give to his friends. "This will help you remember my body," he said. "I'm giving my body for you."

THINK AND TALK
Why do you think Jesus gave thanks? What was he giving thanks for? Who are some of the people you thank most often? Tell about a time when you forgot to thank someone. Did you ever say thank-you to someone, but you were not really thankful for what they did? If so, why were you not thankful, and why did you say thank-you anyway? Do you have to feel thankful to say thank-you?

PRACTICE

You and another person can challenge each other to practice fighting temptation. Do this by taking turns drawing the temptation cards from a bowl. Ask each other person what you would do if you were tempted in that way.

TRY THIS

Make Communion bread. Stir three-fourths teaspoon of salt into one cup of flour (white or whole wheat). In a measuring cup, pour one-fourth cup of vegetable oil plus two and one-half tablespoons of cold water, but don't stir them. Pour the liquid all at once into the flour and salt mixture, and stir. Press this dough out onto a cookie sheet and bake it at 450 degrees for 10 to 12 minutes. What did Jesus have to be thankful for? What do you have to be thankful for?

DAY 5

READ

Romans 1 ("A Letter from Greece," page 702 in the *Day By Day Kid's Bible*)

God is showing his anger... He is against sinful people who hide the truth by their sins. These people know about God. God clearly showed who he is... So there is no reason for people not to believe. These sinful people knew God. But they didn't show how great he was. And they didn't thank him.

THINK AND TALK

What do we show God when we thank him? Why do people not thank God? Why do people sometimes forget to thank each other? Why would someone be ungrateful? What are some things you can do to remind yourself to be thankful?

PRACTICE

Challenge someone to practice fighting temptation. You can take turns drawing the temptation cards from a bowl. Ask each other what you would do if you were tempted in that way.

TRY THIS

Make thank-you notes to keep on hand for times when you need to send them. Fold printer paper in half from top to bottom, then in half again from side to side. Cut a sponge into different shapes. Pour different colors of water-based, washable paint onto paper plates, just using a little of each different color on each plate. Wet the sponge shapes and squeeze them out. Press each one into a different color of paint and then onto the fronts of the folded thank-you cards. Let them dry, then write "Thank You" on front or on the inside.

DAY 6

READ

Ephesians 5 ("Children of the Light," page 742 in the *Day By Day Kid's Bible*)

Don't look at things that make you think about sin. Don't let yourself want more and more things. These things are not right for God's special people. Don't tell dirty jokes. They don't fit you. Instead, talk about what you're thankful for.

THINK AND TALK

Why is it important to talk about what you're thankful for? Have you ever been tempted not to thank someone, even God? What are some things that can distract us and cause us to forget to be thankful?

PRACTICE

Challenge someone to practice fighting temptation. You can take turns drawing the temptation cards from a bowl. Ask each other what you would do if you were tempted in that way.

TRY THIS

Write the letters of the word *thanks* along the left side of a piece of notebook paper. Write the letter *T* on one line. Skip two lines. Write *H*. Skip two lines. Keep writing the letters that spell *THANKS*, skipping two lines between each letter. Now beside the *T*, write something you are thankful for that begins with that letter. Do the same with the other letters on the page.

DAY 7

READ

Psalm 107 ("Love That Lasts Forever," page 469 in the *Day By Day Kid's Bible*)

Give thanks to God. He is good. His love lasts forever. Let the people that God saved say so. He saved people from many lands... So let them thank God for his love that lasts forever. Let them thank him for the wonderful things he does.

THINK AND TALK

The sword for this week tells us to be thankful no matter what happens. How is it possible to be thankful when times are hard, or when we are sad? How can you tell when a person is grateful? How can you tell when a person is ungrateful? What would you suggest to a friend who is tempted to be ungrateful?

PRACTICE

Challenge someone to practice fighting temptation. You can take turns drawing the temptation cards from a bowl. Ask each other what you would do if you were tempted in that way.

TRY THIS

Write your own psalm of thanks to God.

Being Dependable

Your sword of the Spirit for this week is:

A person who is trusted with something must show that he is worthy of that trust. 1 CORINTHIANS 4:2

With the above sword you can fight back when you face this temptation:

You are tempted to be undependable.

DAY 1

READ

Genesis 39:1-6 ("At the Captain's House," page 34 in the *Day By Day Kid's Bible*)

God took care of Joseph. He lived in the captain's house. The captain saw that God helped Joseph. Good things happened when Joseph was around. So the captain put Joseph in charge of everything in his house. With Joseph in charge, the captain didn't worry about anything.

THINK AND TALK

Being *dependable* means doing what you're supposed to do when you're supposed to do it. When you are dependable, people can trust you. What choices did Joseph have? What did he choose to do? Joseph was dependable. Is it always easy to be dependable? Do you think Joseph felt like being dependable every day? Why do you think Joseph was dependable?

PRACTICE

Read the verse. Try to repeat it without looking. Cut a sword shape from paper or cardboard and write the verse on it. You'll want to hang it up in your house where it will remind you of the Spirit's sword from 1 Corinthians 4:2. You can use it to fight against the temptation to be undependable.

DAY 2

READ

Matthew 21:28-31 ("Two Sons and a Grape Garden," page 599 in the *Day By Day Kid's Bible*)
There was once a man who had two sons. The man talked to his first son. "Go work in the grape garden today," he said. His first son said no. Later, he changed his mind. He did go. The man talked to his other son. "Go work in the grape garden today," he said. His other son said, "Yes, sir. I will." But he didn't go.

THINK AND TALK

Both of the man's sons were tempted to be undependable. They were tempted to do the wrong thing. Which son fell for the temptation? Which son won over the temptation? Why does God want us to be dependable? What happens when we are not dependable?

PRACTICE

Challenge a friend or family member (or yourself) to a sword-fight. One person says, "What will you do if you are tempted to be undependable?" The other person answers, "I will be dependable, because it is written, 'A person who is trusted with something must show he is worthy of that trust.'"

DAY 3

READ

1 Samuel 20 ("The Arrow," page 143 in the *Day By Day Kid's Bible*)
Jonathan shot an arrow into the field. The boy ran to where it landed. Jonathan called, "The arrow is far away. It is past you." Then he called, "Hurry and go fast! Don't stop!" The boy picked up

the arrow and ran back to Jonathan... This was a message for David.

THINK AND TALK
Who was depending on Jonathan? Why? Was Jonathan dependable? Was the boy helping Jonathan be dependable? Do you think Jonathan would have chosen that boy to help him if the boy had not been dependable? What might have happened if Jonathan had not been dependable? When is it hardest for you to be dependable?

PRACTICE
Challenge someone to a sword-fight with your sword for this week. Write on an index card: "You are tempted to be undependable." Add this temptation card to the other cards you've collected. Place them in a bowl. The first person draws a card and challenges the second person with that temptation. The second person repeats the sword of the Spirit that she can use to fight the temptation. Then it's her turn to draw a card and challenge the first person.

DAY 4

READ
2 Samuel 23 ("Brave, Strong Men," page 170 in the *Day By Day Kid's Bible*)
There were three strong men who led David's battles. One of them killed 800 men in one fight. Then there was a second man... He kept fighting until his hand got tired. His hand locked around his sword. Then there was a third man. Once the enemy army came together in a field. David's army ran away. But this third man stayed right in the middle of the field. He kept fighting the enemy. God helped his people win.

THINK AND TALK
What choices did David's men have? What did they choose to do? What did David's men do that made them dependable? David could trust them to do what they were supposed to do, when they were supposed to do it. When you choose people to help you, you

want them to be dependable. Tell about someone you know who is dependable. How can you tell that this person is dependable? Tell about ways in which you show that you are dependable.

PRACTICE
You and another person can challenge each other to practice fighting temptation. Do this by taking turns drawing the temptation cards from a bow. Ask each other person what you would do if you were tempted in that way.

TRY THIS
Make an arrow design. Cut two and one-half inches off the bottom of a piece of white printer paper to make it square. Draw a diagonal line across each corner as if making arrowheads, with the corner of the paper being the tip of each arrow. Now use a ruler to make the shafts of these arrows, drawing two lines from one corner arrowhead to the arrowhead in the opposite corner. Do the same thing with the remaining two arrowheads. What weapons do you think David's mighty men used?

DAY 5

READ
1 Samuel 29 ("David Moves to Enemy Country," page 154 in the *Day By Day Kid's Bible*)
David and his 600 men moved to enemy country. They lived in the city of Gath... The enemy king trusted David. One day the king of Gath got his army together. They marched out to fight Saul's army. The king told David, "Come and help us fight... You can be my guard for life."... But the enemy leaders asked, "What about these Jewish people?" "This is David!" said the king. "He has been with me more than a year. He has done nothing wrong."

THINK AND TALK
Why did the king want to depend on David? Why do you think the leaders did not want to depend on David? Who do you depend on? What do you depend on them to do for you? Who depends on you? What do they depend on you to do for them?

PRACTICE
Challenge someone to practice fighting temptation. Do this by taking turns drawing the temptation cards from a bowl. Ask each other what you would do if you were tempted in that way.

TRY THIS
Draw a maze. Give it to a friend and see if your friend can solve the maze. If you are sword fighting with friends or family, ask each person to draw a maze. Then trade mazes and try to work the maze you have been given. David's travels took him in many different directions. How did he show he was dependable?

DAY 6
READ
Matthew 21:1-7 ("A Colt," page 596 in the *Day By Day Kid's Bible*)
Jesus asked two of his 12 special friends to do something. He asked them to go into the next town. "You'll see a donkey with her colt just as you go into town... Untie it, and bring it to me... " Jesus' two friends went to town. They found the colt... Jesus' friends took the colt to Jesus.

THINK AND TALK
What choices did Jesus' friends have? What did they choose to do? Were Jesus' friends dependable? How do you know? What are some things that can cause us to be undependable?

PRACTICE
Challenge someone to practice fighting temptation. Do this by taking turns drawing the temptation cards from a bowl. Ask each other what you would do if you were tempted in that way.

TRY THIS
Make COLT salad. The *C* is for one 12-ounce container of Cottage cheese. The *O* is for one small can of Oranges (mandarin oranges). The *L* is for one 3-ounce package of Lime Jell-O. The *T* is for one can of Tropical fruit. You will also need 4 to 5 ounces of frozen whipped topping. Mix the cottage cheese and dry Jell-O in

a big bowl. Drain the fruits and add them to the mixture. Fold the whipped topping in gently. Chill this in the refrigerator for at least one hour before you eat it. As you eat your COLT salad, recall the story of two dependable men and a colt.

DAY 7

READ

Matthew 25:14-30 ("The Servants and the Money," page 594 in the *Day By Day Kid's Bible*)

Once there was an important man. He had to go to a land far away. He... called ten servants. He gave each of them some money. "Use this money to get more money," he said... The man was made king... Then he came home... The first servant came to him. He said, "Sir, I made more money for you. You gave me one piece of money and I got ten more." "Well done!" said the king. "You are a good servant. I see I could trust you with a little bit. Now you may be in charge of ten cities."

THINK AND TALK

What choices did the servants have? What did they choose to do? Which servants were dependable? Why? Which were undependable? Why? Is it always easy to be dependable? What would you suggest to a friend who finds it hard to be dependable?

PRACTICE

Challenge someone to practice fighting temptation. Do this by taking turns drawing the temptation cards from a bowl. Ask each other what you would do if you were tempted in that way.

TRY THIS

Make a money bank from a margarine tub. Cut a slit in the middle of the lid so that a quarter will fit through it. Cut different colors of Con-Tact paper into small triangles, circles, rectangles, and squares. Stick these or other kinds of stickers onto the lid and sides of the margarine tub. How can you show that you are dependable with your money?

Having Contentment

Your sword of the Spirit for this week is:

Do everything without complaining or arguing.
PHILIPPIANS 2:14

With the above sword you can fight back when you face this temptation:

You are tempted to complain or argue.

DAY 1

READ
2 Kings 5:1-19 ("Dipping Into the River," page 303 in the *Day By Day Kid's Bible*)
Elisha sent a man out to Naaman with this message. "Go to the Jordan River. Dip down into the river seven times. Then your skin will be well." Naaman became angry... "We have better rivers in our land. Can't I be made well if I dip in them?" Then Naaman left.

THINK AND TALK
Being *content* means being happy with what you have. How can you tell if a person is content? How can you tell if a person is not content? At first Naaman was not content with the way Elisha told him to get well. Naaman complained. Why did Naaman change his mind?

PRACTICE
Read the verse. Try to repeat it several times without looking. Cut a sword shape from paper or cardboard and write the verse on it.

You'll want to hang it up in your house where it will remind you of the Spirit's sword from Philippians 2:14. You can use it to fight against the temptation to complain or argue.

DAY 2

READ

Numbers 11 ("Piles of Quail," page 77 in the *Day By Day Kid's Bible*)
Now some of the people wanted different food. "We wish we had meat to eat," they said. "We remember the fish we had in Egypt. We got it free! We ate cucumbers and melons. We had leeks and onions and garlic. But now we don't even like to eat. We don't see any food but this manna!"

THINK AND TALK

What choices did God's people have? What did they choose to do? Why does God want us to be content with what we have? Why does he want us not to complain? Why does he not want us to argue? Is there a difference between pointing out a problem and complaining about it? Explain. Is there a difference between expressing your feelings and complaining? Explain.

PRACTICE

Challenge a friend or family member (or yourself) to a sword-fight. One person says, "What will you do if you are tempted to complain or argue?" The other person answers, "I will not complain or argue, because it is written, 'Do everything without complaining or arguing.'"

DAY 3

READ

Genesis 13 ("Lot Chooses His Land," page 10 in the *Day By Day Kid's Bible*)
Lot's servants took care of Lot's sheep and cows. Abram's servants took care of Abram's sheep and cows. But Lot's servants began to fuss and fight with Abram's servants. Abram told Lot, "Let's not fuss and fight. Let's not allow our servants to fuss and fight. Don't we have all this land around us? Let's live in different places."

THINK AND TALK

What choices did all of these servants have? What did they choose to do? Why were the servants complaining and arguing? Was there a real problem? What could they have done to solve their problem instead of complaining and arguing? How do you feel when someone complains to you? How do you feel when someone argues with you? When is it hardest for you to be content?

PRACTICE
Challenge someone to a sword-fight with your sword for this week. Write on an index card: "You are tempted to complain or argue." Add this temptation card to the other cards you've collected. Place these in a bowl. The first person draws a card and challenges the other person with that temptation. The second person repeats the sword of the Spirit that he can use to fight the temptation. Then it's his turn to draw a card and challenge the first person.

DAY 4

READ
Luke 12:13-21 ("The Rich Man's Barns," page 544 in the *Day By Day Kid's Bible*)
A rich man grew lots of crops on his farm. "What should I do?" said the rich man. I don't have a place to keep all my crops." Then the rich man said, "I know! I'll take down my old barns. I will build bigger barns. Then I can store all my crops... I can eat. I can drink. I can be happy."

THINK AND TALK
What choices did the rich man have? What did he choose to do? The rich man said he'd eat and drink and be happy after he built bigger barns and stored more crops. What was keeping him from being happy and content with what he already had? Are you content with what you have, or do you complain and want more? Will more things make you content? Someone once said, "If you're not happy now, you never will be happy." Is that true? Why or why not?

PRACTICE

You and another person challenge each other to practice fighting temptation. Do this by taking turns drawing the temptation cards from a bowl. Ask each other what you would do if you were tempted in that way, and answer by saying the appropriate verse.

TRY THIS
Start a collection of your choice. You can collect rocks or stamps or hats or pressed flowers or insects or leaves or shells. Why might it be hard for someone with a collection to be content?

DAY 5

READ
1 Timothy 6 ("Loving Money," page 753 in the *Day By Day Kid's Bible*)
Here's what is best. It's being good and being happy with what you have. We didn't bring anything into the world with us. We can't take anything out of the world with us. We should be happy to have food and clothes.

THINK AND TALK
Tell about someone you know who is content. Tell about someone you know who complains and is not content. What are you tempted to complain about? Why would it be wrong to complain about it? Could you talk about it without complaining? If so, how?

PRACTICE
Challenge someone to practice fighting temptation. Do this by taking turns drawing the temptation cards from a bowl. Ask each other what you would do if you were tempted in that way.

TRY THIS
Write one word of your memory onto each of six index cards. Write the Scripture reference Philippians 2:14 onto another index card. Stretch a clothesline or string across a room or outdoors. Then let someone mix up the cards and hang them on the clothesline with clothespins. Time yourself to see how long it takes you to put the cards in order.

DAY 6

READ

1 Kings 21 ("King Ahab and the Grape Field," p. 288 in *Day By Day Kid's Bible*)

King Ahab told Naboth, "I want your grape field. I want to make it into a vegetable garden... " "No," said Naboth. "This field has belonged to my family for many years... " King Ahab went home. He was sad and angry. He lay down on his bed. He wouldn't eat anything. Jezebel, his wife, came in. "Why are you sad and angry?" she asked... "Naboth won't sell me his grape field," said Ahab.

THINK AND TALK

What choices did Ahab have? What did he choose to do? Ahab was tempted to complain to Jezebel. Did he fall for the temptation? What was happening in his heart that caused him to complain? What happened because Ahab chose to complain? What are some attitudes that we might have in our hearts that could lead to complaining or arguing?

PRACTICE

Challenge someone to practice fighting temptation. Do this by taking turns drawing the temptation cards from a bowl. Ask each other what you would do if you were tempted in that way.

TRY THIS

Spread a little bit of purple, water-based, washable paint across a paper plate. Spread some light green paint on another plate. On a third paper plate, you will make grape designs. Press one of your thumbs into the purple paint. Then press that thumb onto the clean paper plate to make a grape. Make lots of purple grapes until you have a bunch of grapes. With your other thumb, you can make green grapes. When your grape painting is dry, write the memory verse for this week on the border around the plate.

DAY 7

READ

Philippians 4:10-13 ("Show Your Joy!," page 748 in the *Day By Day Kid's Bible*)

I've learned how to be happy no matter what. I know what it's like to need things. I know what it's like to have more than enough. I've learned the secret of being happy all the time. I can be happy if I'm well-fed. I can be happy if I'm hungry. I can be happy if I have all I need. I can be happy if I need things. The secret is this. I can do everything with Jesus' help. He makes me strong.

THINK AND TALK

Is it always easy to be content? What are some things you can do to help yourself be content? What would you suggest to a friend who was tempted to complain or argue?

PRACTICE

Challenge someone to practice fighting temptation. Do this by taking turns drawing the temptation cards from a bowl. Ask each other what you would do if you were tempted in that way.

TRY THIS

Get a small box, any kind. Cover it with Con-Tact paper, gift wrap, or plain paper. Cover the lid separately so you can just lift it off to open the box. Or you can paint the box and lid. Write "My Secret" on the box. On a small piece of paper, write the secret that Paul discovered: "I can do everything with Jesus' help." This can be your secret too. Place this secret in your box to remind you of how you can be content.

Being Prayerful

Your sword of the Spirit for this week is:

Never stop praying. 1 THESSALONIANS 5:17

With the above sword you can fight back when you face this temptation:

You are tempted not to pray.

DAY 1

READ

Daniel 6 ("Lions!" page 456 in the *Day By Day Kid's Bible*)

[The] leaders tried to find something wrong with Daniel. But they couldn't. Daniel was someone you could trust. He didn't do wrong... So the leaders went to the king... "We think you should make a law. Tell people to pray only to you for the next 30 days. Anyone who doesn't obey will be thrown into the lions' den" ...So King Darius wrote the law down. Then the men went to see Daniel. They found him praying to God.

THINK AND TALK

Have you ever been someplace where the radio is on all the time? Or maybe there have been times when the weather was stormy and your family kept the radio or TV on all day to hear storm warnings. You were *tuned* in to the radio or TV station. *Prayerfulness* is being tuned in to God. To "never stop praying," you have to know that God is beside you all day, every day. And you talk to him just like you'd talk to a friend, except you might talk to God silently. When do most people pray? Why do you think

Daniel might have been tempted not to pray? What happened because of Daniel's choice to pray?

PRACTICE
Read the verse. Try to repeat it several times without looking. Cut a sword shape from paper or cardboard and write the verse on it. You'll want to hang it up in your house where it will remind you of the Spirit's sword from 1 Thessalonians 5:17. You can use it to fight against the temptation not to pray.

DAY 2

READ
Genesis 24:1-27 ("Looking for a Wife," page 18 in the *Day By Day Kid's Bible*)
The servant prayed. "God," he said. "... I am standing by the well. The women are coming to get water here. I'll speak to one of the girls. I'll ask her to get me some water with her jar. Show me the one you choose, God. Have her give me a drink. Have her say that she will give my camels water, too. Then I'll know you want her to be Isaac's wife." ...Before the servant stopped praying, Rebekah came to the well.

THINK AND TALK
The servant talked to God as if God were his friend standing right beside him. He talked to God about the help he needed. What can we talk to God about? Is there anything we should not talk to God about? Why or why not? Why does God want us to be prayerful? What happens when we're not prayerful?

PRACTICE
Challenge a friend or family member (or yourself) to a sword-fight. One person says, "What will you do if you are tempted not to pray?" The other person answers, "I will pray anyway, because it is written, 'Never stop praying.'"

DAY 3
READ
Matthew 6:5-15 ("Your Secret," page 533 in the *Day By Day Kid's*

Bible)
"Don't pray just so others will see you... This is how you should pray," said Jesus. "Our Father in heaven, your name is wonderful. Bring your kingdom here to earth. We pray that what you want will be done on earth like it is in heaven. Give us the food we need each day. Forgive us for our sin. Forgive us as we forgive people who sin against us. Don't let anyone try to make us do wrong. Save us from Satan, the enemy."

THINK AND TALK
Do you think Jesus was ever tempted not to pray? Why or why not? Lots of times, Jesus went off by himself to pray. Do you have a special place where you go to pray? If you don't, think about where your special place could be. Where else can you pray? Are you ever tempted not to pray? When is it hardest for you to be prayerful?

PRACTICE
Challenge someone to sword-fight with your sword for this week. Write on an index card: "You are tempted not to pray." Add this temptation card to the other cards you've collected. Place these into a bowl. The first person draws a card and challenges the second person with that temptation. The second person repeats the sword of the Spirit that she can use in order to fight that temptation. Then it's her turn to draw a card and challenge the first person.

DAY 4

READ
Nehemiah 1; 2:1-6 ("The Broken Wall" and "Burned Gates," page 489 and 490 in the *Day By Day Kid's Bible*)
These are the words of Nehemiah... One day I took the king's wine to him. The king had never seen a sad look on my face before. So he asked, "Why are you sad?... " I was afraid. But I told the king, "It's because of Jerusalem. It's a pile of sticks and stones. Fire has burned up its gates. That's why I look sad." "What do you want to do about it?" asked the king. I prayed to God. Then I answered the king... "Let me build the city back up." ...He was glad to send me.

THINK AND TALK

Do you think that Nehemiah was ever tempted not to pray? Why would a choose not to pray? Nehemiah didn't even wait until he got home to pray. After the king asked Nehemiah what was wrong, Nehemiah prayed quickly and silently. He knew how to "never stop praying." Is it all right to *practice* praying always? What are some things you can do to help yourself remember to pray always?

PRACTICE

You and another person can challenge each other to practice fighting temptation. Do this by taking turns drawing the temptation cards from a bowl. Ask each other what you would do if you were tempted in that way.

TRY THIS

Try to make a house out of playing cards. Stand the cards on end and slowly, carefully lean them against each other. This may take some practice. If this seems too hard, use old cards with a bit of Play-Doh or clay to stand the cards on. You can build a whole city this way. Remember the city of Jerusalem that was torn down.

DAY 5

READ

2 Kings 20:1-11 ("A Shadow Moves Backward," page 358 in the *Day By Day Kid's Bible*)

King Hezekiah got sick. He was dying. Isaiah went to see him. Isaiah said, "Here's what God says. Get everything ready. You won't get well. You're going to die." Hezekiah turned to the wall. He prayed... Isaiah was leaving when God spoke to him. "Go back to Hezekiah. Tell him that I heard his prayer. I saw him cry. I will make him well."

THINK AND TALK

What choices did Hezekiah have? Why might Hezekiah have been tempted not to pray? What did he choose to do? God answered his prayer right away. If God had not answered right away, do you think Hezekiah would have been tempted to stop praying? Why or why not? When are you tempted to stop praying?

PRACTICE

Challenge someone to practice fighting temptation. Do this by taking turns drawing the temptation cards from a bowl. Ask each other what you would do if you were tempted in that way.

TRY THIS

You can do this indoors or outdoors during the day when the sun is shining. Find a spot where an object is making an interesting shadow. Lay a piece of paper on the most interesting spot and trace around the design the shadow makes on the paper. You can make several shadow tracings this way, using a different piece of paper for each shadow. Now look back at the tracings and see if they remind you of anything. Maybe one looks like a person. Maybe another looks like a strange animal. Color around these tracings to make pictures. Read the whole story of Hezekiah to find out what he learned from a shadow.

DAY 6

READ

1 Timothy 2 ("Listen and Learn," page 750 in the *Day By Day Kid's Bible*)
Pray for everybody. Ask God to give people what they need. Thank God for them. Pray for kings. Pray for anybody who is in charge. Pray that we can be godly and clean in our hearts. Pray so our lives can be full of peace and quiet. When we pray for these things, God is happy. He wants everybody to be saved. He wants everybody to know the truth. There is one God. There is one person who talks to God for people. That's Jesus. He gave his life to buy us back from sin. I want all people to lift up their hands to pray.

THINK AND TALK

First Timothy is a letter that Paul wrote to Timothy. Paul says that God is happy when we pray for the things he listed. Why is God happy when we pray for those things? Name some people and things you normally pray for. Tell about some people you know who are prayerful. How do you know that they are prayerful? What are their prayers like? Do you think they are ever tempted not to pray?

59

PRACTICE

Challenge someone to practice fighting temptation. Do this by taking turns drawing the temptation cards from a bowl. Ask each other what you would do if you were tempted in that way.

TRY THIS

Cut a piece of thin cardboard, posterboard or construction paper into a rectangle one and one-half inches wide and six inches long. This will be a bookmark for your Bible. On this bookmark, write a list of leaders you will pray for. You can also make designs on the bookmark. You can cover it with clear Con-Tact paper if you want.

DAY 7

READ

Psalm 32 ("Not like a Horse," page 216 in the *Day By Day Kid's Bible*)

People are happy when God throws away the list of their sins... I said, "I will tell God about my sins." Then you forgave me. So everyone who loves you should pray to you. You are like a place for me to hide. You give me songs about how you save me.

THINK AND TALK

David wrote this psalm. It's a prayer. It says that everyone who loves God should pray to him. Why should they pray? Do you think David was ever tempted not to pray? Is it always easy to pray? Why or why not? What are some things that can distract us and cause us to forget to pray? What can you do to help yourself remember to pray?

PRACTICE

Challenge someone to practice fighting temptation. Do this by taking turns drawing the temptation cards from a bowl. Ask each other what you would do if you were tempted in that way.

TRY THIS

Decorate the front of a small notebook to make a prayer journal. Inside this journal, write down what you pray about each day. You'll want to put the date beside each item on your list. You can look back in the journal to see how God has answered your prayers.

Showing Optimism

Your sword of the Spirit for this week is:

All things work together for good to them who love God. ROMANS 8:28

With the above sword you can fight back when you face this temptation:

You are tempted to be pessimistic.

DAY 1

READ

2 Kings 6:8-23 ("What Elisha Saw," page 302 in the *Day By Day Kid's Bible*)

Elisha's helper, Gehazi, got up early the next day. He looked out and saw the army around the city. He saw the horses and chariots. "What are we going to do?" he called to Elisha. "Don't be scared," said Elisha. "Our army is bigger than theirs." Then Elisha prayed. He said, "God, let Gehazi see." So God let Gehazi see. He looked out and saw another army all over the hills. It was an army of horses and chariots of fire.

THINK AND TALK

Optimism is looking for what's good in everything that happens. It's expecting that the best will come from whatever happens. It's being cheerful about life. *Pessimism* is looking at all the things that could go wrong in everything that happens. It's expecting that the worst will come from whatever happens. It's being gloomy about life. Why can God's people be optimistic? Why was Gehazi

tempted to be pessimistic? Why could he be optimistic instead?
It's hard to be optimistic unless you're trusting in God.

PRACTICE
Read the verse. Try to repeat it several times without looking. Cut
a sword shape from paper or cardboard and write the verse on it.
You'll want to hang it up in your house where it will remind you of
the Spirit's sword from Romans 8:28. You can use it to fight against
the temptation to be pessimistic.

DAY 2

READ
Matthew 14:22-33 ("On Top of the Water," page 557 in the *Day By
Day Kid's Bible*)
From the hill, Jesus saw his friends in their boat... They were trying
to go one way. But the wind was blowing them the other way.
About three o'clock in the morning, Jesus went out to them. He
walked right on top of the water. Jesus' friends... got scared when
they saw him.... "It's just me," said Jesus. "Don't be afraid." "If it's
really you, tell me to come to you," said Peter. "Let me walk on the
water too." "Come on," said Jesus. So Peter got out of the boat.
He stepped onto the water. He began to walk to Jesus.

THINK AND TALK
If you had been in the boat with Jesus' friends, would you have
been optimistic (expecting the best) about Peter walking to Jesus,
or would you have been pessimistic (expecting the worst)? How
did Peter feel about it? After Peter started walking toward Jesus,
what happened to tempt him to become pessimistic? What are
some things that can tempt us to feel pessimistic about life?

PRACTICE
Challenge a friend or family member (or yourself) to a sword-fight.
One person says, "What if you are tempted to be pessimistic and
think the worst will happen?" The other person answers, "I will not
be pessimistic, because it is written, 'All things work together for
good to those who love God.'"

DAY 3

READ

2 Kings 4:1-7 ("Oil to Sell," page 296 in the *Day By Day Kid's Bible*)
One day a prophet died. His wife went to Elisha, crying. "My husband is dead," she said. "You know how much he loved God. But he owed some money. The man he owed it to wants to take my two boys."... "Go to your neighbors," said Elisha. "Ask them... for lots of jars.... Fill each jar with oil." So the woman left. She did what Elisha said... "Now go and sell the jars of oil," said Elisha. "Pay the man the money your husband owed him."

THINK AND TALK

What tempted the woman to be pessimistic (to expect the worst)? Did she have any reason to be optimistic? Why or why not? How can you tell if a person is optimistic? How can you tell if a person is pessimistic? Why does God want us to be optimistic?

PRACTICE

Challenge someone to a sword-fight with your sword for this week. Write on an index card: "You are tempted to be pessimistic (expect the worst)." Add this temptation card to the other cards you've collected. Place these in a bowl. The first person draws a card and challenges the second person with that temptation. The second person repeats the sword of the Spirit that he can use to fight the temptation. Then it's his turn to draw a card and challenge the first person.

DAY 4

READ

Acts 16:16-36 ("The Earth Shakes," page 663 in the *Day By Day Kid's Bible*)
The Roman leaders had Paul and Silas beaten... Then the leaders had them put in jail... At midnight, Paul and Silas were praying. They were singing songs to God. The other people who had been put in jail were listening. All of a sudden, the earth began to shake hard. The floors of the jail shook. Everybody's chains fell off.

THINK AND TALK

Why might Paul and Silas have been tempted to be pessimistic (to expect the worst)? Did they act like they were pessimistic or optimistic? Why could they be optimistic (expect the best)? Tell about someone you know who is optimistic. Are you optimistic or pessimistic? Why?

PRACTICE

You and another person can challenge each other to practice fighting temptation. Do this by taking turns drawing the temptation cards from a bowl. Ask each other what you would do if you were tempted in that way.

TRY THIS

Fold an index card in half, with the fold at the middle of the long side. Open it up again. On the left half, draw lines from top to bottom to make jail bars. On the right half, close to the center fold line, draw two faces or two figures, one to be Paul and the other to be Silas. Now hold the card in your hand with your arm stretched all the way out in front of you, and look at the center fold line. Keep looking at this line as you bring the card closer and closer to your eyes. As you get closer, you will have to "unfocus" your eyes, but keep them looking at the line. All at once, you will see Paul and Silas in jail.

DAY 5

READ

1 Samuel 23:13-18 ("Hiding Places," page 148 in the *Day By Day Kid's Bible*)

David was staying in the Ziph Desert. He found out that Saul was coming after him. But Jonathan went to see David there. He said, "Don't be scared. Saul won't hurt you. You'll be the king of God's people."

THINK AND TALK

What reason did David and Jonathan have to be pessimistic? Did they choose to be pessimistic or optimistic? How can you tell? Why do you think Jonathan was optimistic? When is it hardest for you to be optimistic?

PRACTICE

Challenge someone to practice fighting temptation. Do this by taking turns drawing the temptation cards from a bowl. Ask each other what you would do if you were tempted in that way.

TRY THIS

With crayons, draw a desert scene on sandpaper. When you are finished, lay a piece of waxed paper across the picture. Place it on some old newspaper on top of an ironing board. Iron over the waxed paper to melt the crayon onto the sandpaper. Be careful with the hot iron. Ask an adult to supervise. Does a desert have to be hot and sandy? Why do you think David chose the desert as his hiding place?

DAY 6

READ

Joshua 10:1-15 ("Sun and Moon Stand Still," page 101 in the *Day By Day Kid's Bible*)

The people of Gibeon sent a message to Joshua. "Come fast! Save us! The kings from the hills are trying to fight us." ... God told Joshua, "Don't be afraid. I'll make you win." Joshua and his army marched all night long. The kings and their armies were surprised to see God's people... God's people chased the kings' armies... That day Joshua prayed, "Let the sun stand still. Let the moon stand still." The sun did stand still. The moon stopped moving across the sky... God really was fighting for his people.

THINK AND TALK

What choices did Joshua have? How could Joshua be optimistic about the battle he was fighting? What are some things that might have tempted him to be pessimistic? What are some things that tempt you to be pessimistic? How do you feel around pessimistic people? How do you feel around optimistic people?

PRACTICE

Challenge someone to practice fighting temptation. Do this by taking turns drawing the temptation cards from a bowl. Ask each other what you would do if you were tempted in that way.

TRY THIS

Make "Sunwiches." Cut a flat square of cheese into a sun shape. Place this on top of a piece of bread and heat it under the broiler in your oven just until the cheese starts to melt and bubble. As you eat your sunwich, think about what would happen if the sun stood still in the sky right now for the length of a day.

DAY 7

READ

Romans 8:35-39 ("More Than Winners," page 708 in the *Day By Day Kid's Bible*)

If God is for us, who can be against us? ...I am sure of this. Death can't keep us from God's love. Life can't. Angels can't. Bad spirits can't. Nothing with us right now can keep God's love away. Nothing that can happen will keep God's love away. No power can keep God's love away, nothing high or low. Nothing in the world can keep God's love from us.

THINK AND TALK

Paul wrote this letter to the Romans. Does it sound as though Paul is optimistic or pessimistic? How can you tell? Is it always easy to be optimistic? What are some things you can do to help yourself be optimistic? What would you suggest to a friend who is pessimistic?

PRACTICE

Challenge someone to practice fighting temptation. Do this by taking turns drawing the temptation cards from a bowl. Ask each other what you would do if you were tempted in that way.

TRY THIS

With a sharp permanent marker, draw the general shapes of the countries onto a large orange as though the orange were a globe. Then stick whole cloves into the orange inside the shapes where the countries are. The cloves form the land and the orange rind that shows is where the oceans are. Let this dry to make a air freshener. It can remind you that nothing in the world can keep God's love from you.

Relying On God

Your sword of the Spirit for this week is:

**Trust in the Lord with all your heart
and lean not on your own understanding;
in all your ways acknowledge him,
and he will make your paths straight.**
PROVERBS 3:5-6

With the above sword you can fight back when you face this temptation:

You are tempted to rely on yourself or something else other than God.

DAY 1

READ
Exodus 16 ("Making a Fuss for Food," page 62 in the *Day By Day Kid's Bible*)
God said to Moses, "Tell the people they will eat meat tonight. Tomorrow morning they'll eat bread. Then they'll know that I am the Lord." That evening fat little birds called quail flew in. They were all over the camp. The next morning... it looked like bits of ice covered the ground. But it wasn't ice. It was thin flakes of bread. "What is it?" the people asked. "It's the bread God sent you," said Moses.

THINK AND TALK
If you *rely* on someone or something, then you depend on them. You count on them. You trust them to take care of things. God's

people were traveling, so they couldn't grow their own food. They were not going through cities, so they couldn't buy their own food. Who did they have to rely on? How did God show that he was *reliable*, that he can be trusted? How has God shown you and your family or friends that he is reliable?

PRACTICE
Read the verse. Try to repeat it several times without looking. Cut a sword shape from paper or cardboard and write the verse on it. You'll want to hang it up in your house where it will remind you of the Spirit's sword from Proverbs 3:5-6. You can use it to fight against the temptation to rely on yourself or something other than God.

DAY 2

READ
1 Kings 17:1-6 ("No Rain, No Food," page 280 in the *Day By Day Kid's Bible*)
Then God told Elijah, "Go east. Hide by the brook there. Drink water from the brook. I have told the birds to bring you food." So Elijah obeyed God. He stayed by the brook. Big, black birds called ravens brought food to him. They brought bread and meat every morning and every evening. Elijah drank water out of the brook.

THINK AND TALK
What choices did Elijah have? What might Elijah have done if he had tried to rely on himself or something other than God? How can you tell when a person is relying on God? How can you tell when a person is not relying on God? What are some things people are tempted to rely on besides God?

PRACTICE
Challenge a friend or family member (or yourself) to a sword-fight. One person says, "What will you do if you are tempted to rely on yourself or something else instead God?" The other person answers, "I will rely only on God, because it is written, 'Trust in the Lord with all your heart and lean not on your own understanding; in all your ways acknowledge him, and he will make your paths straight.'"

DAY 3

READ

Genesis 12:1-9 ("Abram's Travels Begin," page 9 in the *Day By Day Kid's Bible*)

God talked to a man named Abram. God said, "Leave this land. Leave these people... I will show you a new land to live in. I am going to give you a family." ...Abram was 75 years old. But he did what God told him.

THINK AND TALK

Abram didn't have a map. In fact, he didn't even know just where he was going. What would have happened if Abram decided he would rely on himself? What would have happened if Abram decided he would rely on someone else besides God? Why does God want us to rely on him? What happens when we don't rely on God?

PRACTICE

Challenge someone to a sword-fight with your sword for this week. Write on an index card: "You are tempted to rely on yourself." Add this temptation card to the others you've collected. Place these cards in a bowl. The first person draws a card and challenges the second person with that temptation. The second person repeats the sword of the Spirit that she can use to fight the temptation. Then it's his turn to draw a card and challenge the first person.

DAY 4

READ

Genesis 3 ("The Snake's Trick," page 5 in the *Day By Day Kid's Bible*)

Now the snake was tricky. He talked to the woman. "Did God say not to eat fruit from the trees?" "No," she said. "We may eat fruit. Just not from the tree in the middle of the Garden... We'll die if we do." "You won't die," said the snake. "God knows that the fruit will make you wise. Just like God. You will know good and bad." The woman looked at the fruit... Since she thought it would make her wise, she ate some.

THINK AND TALK

What choices did Eve have? If Eve was relying on God to take care of her, why did she think she needed to be wise? Could it be that she didn't quite trust God, so she decided to rely on herself? What happened because of Eve's choice? Why is it hard to rely on God? When is it hardest for you to rely on God?

PRACTICE

You and another person can challenge each other to practice fighting temptation. Do this by taking turns drawing the temptation cards from a bowl. Ask each other what you would do if you were tempted in that way.

TRY THIS

Lay a plate on top of a piece of white paper. Draw around the plate with a pencil. Take the plate off. Place the tip of your pencil at any point on the line you drew to make the circle. Now begin drawing a spiral inside of the circle, making more circles. Each one will get smaller until finally you reach the center of the circle. With your scissors, cut the circle out. Then cut along the spiral line. As it drops away, it will make a figure that looks like a coiled snake. You can tie a string to the inner point of the spiral and hang it up if you want. Why do you think Eve believed the snake?

DAY 5

READ

John 5:1-15 ("At the Pool," page 526 in the *Day By Day Kid's Bible*) Lots of sick people came to the pool. They thought the water could make them well when it bubbled... One man hadn't been able to walk for 38 years... So Jesus asked him, "Do you want to get well?" "Yes," said the man. "But no one will help me into the pool. The water bubbles. Then I try to get in. But somebody else always gets in first." Then Jesus said, "Get up. Pick up your mat. Walk."

THINK AND TALK

Before Jesus found him, who had the lame man been relying on to get well? Part of growing up is realizing that no person is totally reliable. Nothing is totally reliable except God. God will never let us down. He will never leave us. When Jesus told the lame man to walk, the lame man had a choice. Did he choose to rely on Jesus? Was Jesus reliable? Is Jesus still reliable? Tell about a time when you relied on Jesus.

PRACTICE
Challenge someone to practice fighting temptation. You can take turns drawing the temptation cards from a bowl. Ask each other what you would do if you were tempted in that way.

TRY THIS
Make chocolate-cinnamon bubble milk. Pour yourself a mug of milk. Add a chocolate drink mix to it, and heat it in the microwave. Place a stick of cinnamon into your warm chocolate and gently blow, making bubbles to cover the top. If you are going to make these for your family and friends, let each person blow his own bubbles! Can you trust Jesus the way the man at the bubbling pool did?

DAY 6

READ
Proverbs 16:3; 18:2; 18:10; 19:3; 20:24; 28:26; 29:25 ("Trusting," page 232 in the *Day By Day Kid's Bible*)
Let God be in charge of whatever you do. Then your plans will work out for good... How can anybody know what to do? God shows people what to do. People who trust in themselves are foolish. But those who are wise are safe.

THINK AND TALK
Why are people who trust in themselves foolish? Have you ever trusted in yourself instead of God? If so, what happened? Do you think it's possible that sometimes God guides us even when we forget to rely on him? Why or why not? Tell about someone you know who relies on God. Why is God reliable?

PRACTICE
Challenge someone to practice fighting temptation. Do this by

taking turns drawing the temptation cards from a bowl. Ask each other what you would do if you were tempted in that way.

TRY THIS
Make a calendar for next month. Place one piece of white paper over a calendar page. Any month, any year will do, because all you are going to do is trace the squares. When you are finished, look at a calendar that shows you the dates to place in the squares for next month. Write the dates into the squares of your calendar. Write the name of the month above it and design a border for the calendar. As you make your plans for the month, remember to let God be in charge of whatever you do.

DAY 7

READ
Psalm 146 ("Do Not Trust Princes," page 218 in the *Day By Day Kid's Bible*)
Don't trust the leaders of the land to save you. They are only people. When they die, their plans become nothing. But good things come to people who let God be their helper... He always keeps his promises. ...God is King forever. Cheer for God!

THINK AND TALK
Who are some of the people that we rely on? Why do we rely on them? Are they totally reliable? Is it all right to rely on people for some things? Why or why not? Is it always easy to rely on God? What would you suggest to a friend who has a hard time relying on God?

PRACTICE
Challenge someone to practice fighting temptation. Do this by taking turns drawing the temptation cards from a bowl. Ask each other what you would do if you were tempted in that way.

TRY THIS
Look through magazines and cut out pictures of things that people might rely on. Glue these pictures onto a posterboard or piece of paper to make a montage. On this montage, write, "Trust in the Lord with all your heart."

Having Patience

Your sword of the Spirit for this week is:

Be patient, bearing with one another in love.
EPHESIANS 4:2b

With the above sword you can fight back when you face this temptation:

You are tempted to be impatient.

DAY 1

READ

Ecclesiastes 3:1-8 ("A Time for Everything," page 262 in the *Day By Day Kid's Bible*)

There's a time for everything... A time to be born, and a time to die. A time to plant, and a time to pull plants up. A time to kill, and a time to heal. A time to break, and a time to build. A time to cry, and a time to laugh... A time to be quiet, and a time to talk. A time to love, and a time to hate. A time for war, and a time for peace.

THINK AND TALK

Being *patient* means waiting without complaining. If we complain, then we are being *impatient*. What are some things that we can get almost instantly whenever we want them? What are some things that we must wait for? Have you ever said, "I just can't wait until... "? What was it that you couldn't wait for?

PRACTICE

Read the verse. Try to repeat it several times without looking. Cut

73

a sword shape from paper or cardboard and write the verse on it. You'll want to hang it up in your house where it will remind you of the Spirit's sword from Ephesians 4:2b. You can use it to fight against the temptation to be impatient.

DAY 2

READ
Luke 5:1-11 ("Nets Full of Fish," page 522 in the *Day By Day Kid's Bible*)
When Jesus finished talking, he turned to Peter. "Take the boat into deep water now," he said. "Then put your nets out. We can catch some fish." "We fished all night," said Peter. "It was hard work, and we didn't catch anything. But if you say so, I'll put the nets out." The men threw out their nets. Right away, hundreds of fish swam into the nets.

THINK AND TALK
If you've ever gone fishing, tell about the patience a fisherman must have. Jesus asked Peter to go fishing *again*. If you have tried something and it didn't work, it takes patience to try again. Do you think Peter may have been tempted to be impatient? What did Peter choose to do? Why? What happened because of his choice? Tell about a time when you had to be patient.

PRACTICE
Challenge a friend or family member (or yourself) to a sword-fight. One person says, "What will you do if you are tempted to be impatient?" The other person answers, "I will not be impatient, because it is written, 'Be patient, bearing with one another in love.'"

DAY 3

READ
Genesis 29:16-30 ("Working for a Wife," page 26 in the *Day By Day Kid's Bible*)
Now Laban had two daughters. Rachel had a big sister named Leah. But Rachel was prettier than Leah. Jacob loved Rachel. So he said, "Will you let Rachel marry me? If you will, I'll work seven

years for you." "That's fine," said Laban. "You may stay here and work for me." Jacob worked for seven years so he could marry Rachel. But it didn't seem like a long time to Jacob. That's because he loved Rachel so much.

THINK AND TALK
Do you think Jacob might have been tempted to be impatient some time during the seven years when he was working for Laban? Did Jacob choose to be patient or impatient? Why does God want us to be patient? What happens when we are not patient?

PRACTICE
Challenge someone to sword-fight with your sword for this week. Write on an index card: "You are tempted to be impatient." Add this temptation card to the other cards you've collected. Place these cards in a bowl. The first person draws a card and challenges the second person with that temptation. The second person repeats the sword of the Spirit that he can use to fight the temptation. Then it's his turn to draw a card and challenge the first person.

DAY 4

READ
Luke 2:41-52 ("In the Big City," page 510 in the *Day By Day Kid's Bible*)
Once a year, Joseph and Mary went to Jerusalem. They went for the Pass Over holiday. When Jesus was 12 years old, he went too. After the special holiday for God, Joseph and Mary began the trip home. But Jesus stayed in Jerusalem... Then Joseph and Mary began to look for Jesus... He was in the worship house, sitting with the teachers... Everyone was surprised by how much he understood... Jesus went back to Nazareth with Joseph and Mary.

THINK AND TALK
Jesus knew that God was his Father. He knew that he had a special job to do here on earth. But he was 12 years old. He didn't start traveling and teaching until he was 30 years old. How many years did he have to wait in between? Do you think Jesus might

have been tempted to be impatient? How could he be patient? What are some things you can do to help yourself be patient?

PRACTICE
You and another person can challenge each other to practice fighting temptation. Take turns drawing the temptation cards from a bowl. Ask each other what you would do if you were tempted in that way.

TRY THIS
Set up a treasure hunt. Hide some cookies or other goodies. Then place a clue under someone's plate at the dinner table. This clue should lead them to another location. For example, it might say, "At the stop of the stairs, there is a chair. Look around somewhere under there." Under the chair, there should be another clue that leads them to another location. Each location should give your family a new clue until they finally come to the last location where the treat is. Where do you think Mary and Joseph might have looked first when they went back to Jerusalem to find Jesus?

DAY 5

READ
1 Samuel 13 ("Hiding," page 133 in the Day By Day Kid's Bible) Samuel had told Saul to wait seven days for him. Samuel was going to offer gifts to God before the fight. He was going to ask God to help Saul's army. But when Samuel didn't come, Saul's men started leaving him. So Saul said, "Bring me the things to offer to God." Then Saul offered the gifts on the altar. Right after that, Samuel came. "What did you do?" asked Samuel. "My men were leaving," said Saul.... "So I had to offer the gifts to God myself." "That was not wise," said Samuel... "Now your kingdom won't last."

THINK AND TALK
Saul was tempted to be impatient and not to wait for Samuel. What choices did Saul have? What did Saul choose to do?   What happened because of his choice? Tell about a time when you were impatient. When you were patient? When is it hardest for you to

be patient?

PRACTICE
Challenge someone to practice fighting temptation. You can take turns drawing the temptation cards from a bowl. Ask each other what you would do if you were tempted in that way.

TRY THIS
Stand in a circle with friends or family. Toss a ball to one of the people in the circle. When that person catches the ball, he must say the first word of the memory verse. Then he tosses the ball to another person, and this person must say the next word. Keep tossing the ball and letting each person who catches the ball say another word of the verse until the verse has been finished. Then try to go backward, tossing the ball to the person who tossed it to you. This time each person must say the whole verse when he catches the ball.

DAY 6

READ
Proverbs 21:5; 29:20; 14:29 ("Anger, Waiting, and Selfishness," page 241 in the *Day By Day Kid's Bible*)
Good comes from the plans of people who think and act carefully. But people who get in a hurry become poor. Do you see somebody who is in a hurry to talk? There is more hope for a fool than for that person... A person who waits quietly understands many things. But a person who gets angry too fast is a fool.

THINK AND TALK
Patience means waiting quietly. Why would a patient person understand many things? Why is it foolish to get angry too fast? Tell about some you know who is patient. When do people need to be patient with you? How do you feel when someone is impatient with you? How do you feel when someone is patient with you?

PRACTICE
Challenge someone to practice fighting temptation. Do this by

taking turns drawing the temptation cards from a bowl. Ask each other what you would do if you were tempted in that way.

TRY THIS
Cut paper fish out of index cards or paper. Write a number on each fish. Tape a paper clip to the back of each fish. Make a fishing pole by tying one end of a string to a magnet and the other end to an unsharpened pencil, a stick, or a dowel. Take turns catching the fish by letting the magnet stick to a paper clip. Add up the points of the fish that each person catches. The person with the highest score wins. Why does real fishing take patience?

DAY 7

READ
Psalm 37 ("Like the Sun at Noon," page 193 in the *Day By Day Kid's Bible*)
Be with God, and be still. Be quiet and wait for him. Don't worry when sinful people get away with doing wrong... Sinful people will not get God's riches. But people who trust God will get all God has for them. Some day sinful people will be gone... But God's people will always have his riches. They will enjoy peace.

THINK AND TALK
Is it always easy to be patient? Why or why not? What are some things that can tempt us to be impatient? What would you suggest to a friend who is having a hard time being patient?

PRACTICE
Challenge someone to practice fighting temptation. Do this by taking turns drawing the temptation cards from a bowl. Ask each other what you would do if you were tempted in that way.

TRY THIS
You can make a one-minute timer. Use two small plastic cups, the kind used to taking cough medicine or to give young children their medicine. Turn one of the cups upside down on a paper plate and draw around it with a pencil. Now make a square around the circle

you just drew, and cut the square out. Trace around that square onto the paper plate and cut that square out too. Now poke a small hole into the center of the bottom of the cup. Ask an adult to help if you use anything sharp. Place the bottom of the second cup against the bottom of the first one, and poke a hole through the first cup to the bottom of the second one. Holding your finger over this hole, pour salt into it. Place the cup over a bowl and move your finger off of the hole. Let salt drain through the hole for one minute. You may need to add salt to make it last a minute, or make the hole in the cup a bit larger. (If the cup is too small to hold enough salt for a minute, it can be a 30-second timer.) When you've got the salt measured just right in one cup, turn it over and glue the edge around the top of it to one of the squares from the paper plate. When this glue is dry, place the bottom of the second cup onto the bottom of the first cup, matching the holes. Tape the bottoms together with a narrow band of duct tape. Put the measured amount of salt into the open cup. Let it drain into the bottom cup. Then put glue around the edge of the top cup and glue it to the second square. Let it dry. This project will take—patience!

Showing Sympathy

Rejoice with those who rejoice; mourn with those who mourn. ROMANS 12:15

With the above sword you can fight back when you face this temptation:

You are tempted not to care about other people's feelings.

DAY 1

READ

John 11:1-44 ("Out of the Grave," page 589 in the *Day By Day Kid's Bible*)

Mary went to the place where Jesus was. She bowed down at Jesus' feet. "Lord," she said. "If you'd been here, Lazarus wouldn't have died." Mary began to cry. The people who had followed Mary began to cry too. Jesus felt their deep sadness. "Where is the grave?" he asked. "We'll show you," they said. Then Jesus cried too.

THINK AND TALK

Sympathy is sharing another person's feelings. People who don't share the feelings of others could be called *unsympathetic* or *scornful*. They don't care about how other people feel. Did Jesus show sympathy for Mary and her friends or not? If Jesus knew that God was going to bring Lazarus back to life, why did he cry? To *rejoice* means to show your joy. To *mourn* means to show your sadness. Tell why both mourning and rejoicing happened in the story of Lazarus.

PRACTICE

Read the verse. Try to repeat it several times without looking. Cut a sword shape from paper or cardboard. You'll want to hang it up in your house where it will remind you of the Spirit's sword from Romans 12:15. You can use it to fight when you are tempted not to have sympathy.

DAY 2

READ

2 Kings 6:1-7 ("An Ax on the Water," page 298 in the *Day By Day Kid's Bible*)

The prophets told Elisha, "... Let's go to the Jordan River to get logs. Then let's build a new meeting place." ..."All right," said Elisha. So he went with them. They started cutting down trees at the river. But the sharp iron top of one man's ax fell off. It fell into the river. "Oh no!" cried the man. "That's not my ax! It belongs to someone else!" ...Elisha cut a stick. He threw the stick into the water.... Then the heavy iron top of the ax came up. It lay there on top of the water. "Pull it out," said Elisha. The man did.

THINK AND TALK

What choices did the man with the ax have? Could he have been tempted not to care about the feelings of the man who loaned him the ax? What choices did Elisha have? Could Elisha have been tempted not to care about the feelings of the man who lost the ax head? Both of them showed sympathy. How did Elisha show his sympathy? How can you tell if a person has sympathy? How can you tell if a person does not have sympathy?

PRACTICE

Challenge a friend or family member (or yourself) to a sword-fight. One person says, "What will you do if you are tempted not to have sympathy?" The other person answers, "I will have sympathy, because it is written, 'Rejoice with those who rejoice; mourn with those who mourn.'"

DAY 3

READ
Proverbs 9:7-9; 13:1; 23:9 ("Things to Do," page 234 in the *Day By Day Kid's Bible*)
Some people make fun of others. If you tell them they're wrong, they'll make fun of you... A wise child listens to what his father says. But a person who laughs at others doesn't listen... Don't talk to foolish people. They'll make fun of the wise things you say.

THINK AND TALK
Has anyone ever made fun of you, not caring about your feelings? How did you feel? Have you ever made fun of someone else, not caring about their feelings? Why does God want us to have sympathy?

PRACTICE
Challenge each other to sword-fight with your sword for this week. Write on an index card: "You are tempted not to care about others' feelings." Add this temptation card to the other cards you've collected. Place the cards in a bowl. The first person draws a card and challenges the second person with that temptation. The second person repeats the sword of the Spirit that he can use to fight the temptation. Then it's his turn to draw a card and challenge the first person. See if you can go through all the cards this way.

DAY 4

READ
Mark 2:1-12 ("A Hole in the Roof," page 524 in the *Day By Day Kid's Bible*)
Jesus went back to Capernaum.... So crowds started coming to the house where he was staying.... Then four men walked up to the house. They were bringing a friend who couldn't move. They carried him on a mat. But they couldn't get through the crowd. So they dug through the roof. They made a hole right above Jesus.

Then they let the sick man down on his mat.... Jesus saw how much they believed. He told the sick man, "Your sins are forgiven." ...He said, "Get up. Take your mat with you. You can go home now." The man stood up... Everyone was very surprised. They praised God.

THINK AND TALK

What choices did the sick man's friends have? What did they choose to do? Do you find it easy or hard to have sympathy for a person who is sick or handicapped? If you find it hard, what could you do to make it easier to have sympathy for them? The man who couldn't move had friends who cared about him. What happened because of their sympathy? When is it hardest for you to have sympathy for someone?

PRACTICE

You and another person can challenge each other to practice fighting temptation. Do this by taking turns drawing the temptation cards from a bowl. Ask each other what you would do if you were tempted in that way.

TRY THIS

Make chocolate sugar cookies. Mix two-thirds cup brown sugar, one-third cup of white sugar, four tablespoons of softened margarine, one teaspoon of vanilla, and two eggs. In another bowl, mix three-fourths cup of cocoa, three-fourths cup of flour, and a pinch of salt. Mix this into the sugar mixture. Chill this dough for one hour. Make dough balls about one inch around, and place them on a baking sheet. Bake them for 14 to 15 minutes at 350 degrees. While the cookies are still soft and hot, gently press small colored candies (like red hots or M&M's) onto them. Make two eyes and a smile. Think about people you can rejoice with and people you can mourn with.

DAY 5

READ

Luke 15:1-10 ("Lost and Found," page 583 in the *Day By Day Kid's Bible*)

Then Jesus told some stories. "Suppose you're a shepherd. You have 100 sheep. But one of them gets lost... Wouldn't you look for the lost sheep until you found it? ... You'd call all your friends and neighbors. You'd say, 'Be glad with me! I found my lost sheep!'"... "Suppose a woman has 10 silver pieces of money. But she loses one," said Jesus.... "When she finds it, she will call her friends. She will call her neighbors. She will say, 'Be glad with me! I found the money I lost!'"

THINK AND TALK

Why would the shepherd who lost the sheep and the woman who lost the money call their friends and neighbors? Tell about a time when you rejoiced with someone who rejoiced. Tell about a time when you mourned with someone who mourned. Tell about some people who care about how you feel, who rejoice and mourn with you.

PRACTICE

Challenge someone to practice fighting temptation. You can take turns drawing the temptation cards from a bowl. Ask each other what you would do if you were tempted in that way.

TRY THIS

Stuff a small plastic sandwich bag with cotton balls. The fold-top kind of bag will work better than the zipper-locked kind. You can close it with a twist tie. This makes the body of a sheep. Draw the head of the sheep on an index card and cut it out. Clip four clothespins to one of the sides of the sandwich bag to make the legs of the sheep. Tape or staple the head to the twist-tied end of the bag. Glue a cotton ball to the other end to make a tail. Remember how the shepherds friends rejoiced when he found his lost sheep.

DAY 6

READ

Job 2 ("Three Friends," page 439 in the *Day By Day Kid's Bible*)
[Satan] made Job get sores...all over his body. They hurt....Job
had three friends... They heard what happened to Job. So they got
together and went to see him... But they could hardly tell that it was
Job. They began to cry out loud... Then they sat down on the
ground with Job. They sat there for seven days and nights.
Nobody said a thing. That's because they could see how much Job
was hurting.

THINK AND TALK

What choices did Job's friends have? Did they have sympathy for
Job or not? How can you tell? Sometimes when our friends are
sad, they don't need us to say things to try to cheer them up. They
feel better if we just spend time with them and feel sad with them.
Is it always easy to have sympathy for others? What are some
things that could keep us from feeling sympathy with someone?

PRACTICE

Challenge someone to practice fighting temptation. Do this by
taking turns drawing the temptation cards from a bowl. Ask each
other what you would do if you were tempted in that way.

TRY THIS

Make balloon heads. Inflate balloons. Mix flour and water until it
looks and feels like thick paste. Tear old newspapers into strips.
Dip the strips, one at a time, into the flour paste. Gently run the
strip between your thumb and forefinger so that the strip won't have
too much paste on it. Lay the strip across the balloon. Keep
adding strips of dipped paper onto the balloon until the whole
balloon is covered. You can even mold a nose, eyebrows, eyes
and ears onto it. Make several faces, and let the covered balloons
dry completely. Then stick a straight pin into the bottom to pop the
balloon. The popped balloons don't need to come out, but you can
pull it out at the bottom if you want. Paint each face to show a

different emotion. Have you ever felt these ways? Who has sympathy for you?

DAY 7

READ
Hebrews 4:14-16 ("Rest," page 781 in the *Day By Day Kid's Bible*) Jesus understands us. He faced every sin that looks good to us. But he said no every time. He did not sin. So let's go to the kind, loving King in heaven. We can be sure he will understand. He will be kind and loving to us. He will help us when we need him.

THINK AND TALK
Do you think Jesus rejoices when we rejoice? Do you think Jesus mourns when we mourn? Why or why not? Do you ever feel like no one understands or cares how you feel? Who is the one who cares when no one else does? What are some things you can do to help yourself remember to have sympathy for others?

PRACTICE
Challenge someone to practice fighting temptation. You can take turns drawing the temptation cards from a bowl. Ask each other what you would do if you were tempted in that way.

TRY THIS
Make smiling and frowning "masks." Draw a large *U* shape on each of two pieces of construction paper. Draw a line across the top of the *U* to close the shape in. Then cut these shapes out. Fold the shapes down the middle from top to bottom. Close to the fold about halfway down, place a quarter. Trace around the top half of the quarter to make a semicircle that looks like an eyebrow. Move the quarter down about one-half inch and trace another semicircle under the first one. Draw a straight line across the bottom to make an eye. Halfway between the eye and the bottom of the folded *U* shape, make half of a smile. Start at the fold and go up toward the eye. This is the top lip. About one-half inch below that, start at the fold again and make the bottom lip, curving it up to meet the top

one at the corner. Cut around the mouth, and cut out the eye. Open the "mask" up. Now do the same thing with the other mask, but make the eye a half circle with a line straight across the top, and the mouth into a frown. Prepare a drama and act out situations in which you rejoice and mourn.

Obeying

Your sword of the Spirit for this week is:

Obey your leaders and submit to their authority.
HEBREWS 13:17

With the above sword you can fight back when you face this temptation:

You are tempted to disobey.

DAY 1

READ

Exodus 20:1-17; 24 ("Ten Rules," and "On the Mountain with God," page 66 and 68 in the *Day By Day Kid's Bible*)
God told the people, "I am the Lord your God. I took you out of Egypt. I saved you from being slaves. Then God gave them 10 important rules... Moses sent young men to offer gifts on the altar. Moses read from the Law Book. The people said, "We'll do what God said. We'll obey."

THINK AND TALK

Why do you think God gave his people rules? Do we need rules? Why or why not? What does *obey* mean? Are there some people or some times when it would not be right to obey? Explain.

PRACTICE

Read the verse. Try to repeat it several times without looking. Cut a sword shape from paper or cardboard and write the verse on it. Hang it up so it will remind you of the Spirit's sword from Hebrews 13:17. You can use to fight against the temptation to disobey.

DAY 2

READ

Luke 7:1-10 ("The Captain's Servant," page 537 in the *Day By Day Kid's Bible*)

The captain heard that Jesus was in town. So he sent some Jewish leaders...to ask Jesus to come to his house. He wanted Jesus to make his servant well. They met him on his way to see the captain. Jesus went with the leaders. But the captain had sent some friends to Jesus too... They gave Jesus another message. The message said, "Lord, don't bother to come... Just say the word. Then I know my servant will be well again. You see, I know about being in charge," the message said.... "I'm the boss of many other men. I tell one to come, and he comes. I tell another one to go, and he goes."

THINK AND TALK

The captain talked about obeying. He expected the sickness to obey Jesus. Why? Why do people in the army have to obey their commanders? If they don't understand why they are told to do something, do they still have to obey? Why or why not? Who are the people that God wants you to obey?

PRACTICE

Challenge a friend or family member (or yourself) to a sword fight. One person says, "What will you do if you are tempted to disobey?" The other person answers, "I will not disobey, because it is written, 'Obey your leaders and submit to their authority.'"

DAY 3

READ

Jeremiah 35 ("A Family That Obeyed," page 392 in the *Day By Day Kid's Bible*)

God told Jeremiah, "Go to Recab's family. Ask them to come to the worship house... Then give them some wine to drink." So Jeremiah went to Recab's family. He took them to God's worship house... He set out bowls of wine. He set out cups. Then he said, "Drink some wine." But they said, "We don't drink wine. Our father said our family should never drink wine... We obeyed." ...Then God told

90

Jeremiah to say these words to the people of Judah. "Learn a
lesson. Learn to obey me."

THINK AND TALK
What choice did Recab's family have? What did they choose to
do? Do you think that some people in Recab's family were tempted
to drink the wine that Jeremiah offered them? Why does God want
us to obey? What happens when we don't? When is it hardest for
you to obey?

PRACTICE
Challenge someone to a sword-fight with your sword for this week.
Write on an index card: "You are tempted to disobey." Add this
temptation card to the other cards you've collected. Place these in
a bowl. The first person draws a card and challenges the second
person with that temptation. The second person repeats the sword
of the Spirit that he can use to fight the temptation. Then it's his
turn to draw a card and challenge the first person.

DAY 4

READ
Matthew 17:24-27 ("Fishing for Money," page 566 in the *Day By
Day Kid's Bible*)
Some tax men... came up to Peter. They said, "Doesn't Jesus pay
the worship-house tax?" "Yes, he does," said Peter. Then Peter
went to Jesus. But Jesus talked first. "What do you think, Peter?"
he said. "Who do kings get taxes from?"..."From other people,"
said Peter. "Then their own family doesn't pay taxes," Jesus said.
... "Take the first fish you catch. Open its mouth and look inside.
You'll find money in there. Then you can pay our taxes."

THINK AND TALK
What choices did Jesus have? What did he choose to do? Who
was it that Jesus obeyed? Why did Jesus obey? Why is it
important to obey God? How do we know what God wants us to
do? Talk about times when you have obeyed, even though it was
hard. Tell about a time when you disobeyed, and tell what
happened because of your choice.

PRACTICE

You and another person can challenge each other to practice fighting temptation. Do this by taking turns drawing the temptation cards from a bowl. Ask each other what you would do if you were tempted in that way.

TRY THIS

Make numeral cards on 32 slips of paper or index cards by writing 0 on three cards, 1 on three cards, 2 on three cards and so on through the numeral 9. Put a decimal point on one card and a dollar sign on another. Make three different stacks of cards 1-9, and shuffle each stack, placing them face down in a row. Place the dollar sign to the left of the three stacks and the decimal point between the first stack and the second stack. Get several coins of each kind: pennies, nickels, and quarters, plus some dollar bills. You can use play money if you need to. Turn over the top card on each stack. Pretend that is the price you must pay for something you are buying. Lay down enough bills to pay for it. Then you can make your own change, or if you're playing this with someone else, that person can make change for you. He starts by saying the price of the pretend object that is being bought. He adds change onto that price until he reaches the amount of money he was given. What is tax, and why do we pay it?

DAY 5

READ

Joshua 6 ("Falling Walls," page 98 in the *Day By Day Kid's Bible*)
God told Joshua, "I'm giving you the city of Jericho. Take your army. March around the city one time every day. Do that for six days... On day seven, march around the city seven times. The priests should blow their horns... When the people hear the horns, they should shout. The city will fall down. Your people can go right in."

THINK AND TALK

God didn't say why he wanted the people to march around the walls one time every day for six days and then seven times on the seventh day. Do you think the people understood why? What choice did the people have? Do you think some of the people were tempted not to do it God's way? Should we obey God ourselves even when we don't understand?

PRACTICE
Challenge someone to practice fighting temptation. You can take turns drawing the temptation cards from a bowl. Ask each other what you would do if you were tempted in that way.

TRY THIS
Build a wall from paper cups turned upside down. See how tall you can get this wall before it falls. What do you think would have happened if God's people had not obeyed God by marching around Jericho?

DAY 6

READ
Hebrews 13:17 ("Yesterday, Today, and Tomorrow," page 791 in the *Day By Day Kid's Bible*)
Obey your leaders. Let them lead you. They watch over you. They have to answer for what happens to you. Obey them. That way they'll be happy with their work. Their work won't be too hard for them. If their work's too hard, that's not good for you.

THINK AND TALK
Is it always easy to obey? What are some things that might tempt a person to disobey? What would you suggest to a friend who was having a hard time obeying?

PRACTICE
Challenge someone to practice fighting temptation. Do this by taking turns drawing the temptation cards from a bowl. Ask each other what you would do if you were tempted in that way.

TRY THIS
Peel four small, ripe bananas and break them in half across the middle. Then cut them in half lengthwise. In a small bowl, mix one-fourth cup of orange juice and one-third cup of brown sugar. Melt two tablespoons of margarine in a skillet. Add the brown sugar and orange juice. Stir in one-eighth teaspoon of cinnamon. Add the

bananas. Keep stirring and cooking this sauce for two minutes until it starts to get thick. Serve this over ice cream. Why do we obey recipes? What other kinds of instructions must we obey?

DAY 7

READ

Acts 4:1-20 ("Plain Men and Proud Leaders," page 636 in the *Day By Day Kid's Bible*)

Peter and John were saying Jesus was alive again. So the leaders put Peter and John in jail... The next day, the leaders met together. They brought Peter and John in... Then they told them not to teach about Jesus. But Peter and John had an answer for the leaders. "What do you think God would say? Is it right to obey you or God?" they asked. "We can't stop talking about what we saw and heard."

THINK AND TALK

What choices did Peter and John have? What did they choose to do? Because Peter and John chose to obey God, they got in trouble with the leaders. Who are your leaders? Are you supposed to obey all of them all the time? What should you do if you think that something a leader tells you to do is not right?

PRACTICE

Challenge someone to practice fighting temptation. Do this by taking turns drawing the temptation cards from a bowl. Ask each other what you would do if you were tempted in that way.

TRY THIS

Trace around your foot on eight pieces of construction paper. If you are doing this as a group, trace a different person's foot on each piece of paper. Cut these footprints out and write one word of the memory verse on each foot. Lay them on the floor to make a path, putting the words of the verse in order. Stand at the beginning of the path and toss a coin or a button down the path. Hop to the footprint that the coin or button lands closest to. Hop beside the feet, not on them. As you get to each footprint, say the word of the verse that's on the foot. When you stop, say the rest of the verse. Or, if you are playing with others, the second person must say the rest of the verse. Then it is that person's turn.

Being Generous

Your sword of the Spirit for this week is:

God loves a cheerful giver.
2 CORINTHIANS 9:7

With the above sword you can fight back when you face this temptation:

You are tempted not to give.

DAY 1

READ

1 Samuel 18:1-4 ("A Friend, a Spear, and a Wife," page 140 in the *Day By Day Kid's Bible*)

Jonathan and David made a promise to be special friends. Jonathan took off his own robe. He gave it to David. Jonathan also gave David his long shirt and his belt. He gave David his sword and his bow for shooting arrows.

THINK AND TALK

Why do you think Jonathan gave David so *many* things? Wouldn't one of those things have been enough to show friendship? When someone gives what seems to be more than a person would normally give, that's *generosity*. The giver is being *generous*. A person who does not give, or who holds back some of what he ought to give, is *stingy*. Jonathan was generous.

PRACTICE

Read the verse. Try to repeat it several times without looking. Cut a sword shape from paper or cardboard and write the verse on it.

You'll want to hang it up in your house where it will remind you of the Spirit's sword from 2 Corinthians 9:7. You can use it to fight against the temptation to be stingy.

DAY 2

READ

John 6:1-14 ("Bread for Everyone," page 556 in the *Day By Day Kid's Bible*)

Jesus looked at the crowd of people... "Where can we get bread for these people?" he asked... "Look at this little boy," said Andrew. "He has five rolls and two small fish. But that won't feed many people." ....Jesus took the five rolls and the two fish. He looked up to heaven. He thanked God. Then he began to hand out the rolls... There was more than enough! All of the people got to eat as much as they wanted.

THINK AND TALK

Two people chose to be generous in the story. Who were they? How much did the little boy give? How much did Jesus give to the people? How can you tell when someone is being generous? How can you tell when someone is being stingy? Which person would you rather have for a friend: a generous person or a stingy person?

PRACTICE

Challenge a friend or family member (or yourself) to a sword-fight. One person says, "What will you do if you are tempted to be stingy?" The other person answers, "I will not be stingy, because it is written, 'God loves a cheerful giver.'"

DAY 3

READ

Genesis 14 ("War!" page 10 in the *Day By Day Kid's Bible*)

Then the king of Salem prayed for Abram... Abram took one of every 10 things he got from the war. He gave that to the king of Salem. The king of Sodom told Abram, "Just give me back my people. You can keep everything else." "No," said Abram. "I promised God I wouldn't take anything that was yours."

THINK AND TALK

Who were the generous people after the war that Abram and his men fought? How can you tell that they were generous? The first part of 2 Corinthians 9:7 tells us not to give "relunctantly or under compulsion." What does the word *reluctantly* mean? What does *under compulsion* mean? Why does God want us to be cheerful givers?

PRACTICE

Challenge someone to a sword-fight with your sword for this week. Write on an index card: "You are tempted to be stingy." Add this card to the other temptation cards you've collected. Place these in a bowl. The first person draws a card and challenges the second person with that temptation. The second person repeats the sword of the Spirit that she can use to fight the temptation. Then it's her turn to draw a card and challenge the first person. See if you can remember all the swords from the previous weeks.

DAY 4

READ

2 Chronicles 9:1-12 ("Riches for a Wise King," page 228 in the *Day By Day Kid's Bible*)

The queen of Sheba heard about Solomon. She heard that he obeyed God. So she came to see Solomon... The queen brought a long line of camels with her. They carried spices, gold, and beautiful stones. The queen of Sheba asked Solomon many questions... There was no question too hard for him... "What I heard about you is true," she said.... "You are wiser and richer than what I was told." ...King Solomon gave the queen of Sheba everything she wanted. Then she went back home.

THINK AND TALK

In what way was the queen of Sheba generous? How was Solomon generous to her? Why do you think Solomon was generous to the queen of Sheba? Why do you think God wants us to be generous? What happens when we are not generous?

PRACTICE

You and another person can challenge each other to practice fighting temptation. Do this by taking turns drawing the temptation cards from a bowl. Ask each other what you would do if you were tempted in that way.

TRY THIS

Mix one 18-ounce jar of orange breakfast drink mix, three-fourths cup of sugar, one-half cup of presweetened lemonade mix, one-half cup instant decaffeinated tea, one three-ounce package of orange gelatin, two and one-half teaspoons of cinnamon, and one-half teaspoon of ground cloves. Divide this orange tea mix into small jars or zipper-locked plastic bags. Give them as gifts. To mix this tea, place one heaping teaspoonful of mix into a teacup and stir in one cup of hot water. What would you have given King Solomon?

DAY 5

READ

John 12:1-11 ("A Jar of Perfume," page 595 in the *Day By Day Kid's Bible*)

Mary took out a jar of nard. It was perfume that cost a lot of money. She tipped the jar over. She let perfume flow out onto Jesus' feet. Then she wiped his feet with her hair. The air was filled with the sweet perfume smell.

THINK AND TALK

How did Mary show generosity? Does being generous have to cost money? What else can you give besides things that cost money? Tell about someone you know who is generous. Tell about a time when you were generous. How does it feel to be generous?

PRACTICE

Challenge someone to practice fighting temptation. You can take turns drawing the temptation cards from a bowl. Ask each other what you would do if you were tempted in that way.

TRY THIS

Make potpourri by mixing thinly sliced oranges and lemons. (Ask an adult to do the slicing.) Add whole cloves, cinnamon sticks, and bay leaves. To make your house smell good, put two cups of water in a pot. Bring it to a boil. Add the potpourri and turn the heat to low. Simmer this mixture as long as you want, adding more water as the water level in the pot gets low. Real perfume is very expensive. Why? What would you have given Jesus?

DAY 6

READ

Nehemiah 5 ("Money for Grain," page 493 in the *Day By Day Kid's Bible*)

Now the people began fussing at each other... "We need money to buy grain. Nothing will grrow in the fields now. We give our fields and houses to our leaders. Then they lend us the money." ...I talked to the leaders. "You're taking things from your own people!" I said.... "You ask for their houses before you'll lend them money. This has to stop! Give their houses back. Give their fields back."

THINK AND TALK

Were these leaders of God's people being stingy or generous? When is it hardest to be generous? Are there some times when you should not give to someone? If so, when? Are there ever some things you should not give? If so, what?

PRACTICE

Challenge someone to practice fighting temptation. You can take turns drawing the temptation cards from a bowl. Ask each other what you would do if you were tempted in that way.

TRY THIS

Make braided belts. For each belt, cut three strips of fabric one inch wide and two yards long. Lay the three strips on top of each other tie them into a knot at one end. If you are working by yourself, place the knotted end of the strips into a drawer and close the drawer to hold the strips in place. If you work with a friend, one of you can hold the knotted end. Now separate the three strips close to the knotted end. Bring the right strip over the center strip. Now the right strip has become the center strip. Bring the left strip over the new center strip. Now it becomes the center. Pull all of this until it is firm, not too tight or too loose. With some practice you'll get it just right. Keep braiding right over center, left over center, right over center, left over center, until you reach the end of the strips. Tie this end into a knot. Give the belts as gifts.

DAY 7

READ
Psalm 112 ("Even in the Dark," page 198 in the *Day By Day Kid's Bible*)
God brings good things to the families of people who do right... Even in the dark, light will shine for people who do what's right. They are kind and good. They give to others. They are fair in business... Their hearts will keep on trusting God... They give to poor people. They will always do what's right.

THINK AND TALK
Is it always easy to give? When you give, it is always easy to be generous? Why or why not? What are some things that would tempt you not to give, or not to be generous? What would you suggest to a friend who was tempted to be stingy?

PRACTICE
Challenge someone to practice fighting temptation. You can take turns drawing the temptation cards from a bowl. Ask each other what you would do if you were tempted in that way.

TRY THIS
Design a coin. Cover a small styrofoam plate with aluminum foil. With a pencil, gently draw a design in this as if it were a coin. When is it good to give money? When is it good to give something other than money?

Putting First
Things First

Your sword of the Spirit for this week is:

**Set your mind on God's kingdom
and his justice before everything else,
and all the rest will come to you as well.**
MATTHEW 6:33

With the above sword you can fight back when you face this temptation:

You are tempted not to put God first.

DAY 1

READ

Genesis 19:1-29 ("Angels in Sodom,'" p. 14 in the *Day By Day Kid's Bible*)

The angels turned to Lot.... "God has sent us here to get rid of the city... Run for your lives! Don't look behind you. Don't stop until you get to the mountains!"...The sun was up when Lot got to Zoar. Then God sent fire from heaven. Fire fell like rain on Sodom.... Lot's wife looked back. She turned into a post made of salt.

THINK AND TALK

Part of putting God first is obeying him. The city was important to Lot's wife. In fact, it was more important than what God had told her to do. What had God told her to do? What did she choose to do? What does it mean to put God first?

PRACTICE

Read the verse. Try to repeat it several times without looking. Cut a sword shape from paper or cardboard. Write the verse on it. You'll want to hang it up in your house where it will remind you of the Spirit's sword from Matthew 6:33. You can use it to fight back when you're tempted not to put God first.

DAY 2

READ

Genesis 25:19-34 ("Twins," page 21 in the *Day By Day Kid's Bible*)
One day Jacob cooked some soup. Esau came in from his time in the fields. And he was hungry. "I'm so hungry, I'm about to die!" said Esau. "Hurry and give me some of that red soup!" "First you must promise me something," said Jacob. "When our father dies, he will leave most of what he owns to you. Promise me that you'll let me have it all." "All right," said Esau. "After all, I'm about to die of hunger!"

THINK AND TALK

Esau was supposed to have what his father owned. That was more important than soup. Why was Esau tempted to give up something important to get some soup? What does it mean to put first things first? How can you tell what's important and what's not as important in your life? Name some very important things in your life. Name some things that are not as important.

PRACTICE

Challenge a friend or a family member (or yourself) to a sword-fight. One person says, "What will you do if you are tempted not to put God first?" The other person answers, "I will put God first, because it is written, 'Set your mind on God's kingdom and his justice before everything else, and all the rest will come to you as well.'"

DAY 3

READ

Daniel 3 ("The Big, Burning Oven," page 431 in the *Day By Day Kid's Bible*)
"King Nebuchadnezzar," said Shadrach, Meshach and Abednego.

102

"We don't need to tell you we're right. Our God can save us if we're thrown into the burning oven. Even if he doesn't save us, you should know this. We won't obey your gods. We won't worship the gold idol you set up."

THINK AND TALK
What choice did Shadrach, Meshach and Abednego have? Why might they have been tempted not to put God first? Would you have been tempted to put King Nebuchadnezzar's wishes first? The three young men's choice to put God first was a choice between life and death. Most decisions we make are not that serious. How can you tell if someone is putting God first? How can you tell if someone is not putting God first?

PRACTICE
Challenge someone to a sword-fight with your sword for this week. Write on an index card: "You are tempted not to put God first." Add this temptation card to the other cards you've collected. Place these in a bowl. The first person draws a card and challenges the second person with that temptation. The second person repeats the sword of the Spirit that he can use to fight the temptation. Then it's his turn to draw a card and challenge the first person.

DAY 4

READ
1 Kings 3:1-15 ("The First Days of King Solomon," page 222 in the *Day By Day Kid's Bible*)
That night God came to Solomon in a dream. "Ask me for whatever you want," God said. "You have been very kind to me," said Solomon.... "Make me wise enough to be their king. Help me understand what's right and what's wrong." God was glad to hear Solomon ask to be wise. "You didn't ask for a long life," said God. "You didn't ask for riches for yourself... You asked to be wise. So I'll give you what you asked for. "

THINK AND TALK
What choices did Solomon have? What would most kings be tempted

to ask for? What did Solomon think was the most important? Do you think he was right? Why or why not? What happened because of the choice Solomon made? Why does God want us to put him and his kingdom first? What happens when we don't?

PRACTICE
You and another person can challenge each other to practice fighting temptation. Take turns drawing the temptation cards from a bowl. Ask each other what you would do if you were tempted in that way.

TRY THIS
Make a pillow. Cut a 12-inch by 24-inch piece of fabric. Use smaller pieces for smaller pillows. Fold the fabric in half with the back of the fabric on the outside. Sew along two sides and three-fourths of the way along the third side. Turn the fabric right side out and stuff it with pillow stuffing. You can get this at craft stores, at fabric stores, or at some discount stores in the sewing section. Remember Solomon's dream.

DAY 5

READ
2 Chronicles 20:1-30 ("Facing the Enemy," page 291 in the *Day By Day Kid's Bible*)
One day some men came to see King Jehoshaphat. "A big army is coming this way!" they said.... Jehoshaphat prayed... "We are not strong enough to win." ...Then God's Spirit came on one of the men... "Here's what God says. 'Don't be scared. Don't give up. The fight isn't yours. It's God's.'" ...Jehoshaphat talked to the leaders. Then he chose singers to sing to God. They praised God. Then they led the army. They sang, "Give thanks to God. His love lasts forever." ...Then God began to work out his plan against the enemies.

THINK AND TALK
Who led the army? Why were the singers chosen to be the most important? Do you think King Jehoshaphat might have been tempted to put someone else first? Why or why not? Tell about someone you know who puts God first.

PRACTICE

Challenge someone to practice fighting temptation. You can take turns drawing the temptation cards from a bowl. Ask each other what you would do if you were tempted in that way.

TRY THIS

Get a group of friends and play Dodge and Capture. This is like the game that some people call Prison Ball. Play this in a gym or in a yard outdoors. Form two teams. Make two lines at opposite sides of the playing area. The leader of each team is behind his team's line. The other players are in the area between the lines. The leader of Team 1 starts the play by throwing a beach ball at someone from Team 2. If the ball hits a person from Team 2, that person has to go behind Team 1's line. The Team 1 leader continues to throw the ball. If she misses, the opposite team's leader gets to throw the ball. If a captured team mate catches one of the balls thrown by his team leader, he gets to go back into the game. How would you have felt like if you had been one of the singers chosen to lead the army against the enemy?

DAY 6

READ

Matthew 13:44-46 ("Seeds, Yeast, Pearls, and Nets," page 549 in the *Day By Day Kid's Bible*)

"God's kingdom is like riches in a field," said Jesus. "The riches were hidden under the ground. A man who was digging found them... So he sold everything he owned to buy that field. God's kingdom is like a man shopping for fine pearls. One day, he found a very special pearl... So the man sold everything he owned. He bought the pearl."

THINK AND TALK

Why did the man buy the field? Why did the man buy the pearl? Is there anything in life that's worth giving everything else up just so you can have it? If so, what is it? What does God promise to do if we make his kingdom the most important?

PRACTICE

Challenge someone to practice fighting temptation. You can take turns drawing the temptation cards from a bowl. Ask each other what you would do if you were tempted in that way.

TRY THIS

Play Hide the Treasure with a group of friends. Choose an unbreakable object to be your treasure. Send everyone out of the room while you hide it. Then call everyone into the room and let them look for the treasure. The one who finds it gets to hide the treasure next. What are some of the things that you consider to be your treasures? Why are they treasures to you?

DAY 7

READ

Mark 12:28-34 ("More Tricks," page 601 in the *Day By Day Kid's Bible*) One teacher of God's laws... said, "There are many rules. Which one is the most important?" "The most important rule is this one," said Jesus. "The Lord is the only God. Love the Lord with all your heart. Love the Lord with all your soul. Love him with all your mind. Love him with all your strength."

THINK AND TALK

Is it always easy to put God first? What are some things that people put in first place ahead of God? How can you love the Lord with all your heart and soul? How can you love the Lord with all your mind? How can you love the Lord with all your strength?

PRACTICE

Challenge someone to practice fighting temptation. You can take turns drawing the temptation cards from a bowl. Ask each other what you would do if you were tempted in that way.

TRY THIS

Write the memory verse for this week on a large piece of paper or on poster board. Cut the paper or poster board into large pieces of different shapes to make a jigsaw puzzle. Mix the pieces up and see how long it takes you to put it back together again. Give the pieces to someone else and see if they can put it together.

Being
Considerate

Your sword of the Spirit for this week is:

Each of you should look not only to your own interests, but also to the interests of others.
PHILIPPIANS 2:4

With the above sword you can fight back when you face this temptation:

You are tempted to be rude.

DAY 1

READ
Ruth 2 ("In the Grain Fields," page 112 in the *Day By Day Kid's Bible*)
When Ruth went back to the field, Boaz talked to his workers. "Let her get the grain wherever she wants. Even if she gets it from around the piles you gathered. Don't make her feel bad about it. In fact, pull some grain out of the piles for her. Leave it for her to pick up. Don't get mad at her."

THINK AND TALK
Being *considerate* means being thoughtful of other people's feelings. Ruth was not Jewish. She was a foreigner living in Bethlehem.   Some people are rude to people from other countries. Why?   What did Boaz do that showed he was considerate? Have you ever had a chance to be considerate to someone from another country? If so, tell about it.

PRACTICE

Read the verse. Try to repeat it several times without looking. Cut a sword shape from paper or cardboard and write the verse on it. You'll want to hang it up in your house where it will remind you of the Spirit's sword from Philippians 2:4. You can use it to fight against the temptation to be rude.

DAY 2

READ

2 Samuel 9 ("Jonathan's Son," page 164 in the *Day By Day Kid's Bible*)

"Is anybody from Saul's family still alive?" asked David. "Is there someone I can be kind to because of Jonathan?" "There is Jonathan's son," the servant said. "He can't walk." ... So David sent for Jonathan's son... "Your father, Jonathan, was my best friend. I'll give you all the land that Saul, your grandfather, owned. I'll always let you eat at my table."

THINK AND TALK

What choices did David have? What are some reasons that David might *not* have wanted to be considerate to anyone from Saul's family? Why did David choose to be considerate? What were some of the good things that may have happened because David "looked to the interests of others"? How can "looking to the interests of others" help bring peace in your life?

PRACTICE

Challenge a friend or family member (or yourself) to a sword-fight. One person says, "What will you do if you are tempted to be rude?" The other person answers, "I will not be rude, because it is written, 'Each of you should look not only to his own interests, but also to the interests of others.'"

DAY 3

READ

Mark 10:13-16 ("A Camel and a Needle," page 591 in the *Day By Day Kid's Bible*)

People started bringing little children to Jesus. They wanted Jesus to touch them and pray for them. But Jesus' friends got mad at the people. Jesus saw this, and he was upset. He said, "Let the little children come to me. Don't stop them."

THINK AND TALK

What choice did Jesus have when he saw his friends send the children away? Jesus' disciples were not thinking of the children's interests, so they were rude. But Jesus was considerate. Tell about a time when you were considerate of someone, or when someone was considerate of you. What happened because of the choice to be considerate?

PRACTICE

Challenge someone to a sword-fight with your sword for this week. Write on an index card: "You are tempted to be rude." Add it to the other temptation cards you've collected. Place these in a bowl. The first person draws a card and challenges the second person with that temptation. The second person repeats the sword of the Spirit that he can use to fight the temptation. Then it's his turn to draw a card and challenge the first person.

DAY 4

READ

Luke 10:25-37 ("The Neighbor," page 578 in the *Day By Day Kid's Bible*) There once was a man who was on a trip. He was going from Jerusalem to Jericho. But robbers jumped out at him. They took his clothes. They beat him. Then they left. There the man was, lying by the road. He was half dead. Soon a priest came down the road. He saw the hurt man. But he moved to the other side of the road. He just passed by.

THINK AND TALK

What choices did the priest have? Why do you think the priest was so rude that he walked past a man who needed his help? Could being considerate to someone put us in danger? If so, how? Are there ever people we shouldn't help? Explain.

PRACTICE

You and another person can challenge each other to practice fighting temptation. Do this by taking turns drawing the temptation cards from a bowl. Ask each other what you would do if you were tempted in that way.

TRY THIS

Read about first aid in a book or look it up in an encyclopedia. Find out how to help if someone gets cut or has a nosebleed or gets hurt in other ways. Tell about how you helped someone who was hurt, or about how someone helped you when you were hurt.

DAY 5

READ

Titus 3 ("Making Us New," page 756 in the *Day By Day Kid's Bible*) Help people remember to obey the rulers in charge. People need to be ready to do good. They shouldn't say bad things about others. They should make peace. They should be thoughtful. They should treat other people as the important ones.

THINK AND TALK

Why does God want us to be considerate? How can you tell when a person is considerate? How can you tell when a person is rude? Which would you rather have as a friend?

PRACTICE

Challenge someone to practice fighting temptation. You can take turns drawing the temptation cards from a bowl. Ask each other person what he would do if he were tempted in that way.

TRY THIS

Take a walk around your neighborhood with a friend. Take a trash bag with you and pick up any trash you find on your walk. Why is this a considerate thing to do?

DAY 6

Acts 26 ("You're Out of Your Mind!" page 727 in the *Day By Day Kid's Bible*)
Then Festus shouted, "You're out of your mind, Paul! You've learned so much, your mind is gone!" "I'm not out of my mind," said Paul. "I'm telling the truth. It makes sense."

THINK AND TALK

What choices did Festus have? Festus chose to speak rudely to Paul. What would have happened if Paul had spoken rudely back to Festus? What happens when we are rude to people? What happens when we are considerate of people? Is it easy to be considerate toward people who are being rude to you? Talk about some examples of this.

PRACTICE

Challenge someone to practice fighting temptation. You can take turns drawing the temptation cards from a bowl. Ask each other what you would do if you were tempted in that way.

TRY THIS

Make a "blue ribbon" from a piece of blue construction paper. Write on it, "You First." Wear this blue ribbon, and for a whole day try to remember to *always* let someone else go ahead of you.

DAY 7

READ

Matthew 25:31-45 ("Sheep and Goats," page 605 in the *Day By Day Kid's Bible*)
"I'll come back," said Jesus... "The people who did what's right will wonder. They'll say, 'Lord, when did we see you hungry? When did we give you food?' ...Then I'll say, 'You did these things for ...people who don't seem important at all. That's when you did them for me.'"

THINK AND TALK
What is Jesus saying here about being considerate of others? When are you most tempted to be rude? What kinds of people are you most tempted to be rude to? Why is it so important to look to the interests of others?

PRACTICE
Challenge someone to practice fighting temptation. You can take turns drawing the temptation cards from a bowl. Ask each other what you would do if you were tempted in that way.

TRY THIS
Make a special drink to serve to friends or family. For each serving of this drink, you will need six ounces of pineapple juice, one eight-ounce container of strawberry yogurt, and one ripe, sliced banana. Mix all of this in a blender, pour the drink into a glass, and serve it to someone. Is it easier to be considerate to someone you think deserves it than to someone you think doesn't deserve it? Why?

Being Willing

Your sword of the Spirit for this week is:

Grant me a willing spirit, to sustain me.
PSALM 51:12

With the above sword you can fight back when you face this temptation:

You are tempted to be stubborn.

DAY 1

READ

2 Samuel 24:18-25 ("The Angel at the Barn," page 182 in the *Day By Day Kid's Bible*)

The angel was standing at the farmer's work place. David looked up and saw the angel... His sword was out. It was pointing to Jerusalem. So David went toward the work place. The farmer was working. His four sons were with him... He and his sons saw the angel too... David said, "Sell me your work place. I want to build an altar to God here." ..."Take my barn for free," said the farmer... "No," said King David. "I'll pay you for it... I won't give God something that cost me nothing."

THINK AND TALK

Willingness is choosing to be ready to do something if you are asked to do it or if you need to do it. *Stubborness* is choosing not to do something no matter how many times you are asked and no matter how much you need to do it. The farmer was willing to give his barn to David for free. David ended up paying for it, but

113

the farmer was willing. In a family, people need to be willing and ready to do many things. What are some things you are willing to do in your family if you need to?

PRACTICE
Read the verse. Try to repeat it several times without looking. Cut a sword shape from paper or cardboard. Write the verse on it. You'll want to hang it up in your house where it will remind you of the Spirit's sword from Psalm 51:12. You can use it to fight against the temptation to be stubborn.

DAY 2

READ
2 Corinthians 9:2-7 ("The Big Gift," page 699 in the *Day By Day Kid's Bible*)
You're ready to help. I've been bragging about it to the people in Macedonia. I told them you've been ready to give for a year. They know you want to give, so most of them are giving too.

THINK AND TALK
A *willing* heart is a heart that is open to God. A *stubborn* heart is a heart that is closed to God. Paul was writing to some people in Corinth. What were they willing to do? How did that affect the people in Macedonia? If you are willing to follow God, other people may choose to be willing to follow God too. What are some things you think God wants you to be willing to do?

PRACTICE
Challenge a friend or family member (or yourself) to a sword fight. One person says, "What will you do if you are tempted to be stubborn?"   The other person answers, "I will not be stubborn, because it is written, 'Grant me a willing spirit to sustain me.'"

DAY 3

READ
Jeremiah 26:1-16 ("Jeremiah Should Die!" page 389 in *Day By Day Kid's Bible*)
These are the words God told Jeremiah to say. "Listen to me.

114

Obey my laws. Listen to my prophets. I sent prophets to you over and over again. I sent them, even though you didn't listen. What if you still don't listen? Then I'll tear down this worship house. There will be nothing good left to say about this city."

THINK AND TALK
Does it sound as though God's people are willing to listen to him, or are they stubborn about thinking what they want to think? The sword for this week was written by David. "Grant me a willing spirit to sustain me." To sustain means to support or hold up under pressure. How could a willing spirit support us or hold us up in hard times?

PRACTICE
Challenge someone to a sword-fight with your sword for this week. Write on an index card: "You are tempted to be stubborn." Add this temptation card to the other cards you've collected. Place these cards in a bowl. The first person draws a card and challenges the second person with that temptation. The second person repeats the sword of the Spirit that he can use to fight the temptation. Then it's his turn to draw a card and challenge the first person. See if you can use all the swords you've learned so far.

DAY 4

READ
Mark 5:1-20 ("The Man Who Lived by Graves," page 551 in the *Day By Day Kid's Bible*)
Jesus and his friends landed their boat. Jesus got out. A man came up to meet him. This man was controlled by a bad spirit... Jesus said, "You bad spirit, come out of this man!" ...Pigs were eating on a hill nearby... The spirits went into them. Then all the pigs ran down the hill. They jumped into the lake and drowned. The people who had been taking care of the pigs... told everyone in town what had happened... The people were scared. They begged Jesus to leave their land.

THINK AND TALK
Were the people from the city willing to get to know Jesus? Why? What are some things that could keep a person from being willing

115

to believe in Jesus or follow him? Are you willing to believe in Jesus and follow him?

PRACTICE
You and another person can challenge each other to practice fighting temptation. Take turns drawing the temptation cards from a bowl. Ask each other what you would do if you were tempted in that way.

TRY THIS
Make "Pigs in a Blanket." Use canned crescent-roll dough. Cut frankfurters in half. On each slice of dough, place a half of a frank and a small slice of cheese. Roll these up inside the dough. Bake it the way the instructions tell you to. Jewish people do not eat pig meat. Can you find out why?

DAY 5

READ
Mark 3:1-5 ("On the Worship Day," page 528 in the *Day By Day Kid's Bible*)
There was a man in the worship house. His right hand was small and twisted... "Stand up in front of everyone," said Jesus. Then Jesus turned to the people. "Should we do good or bad on the worship day?" ...Nobody answered. The people were all quiet. Jesus looked around. He was very upset because their hearts were hard. They didn't care about God.

THINK AND TALK
One way to describe a stubborn person is to say his heart is hard. How can you tell when a person is willing—open to God and God's will? How can you tell when a person is stubborn—closed to God and God's will? What would you suggest to a friend who was tempted to be stubborn about God and God's will?

PRACTICE
Challenge someone to practice fighting temptation. You can take turns drawing the temptation cards from a bowl. Ask each other what you would do if you were tempted in that way, and answer by saying the appropriate verse.

TRY THIS

Ask someone to tape the thumb of your right hand to your right palm with bandage tape or tie a bandanna around your hand to keep your thumb close to your palm. If you are left handed, do this with your left hand. Now try to go through your normal activities without using your thumb. What is it like? Who will help you? Someone with a stubborn or a willing spirit?

DAY 6

READ

Acts 18:12-28 ("A Judge and a New Jewish Teacher," page 673 in the *Day By Day Kid's Bible*)

While Paul was traveling, a man named Apollos went to Ephesus. He was Jewish. He was very smart. He knew God's Word well. Apollos told people about Jesus. But he only knew about baptizing like John did. Apollos talked in the town's worship house. Aquila and Priscilla heard him. They asked him to come home with them. They taught him more about Jesus.

THINK AND TALK

What was Apollos willing to do? Sometimes it's hard for smart people to be willing to learn. Why? What were Aquila and Priscilla willing to do? What are some things you must be willing to do if you want to get to know Jesus better? Is it always easy to be willing and open to God and what he wants? What are some things that could cause us to be stubborn?

PRACTICE

Challenge someone to practice fighting temptation. You can take turns drawing the temptation cards from a bowl. Ask each other what you would do if you were tempted in that way.

TRY THIS

Make a pencil holder from a can. You might use a can that vegetables come in. Cut pages out of a magazine and trim them so that they are about six inches wide. Roll each page into a small roll around a pencil. Tape the end of the paper to keep it rolled. Slide the pencil out. Ask an adult to supervise as you hot-glue the roll of paper onto the can. Keep making rolls of paper and gluing them onto the can, side by side, until the whole can is covered with these colorful columns. Now it's ready to hold your pencils. What other supplies do you use when you learn? Are you willing to please God by learning new things?

DAY 7

READ

Ezekiel 3:4-9 ("Hard Hearts," page 404 in the *Day By Day Kid's Bible*) Then God said, "Go to my people. Tell them my words. They speak your language. They understand your words. But they won't want to listen to you. That's because they don't want to listen to me. They have hard hearts. But I'll make you as strong as they are. I'll make your forehead as hard as stone. It will be harder than rock. So don't be scared of them."

THINK AND TALK

Were God's people stubborn or willing? How can you tell? Their hearts were turned against God. Is there ever a good kind of stubbornness and a bad kind of willingness? What does God say he is going to do with Ezekiel? Does it sound like Ezekiel was going to be a good kind of stubborn in keeping his heart open to God? Was it good that he was not willing to close his heart to God? If God wants us to be willing, what does he want us to be willing to do?

PRACTICE

Challenge someone to practice fighting temptation. You can take turns drawing the temptation cards from a bowl. Ask each other what you would do if you were tempted in that way.

TRY THIS

Take some paper outdoors. You'll need a piece of black construction paper and a piece of white paper. Gather some rocks and try to write on the paper with each rock. What happens? Can you find any rocks that make marks on the paper? What do you think God meant when he told Ezekiel that he would make Ezekiel's forehead as hard as stone, harder than rock? Have you ever heard people call a stubborn person "hardheaded"?

Having Faith

Your sword of the Spirit for this week is:

Now faith is being sure of what we hope for and certain of what we do not see.
HEBREWS 11:1

With the above sword you can fight back when you face this temptation:

You are tempted not to believe God.

DAY 1

READ

Hebrews 11 ("Faith," page 786 in the *Day By Day Kid's Bible*)

We have faith. So we understand that God made the world and all of space. He told it to happen, and it happened. He made things we see out of things we don't see... People who come to God have to believe two things. First, they must believe that God really lives. Then they must believe that God brings good to people who look for him.

THINK AND TALK

Faith is strongly believing and trusting something you can't see. Can you see gravity? If you drop a ball from an upstairs window, will it go up or down? How do you know? You can't see gravity, but you can see what it does. We can't see God, but we can see what he does. The opposite of faith is *sight*. If we see something, we don't need to have faith that it is real. What are some things that people put their faith in?

PRACTICE

Read the verse. Try to repeat it several times without looking. Cut a sword shape from paper or cardboard and write the verse on it. You'll want to hang it up in your house where it will remind you of the Spirit's sword from Hebrews 11:1. You can use it to fight against being tempted not to believe God.

DAY 2

READ

Psalm 19 ("God's Way," page 201 in the *Day By Day Kid's Bible*) The sky shows how great God is. Every day it tells about God. Every night it shows what he is like. No matter what language people speak, they can understand what the sky tells. All over the world, people can see it... God's way is the best. It keeps us strong. We can trust God's rules... God's commands shine clearly, giving our spirits light.

THINK AND TALK

What are some things in nature that show you God's greatness, power, and wisdom? Why do you think some people see and study nature and still don't have faith in God?

Paul wrote, "God clearly showed who he is. He showed his greatness. People can see his greatness by looking at what he made. So there is no reason for people not to believe" (Romans 1:20, page 703 in the *Day By Day Kid's Bible*).

PRACTICE

Challenge a friend or family member (or yourself) to a sword-fight. One person says, "What will you do if you are tempted not to have faith in God?" The other person answers, "I will not lose my faith, because it is written, 'Now faith is being sure of what we hope for and certain of what we do not see.'"

DAY 3

READ

John 20:24-29 ("In a Locked Room," page 628 in the *Day By Day Kid's Bible*)

Jesus came again. He stood with his friends. "Be at peace!" he said. Then he turned to Thomas... "Touch my side. Look at my hands. Stop thinking that this is just a story. Believe!" "My Lord and my God!" said Thomas. "You believe because you see me," said Jesus. "Some people don't see me. They believe anyway. God will send good things to them."

THINK AND TALK

How can you tell if someone has faith in Jesus? How can you tell if someone does not have faith in Jesus? Why do you think God doesn't show himself to us? If God showed himself to us and we could see him, would we have to have faith? Even though people in Bible times could see Jesus, did everyone believe? How do you show your faith?

PRACTICE

Challenge someone to a sword-fight with your sword for this week. Write on an index card: "You are tempted not to believe in God." Add this temptation card to the other cards you've collected. Place these cards in a bowl. The first person draws a card and challenges the second person with that temptation. The second person repeats the sword of the Spirit that she can use to fight the temptation. Then it's her turn to draw a card and challenge the first person.

DAY 4

READ

Matthew 9:27-31 ("Two Men Who Could Not See," page 553 in the *Day By Day Kid's Bible*)

Two men who could not see began to follow Jesus. They called out, "Jesus, be kind to us. Make us well!"... "Do you believe I can do this?" Jesus asked. "Yes, Lord," they said. Then Jesus touched their eyes. He said, "You believe. So you will see."

121

THINK AND TALK

What choice did the blind men have? What did they choose? What happened because of their choice? Have you ever heard anyone say, "Seeing is believing"? In the case of the two blind men, believing was seeing! Why do you think God wants us to have faith instead of seeing everything? What happens when we don't have faith?

PRACTICE

You and another person can challenge each other to practice fighting temptation. Do this by taking turns drawing the temptation cards from a bowl. Ask each other what you would do if you were tempted in that way.

TRY THIS

On a piece of paper, trace around two dimes placed side by side with a little space between. These will be cartoon eyes. Make four sets of eyes. For the first set, draw a line across the middle of each eye. Make a black dot in the half of each eye below the line. For the second set of eyes, make a black dot in each eye right at the center top of the circle. For the third set, place the black dot right in the center of each. For the fourth set, put the black dots at the center bottom of the circle. Then make a diagonal backslash line across the upper right of the right eye and a diagonal slash crossing the left side of the left eye. Eyes not only allow us to see, but they also allow us to express emotions. Try making other eyes with different expressions. Do you have to see everything, or do you have faith?

DAY 5

READ

Romans 4:18-25 ("Believing the Promise," page 705 in the *Day By Day Kid's Bible*)

Abraham knew he was too old to have children. In fact, he was almost 100 years old. He knew his wife, Sarah, was old too. But he believed God's promise anyway. Abraham's faith was strong. He believed God had the power to do what he promised. That's why God said Abraham was right with him... We can believe in God also. When we do, God says we are right with him.

THINK AND TALK
What choice did Abraham have? What fact tempted Abraham not to believe God? What are some things that tempt you not to believe God? When is it the hardest for you to believe God?

PRACTICE
Challenge someone to practice fighting temptation. You can take turns drawing the temptation cards from a bowl. Ask each other what you would do if you were tempted in that way.

TRY THIS
Trick your eyes. With your left hand hold a cardboard tube from a roll of paper towels. Look through the tube with your left eye. Keep your right eye open too. Now place your right hand up, resting against the side of the tube, with your palm toward your face. Slowly bring your hand toward you or move it away until you see a hole in your hand. But this is just a trick, an illusion. At this moment, you believe what you *can't* see—you believe your hand has no hole. What other things do you believe that you can't see?

DAY 6

READ
Romans 10 ("Beautiful Feet," page 710 in the *Day By Day Kid's Bible*)
God's Word is near you. It's in your mouth. It's in your heart. That's the faith we're talking about. So say it with your mouth. "Jesus is Lord." Believe that God made him come back to life again. Then you will be saved. When you believe with your heart, it's just as if you'd never sinned. When you say with your mouth that you believe, you are saved.

THINK AND TALK
What is it that God wants us to believe before we can be saved? What are we saved from? Why do we have to have faith to be

saved? Is it always easy to have faith? Why or why not?

PRACTICE
Challenge someone to practice fighting temptation. You can take turns drawing the temptation cards from a bowl. Ask each other what you would do if you were tempted in that way.

TRY THIS
You will need 19 index cards. Write one word from the memory verse in the center of each card, with the reference on the last one. Line the cards up in order from end to end. Now design a border to the right of the first word (now), and make the same side border to the left of the second word (faith). Draw a different design at the right border of the card with the word *faith* and the same border to the left of the card that says *is*. Keep designing these cards so that the right border of a word matches the left border of the word that comes after it. You are making dominoes. When the cards are finished, mix them up. Find a person to put the cards in order by matching their borders. Since a person doesn't have to read to do this, you could do this with a young brother, sister, or friend. Then you can read the sentence to this person.

DAY 7

READ
2 Thessalonians 1 ("Bright Fire and Strong Angels," page 671 in the *Day By Day Kid's Bible*)
We should always thank God for you. That's because your faith is growing more and more... We talk about how you keep going in hard times. We talk about how you keep believing. It just shows what God does is right... People give you a hard time for believing in God. But God is fair. He will give trouble to people who give you trouble. And he will take our troubles away. That will happen when Jesus comes back.

THINK AND TALK
Are there things we can do to help our faith grow? If so, what can we do? Have people ever given you a hard time for believing in

124

God? What happened? All people have faith in something. What are some things people put their faith in? Why would it be better for them to put their faith in God?

PRACTICE
Challenge someone to practice fighting temptation. You can take turns drawing the temptation cards from a bowl. Ask each other person what you would do if you were tempted in that way.

TRY THIS
Make Faith Rolls. In a big bowl, mix three cups of flour, one package of quick-rising yeast, one-half teaspoon of salt, and one-third cup of sugar. In a saucepan, mix one-half cup of butter or margarine cut into slices, one-half cup of milk, and one-half cup of water. Heat the milk mixture until bubbles just start to form around the edges and the butter is melting. Then pour it all at once into the flour mixture and stir it in. In a small bowl, lightly beat one egg with a fork. Add it to the batter and mix it in well. Add flour a little at a time, up to one cup more, mixing well after you add it, even if you have to mix it with your hands. But add just enough so the dough is not sticky. Then cover the bowl with a clean kitchen towel and let it rest for 10 minutes. Grease a baking sheet. Next, grab a handful of dough and shape it into the letter *F*. With another handful of dough, shape the letter *A*. Shape an *I*, a *T*, and an *H*. What have you spelled? Place all the rolls on the baking sheet. Cover them again with the towel and let them rise for 30 minutes. Heat the oven to 400 degrees. Bake the rolls for 15 minutes. You'll see the dough rise while it sits and while it bakes, so you'll "see FAITH grow." How does real faith grow?

Showing Selflessness

Your sword of the Spirit for this week is:

Do nothing out of selfish ambition or vain conceit. PHILIPPIANS 2:3a

With the above sword you can fight back when you face this temptation:

You are tempted to be selfish.

DAY 1

READ

Luke 21:1-4 ("The Most Money," page 602 in the *Day By Day Kid's Bible*)

Jesus sat down at the worship house. He was across from the place where people gave money... Lots of rich people came by. They threw in lots of money. Then a poor woman... dropped in two small pennies. "Look!' said Jesus... "This woman put the most money into the offering box... The other people gave only part of their riches. This poor woman gave all the money she had."

THINK AND TALK

Being *selfless* is doing what is best for others, even if it's not what you really want to do. What choice did the woman have? Would it have been selfish for her to give only one penny? Why or why not? Why do you think she gave her last two pennies? Have you ever known someone who gave away something they really liked? Why did they do it? What happened?

PRACTICE

127

Read the verse. Try to repeat it several times without looking. Cut a sword shape from paper or cardboard and write the verse on it. You'll want to hang it up in your house where it will remind you of the Spirit's sword from Philippians 2:3a. You can use it to fight against the temptation to be selfish.

DAY 2

READ
Mark 9:33-35 ("Who Is the Greatest?" page 567 in the *Day By Day Kid's Bible*)
Jesus and his friends were walking down the road. His friends began fussing with each other. So Jesus asked them, "What are you fussing about?" Jesus' friends didn't answer. They had been fussing over who was the greatest. Jesus sat down. "Do you want to be first?" he asked. "Then make yourself last. Serve others."

THINK AND TALK
When do you most want to be first? Have you ever seen people, even grown people, fussing over who gets to be first? Why do they want to be first? How can you tell if someone is selfish? How can you tell if someone is selfless? Which person would you rather have as a friend?

PRACTICE
Challenge a friend or family member (or yourself) to a sword-fight. One person says, "What will you do if you are tempted to be selfish?" The other person answers, "I will not be selfish because it is written, 'Do nothing out of selfish ambition or vain conceit.'"

DAY 3

READ
Luke 16:19-31 ("Lazarus and the Rich Man," page 585 in the *Day By Day Kid's Bible*)
"Once there was a rich man," said Jesus.... "A beggar named Lazarus sat at his gate... Little bits of food fell off the rich man's table. Lazarus would have loved to eat those bits. One day, Lazarus died. Angels came and got him.... The rich man looked

up. He saw Abraham far away. Lazarus was sitting beside him. 'Father Abraham!' he cried…. 'All this fire is too much for me!' But Abraham said, 'Remember the way you lived. You got your good things on earth. Lazarus got bad things. But now he is feeling good and you're not.'"

THINK AND TALK
What choices did the rich man have before he died? What did he choose to do? Why does God want us to be selfless? What does *selfish ambition* mean? Have you ever known someone, or seen a character in a book or video, who had selfish ambition? What happened to that person in the story? What happens to people who are like that in real life? What happens when we are selfless?

PRACTICE
Challenge someone to a sword-fight with your sword for this week. Write on an index card: "You are tempted to be selfish." Add this temptation card to the others you've been collecting. Place these cards in a bowl. The first person draws a card and challenges the second person with that temptation. The second person repeats the sword of the Spirit that he can use to fight the temptation. Then it's his turn to draw a card and challenge the first person.

DAY 4

READ
Genesis 18:1-15 ("Abraham's Visitors," page 13 in the *Day By Day Kid's Bible*)
Abraham looked up and saw three men. So he got up and went to meet them... Abraham bowed down. "Stay here for a while," he said. "Rest in the shade of the tree. My servants will get water so you can wash your feet. I'll get some food so you can eat. You can go on after you rest."

THINK AND TALK
Did Abraham choose to be selfish or selfless toward his three visitors? What might Abraham done if he had been selfish? What is *vain conceit*? One meaning is "foolish and prideful over what

you've done." Abraham had done some great things. Why do you think he was not prideful?

PRACTICE
You and another person can challenge each other to practice fighting temptation. Do this by taking turns drawing the temptation cards from a bowl. Ask each other what you would do if you were tempted in that way.

TRY THIS
Shine a bright light onto a wall. Make hand shadows. Try to make a camel. One hand can be the head of the camel. Try using your other hand to make the hump. Try a paper-plate shadow to make the hump. Try a small pillow. What other objects could you try? If a friend is with you, use your friends hands to help you. If you had lived in Abraham's time, what kind of transportation would you have wanted to use when you traveled?

DAY 5

READ
1 Samuel 25 ("The Man Whose Name Means 'Fool'," page 151 in the *Day By Day Kid's Bible*)
[David] sent 10 young men to Nabal. David said, "Tell Nabal hello for me. Tell him we pray for good things for him and his family. Then tell him that his shepherds were with us for a while. We were good to them... Then ask Nabal to give us whatever he can." So David's men went to Nabal... "Who is David?" said Nabal.... "Why should I give bread and water to him? I have meat for my workers. Why should I give it to David?"

THINK AND TALK
What choices did Nabal have? Did Nabal choose to be selfish or selfless? Why? What happened after that? What does it feel like to be selfish? What does it feel like to be selfless?

PRACTICE

Challenge someone to practice fighting temptation. You can take turns drawing the temptation cards from a bow. Ask each other what you would do if you were tempted in that way.

TRY THIS
Make raisin cakes. (Read the whole story of David and Naboth to find out why raisin cakes are in this story.) In a pan on the stove, heat one-fourth cup of sugar, one tablespoon of cornstarch, one cup of water and two cups of raisins. When this mixture is thick, take it off the stove and let it cool. Now mix one-half cup of softened margarine and one cup of brown sugar. In another bowl, mix one and one-half cups of flour, one-half teaspoon of baking soda, and one-half teaspoon of salt. Add this flour mixture to the margarine mixture. Now stir in one and one-half cup of oats and one tablespoon of water. Press half of this dough into a 13-inch by 9-inch baking pan. Spread the raisin mixture over it. Then spread the other half of the dough on top. Bake it at 350 degrees for 35 minutes.

DAY 6

READ
Ruth 1 ("Going Home," page 111 in the *Day By Day Kid's Bible*)
One man left Judah. He moved with his wife and family to the land of Moab. He had two sons. His wife's name was Naomi. After they moved, the man died... When Naomi's sons were old enough, they got married. One married a young woman named Orpah. One married a young woman named Ruth. But ... both of Naomi's sons died... One day Naomi... decided to go back home... Naomi kissed Orpah and Ruth good-bye and went home… Orpah kissed Naomi. She said good-bye and went home... "Don't tell me to leave you," said Ruth. "I'll go where you go. I'll stay where you stay... I won't leave you as long as I live."

THINK AND TALK
What choices did Orpah and Ruth have? What did they choose to do? Why do you think Ruth would leave her own land and family to go with Naomi? Read further in the book of Ruth to find out how

selfless Ruth was as she served Naomi. Do you think it was always easy for Ruth to be selfless? Why or why not? Tell about someone you know who is selfless.

PRACTICE
Challenge someone to practice fighting temptation. You can take turns drawing the temptation cards from a bowl. Ask each other what you would do if you were tempted in that way.

TRY THIS
Ask friends or family to play Pack My Bag with you. Sit in a circle. Choose one person to start the game. This person says, "I'm going to (he names a place that starts with the letter *A*) and I'm going to pack an (he names a thing that starts with the letter *A*)." The next person says the same thing except she must name a place that starts with *B* and a thing that starts with *B*. Continue this way with each person naming a place and a thing that starts with the next letter of the alphabet. If you were moving to a new place like Ruth was, what is the one thing you would want to take with you?

DAY 7

READ
Matthew 16:21-24 ("What's Coming," in the *Day By Day Kid's Bible*) Jesus now began to get his friends ready. He let them know what was going to happen... He said he would be killed. But he'd come alive again on the third day. Peter pulled Jesus to one side. "Never, Lord," he said. "This will never happen to you." "Get out of my way, Satan!" said Jesus. "This does not help me. You're not thinking of what God wants. You're thinking of what you want... Do you want to be with me? Then you'll have to give up what you want. You'll have to do what God chose you to do."

THINK AND TALK
It sounded like Peter was trying to think of what was good for Jesus. Why wasn't it good? Is it always easy to be selfless? What are some things that can tempt you to be selfish? When is it hardest for you to fight the temptation to be selfish? What can you

do to help yourself be selfless?

PRACTICE
Challenge someone to practice fighting temptation. You can take turns drawing the temptation cards from a bowl. Ask each other what you would do if you were tempted in that way.

TRY THIS
Play balloon volleyball with at least one other person. Stretch a string or clothesline across a room or yard. Make it about five feet off the ground. You can make it higher or lower it if you need to. Or if you have a volleyball net or badminton net, you may use it instead of a string. Blow up a large balloon. Bat it back and forth across the net, playing volleyball with the balloon. You may want to have some extra balloons handy in case the first one pops. Is it possible to be selfless in sports? If so, how? If not, why?

Accepting Those Who Are Different

Your sword of the Spirit for this week is:

In humility consider others better than yourselves. PHILIPPIANS 2:3b

With the above sword you can fight back when you face this temptation:

You are tempted to reject someone who is different.

DAY 1

READ

Mark 10: 46-52 ("By the Side of the Road," page 593 in the *Day By Day Kid's Bible*)

A man was sitting by the side of the road. He could not see. His name was Bartimaeus... Bartimaeus heard people say that Jesus was coming. So he started shouting, "Jesus! Be kind to me." Lots of people got mad at him. They told him to be quiet... Jesus stopped walking... "What do you want me to do?" Jesus asked. "I want to see!" said Bartimaeus. "All right," said Jesus. "You are well because you believe in me!" Right away, Bartimaeus could see.

THINK AND TALK

Accepting others means receiving them kindly, treating them as important people. *Rejecting* others means ignoring them or making fun of them. Bartimaeus was a blind beggar. The people were tempted to reject Bartimaeus. Why? Did they fall for the temptation? Did Jesus fall for the temptation? Some people are tempted to reject a person who is blind or who has another handicap. Why? If you have accepted a handicapped person as a friend, tell about it. If you are handicapped, are you tempted to reject other people? Why or why not?

PRACTICE
Read the verse. Try to repeat it several times without looking. Cut a sword shape from paper or cardboard and write the verse on it. You'll want to hang it up in your house where it will remind you of the Spirit's sword from Philippians 2:3b. You can use it to fight against the temptation to reject people who are different.

DAY 2

READ
Luke 19:1-10 ("Up in a Tree," page 593 in the *Day By Day Kid's Bible*)
Zacchaeus heard that Jesus was coming. He wanted to see who Jesus was. But Zacchaeus was a short man. So he couldn't see around the crowd... He climbed up into a tree... Jesus did come that way. When he got to the tree, he stopped.... "Zacchaeus!" he called. "Come down right away. I need to stay at your house today." ...The other people began to make a fuss. "Jesus has gone to stay with a sinner!" they said.

THINK AND TALK
Who was tempted to reject Zacchaeus? Why? Have you ever been tempted to reject someone who was too short or too tall or too fat or too thin? Why does God want us to accept people? What happens when we don't accept people? List some of your friends who are taller, shorter, larger or thinner than you. List some of the blessings you have received by having friends like these.

PRACTICE
Challenge a friend or family member (or yourself) to a sword fight. One person says, "What will you do if you are tempted to reject someone?" The other person answers, "I will not reject people,

because it is written, 'In humility consider others better than yourselves.'"

DAY 3

READ

1 Samuel 16:1-13 ("Choosing the Next King," page 137 in the *Day By Day Kid's Bible*)

God spoke to Samuel... "Put oil in your jar. Go to see Jesse in Bethlehem. One of his sons will be the next king." ...So Samuel went to Bethlehem... Samuel saw Jesse's first son. "This must be the one God chose," he thought. But God said, "Don't choose someone by his looks. Don't choose by how tall he is. I don't look at people the way you do. People only see what others look like. I see what's in their hearts."

THINK AND TALK

Has anyone ever rejected you? Why? How did it feel? Does God ever reject you? Sometimes God surprises and uses people we never would have chosen to carry out his plans. If you know someone like this, tell about it. Is God using you in ways that people never would have thought of? If someone has rejected you, you must forgive them in your heart before God can completely fulfill his plans for you. Why?

PRACTICE

Challenge someone to a sword-fight with your sword for this week. Write on an index card: "You are tempted to reject someone." Add this temptation card to the other cards you've collected. Place these in a bowl. The first person draws a card and challenges the second person with that temptation. The second person repeats the sword of the Spirit that she can use to fight that temptation. Then it's her turn to draw a card and challenge the first person.

DAY 4

READ

Acts 10 ("Animals in a Big Sheet," page 646 in the *Day By Day Kid's Bible*)

There was a Roman army captain named Cornelius... Peter went to see Cornelius at his house... Peter began to talk... "You know the law of Jewish people. We're not supposed to visit someone who is not Jewish. But God showed me that it's all right with him... God doesn't love one person more than another. He loves people from every nation."

THINK AND TALK

Because God had chosen the Jewish people to be his people, they often rejected people of other nations. Why was Peter tempted to reject Cornelius? Why did he choose to accept Cornelius? Why might we be tempted to reject people of other nations today? If you have a friend from another nation, list some of the blessings that you have received by having this friend.

PRACTICE

You and another person can challenge each other to practice fighting temptation. Do this by taking turns drawing the temptation cards from a bowl. Ask each other what you would do if you were tempted in that way.

TRY THIS

Adopt a nation. Choose a nation you want to pray for. Make a poster for this nation. At the top of the poster, write, "God loves people from every nation." Then write the name of the nation you chose. Look it up in the encyclopedia. Draw a map of it. List the climate and some of the customs, the main crops, the religions, and any other interesting information you find. Put this poster in a place where it will remind you to pray for this nation.

DAY 5

READ

John 4:3-42 ("Water from a Well," page 518 in the *Day By Day Kid's Bible*)

Jesus was on his way to Galilee. He went through the land of Samaria. He was tired. So he stopped at a well and sat down... It wasn't long before a woman came to the well... "Would you give me a drink?" Jesus asked her. Now Jews don't like people from Samaria. So the woman said, "Why are you asking me for a drink? You are a Jew. I'm from Samaria."

THINK AND TALK

Why was the woman surprised that Jesus talked to her? Sometimes we are tempted to think that we are better than people from other countries. Why? How can you tell if a person is good at accepting others who are different? How can you tell if a person does not accept others who are different? Which person would you rather have as a friend? Why?

PRACTICE

Challenge someone to practice fighting temptation. You can take turns drawing the temptation cards from a bowl. Ask each other what you would do if you were tempted in that way.

TRY THIS

Put your foot to your forearm with your heal at your elbow. Where do your toes come to? Ask friends or family to try this. What did you find out about the size of a person's foot compared to his forearm? Now place a hand in front of your face, with the base of your palm at your chin, fingers pointing upward, covering your nose. Where does the tip of your middle finger come to? Ask other people to try this. What did you find out about the size of a person's face compared to the size of his hand? Look carefully at people's faces from the front. Where do the tops of their ears come to compared to where their eyes are? Where do the bottoms of their ears come, compared to where their lips are? People are different in many ways. But in many ways, people are alike. What are some other ways that we are alike?

DAY 6

READ

Galatians 3:24-28 ("Believing What You Heard," page 659 in the *Day By Day Kid's Bible*)

You are all God's children. That's because you believe in Jesus. You were baptized into Jesus, soaked in him, covered with him. Being Jewish or not Jewish doesn't matter. Being a slave or being free doesn't matter. Being a man or a woman doesn't matter. Everyone is together in Jesus.

THINK AND TALK

Why would some people be tempted to reject a person because he is a boy or a man? Why would some people be tempted to reject a person because she is a girl or a woman? Did Jesus reject men? Did Jesus reject women? Read or say our sword verse for this week. What does "in humility" mean? How can we show that we "consider others better" than ourselves?

PRACTICE

Challenge someone to practice fighting temptation. You can take turns drawing the temptation cards from a bowl. Ask each other what you would do if you were tempted in that way.

TRY THIS

Are you short-waisted, long-waisted, or neither? Stand straight with your arms by your sides. Now bend your forearms up, keeping your upper arms at your sides so that your elbows are pointing down. If your elbows come above your waist, you are long-waisted. If your elbows come below your waist, you are short-waisted. If your elbows come exactly to your waist, you are neither long-waisted nor short-waisted. You probably choose your friends without caring whether they are short-waisted or long-waisted. In what other ways are your friends different from you? Does that difference matter? Why?

DAY 7

READ

1 Samuel 30 ("Saving Wives and Children," page 155 in the *Day By Day Kid's Bible*)

David's men found a man from Egypt in a field. They took him to David. He hadn't eaten anything for three days and three nights. So they gave him part of a fig cake and two raisin cakes. They gave him some water to drink... "I'm from Egypt," he said. "I'm a slave. My master left me here because I got sick."

THINK AND TALK

Why had the slave's master rejected him? Why would someone be tempted to reject someone who was sick? Is it always easy to accept people who are different? When is it hardest for you to accept someone who is different? How can you help yourself become a person who accepts different people? Is it ever right to reject people? Why or why not?

PRACTICE

Challenge someone to practice fighting temptation. You can take turns drawing the temptation cards from a bowl. Ask each other what you would do if you were tempted in that way.

TRY THIS

David's men gave the man from Egypt some figs to eat. Eat some figs or some fig cookies. Then you can make up a limerick about figs. A limerick is a poem written in a rhythm and rhyme like this one:

There once was a man who found figs
In his garden among the tree twigs.
But he sat down and said,
I like carrots instead.
And he fed all the figs to his pigs.

You may use the opening line of this limerick to start your own.

Encouraging Others

Your sword of the Spirit for this week is:

Think of ways to encourage one another to outbursts of love and good deeds.
HEBREWS 10:24

With the above sword you can fight back when you face this temptation:

You are tempted to discourage someone.

DAY 1

READ
Numbers 14 ("Scared of the People," page 80 in the *Day By Day Kid's Bible*)
That night God's people cried... "Let's go back to Egypt." ...Joshua and Caleb were two of the 12 men who looked around Canaan. They said, "The land is very good. If God is happy with us, he will lead us there... We'll win over those people... Don't be scared of them. God is with us."

THINK AND TALK
When you *encourage* someone, you give them hope and courage. When you *discourage* someone, you tempt the person to be afraid and to give up. When Joshua and Caleb and the other men saw the people of Canaan, they were tempted to discourage the rest of the people. Why? What did they choose to do? How did Joshua and Caleb try to encourage the people? If you had been one of God's people, would you have been discouraged or encouraged?

143

PRACTICE

Read the verse. Try to repeat it several times without looking. Cut a sword shape from paper or cardboard and write the verse on it. You'll want to hang it up in your house where it will remind you of the Spirit's sword from Hebrews 10:24. You can use it to fight against the temptation to discourage someone.

DAY 2

READ

Matthew 9:9-13 ("A Party at Matthew's," page 525 in the *Day By Day Kid's Bible*)

Matthew was sitting at his tax table... He took the tax money that people had to pay. "Follow Me," Jesus said to Matthew. So Matthew followed Jesus. He even gave a big dinner party for Jesus... Tax workers and many other people came to his party... The leaders talked to Jesus' friends... "Why are you eating and drinking with these tax workers? They are sinners."

THINK AND TALK

Why was Jesus eating and drinking with the tax workers? Who was discouraging to Matthew and his friends? Who was encouraging? Why do you think God wants us to encourage others? What happens when we don't encourage others?

PRACTICE

Challenge a friend or family member (or yourself) to a sword-fight. One person says, "What will you do if you are tempted to discourage someone?" The other person answers, "I will not discourage people, because it is written, 'Think of ways to encourage one another to outbursts of love and good deeds.'"

DAY 3

READ

Exodus 18 ("Jethro's Good Idea," page 64 in the *Day By Day Kid's Bible*)

Jethro watched Moses. Then he said,... "Why are you the only judge for all these people? It takes you all day... You're going to get too tired. It's too much work... Choose some men to help you... They can be the judges of the easy problems. They can bring the hard problems to you. That way you'll be able to do this hard job. And the people will be taken care of."

THINK AND TALK

Why might Moses have been discouraged? Did you ever have a job that seemed too difficult or too tiring for you? If so, did someone encourage you? How? How did Jethro encourage Moses? Was Jethro's advice good? How does it feel to be discouraged? How does it feel to be encouraged?

PRACTICE

Challenge someone to a sword-fight with your sword for this week. Write on an index card: "You are tempted to discourage someone." Add this temptation card to the others you've collected. Place these cards in a bowl. The first person draws a card and challenges the second person with that temptation. The second person repeats the sword of the Spirit that he can use to fight the temptation. Then it's his turn to draw a card and challenge the first person.

DAY 4

READ

2 Corinthians 8 ("The First to Give," page 698 in the *Day By Day Kid's Bible*)
You do a great job in everything. You're good at believing. You're good at talking. You're good at knowing things. You're good at wanting to do right. You're good at loving us. So do a great job in your giving, too.

THINK AND TALK

These are words that Paul wrote to God's people who lived in the city of Corinth. What makes these words encouraging? Tell about someone you know who encourages you. How do they encourage you? Is there a time when we *should* discourage someone? If so, when?

145

PRACTICE

You and another person can challenge each other to practice fighting temptation. Do this by taking turns drawing the temptation cards from a bowl. Ask each other what you would do if you were tempted in that way, and answer by saying the appropriate verse.

TRY THIS

Make encouragement cards by writing "Great Job!" on some index cards. Write "You Can Do It!" on some of the cards. Make designs on the cards and color them. Or decorate your cards with stickers that give encouraging messages. Give these cards to people who have worked hard. For example, give "Great Job!" to your mom after she makes a meal, or give it to your little sister after she cleans her room. Give a "You Can Do It!" card to a friend who is studying hard.

DAY 5

READ

Acts 27:27-44 ("Stormy Seas!" page 728 in the *Day By Day Kid's Bible*)

The storm kept blowing... At last, they gave up. They all thought they'd die. The men had not eaten for a long time. Finally Paul stood up... "Be brave," said Paul. "I believe in God" ...Paul tried to talk everyone into eating... "Please eat something. You'll need food to stay alive. No one will lose even one hair from his head." Then Paul picked up some bread... He started eating. The men felt better when they saw Paul eat. They ate some food too.

THINK AND TALK

What choices did Paul have during the storm? Do you think Paul was tempted to be discouraged? How would you have felt if you had been on the ship with Paul? What did Paul *say* to encourage the men on the ship? What did he *do* to encourage them? Tell about a time when you encouraged someone or when someone encouraged you.

PRACTICE

Challenge someone to practice fighting temptation. You can take turns drawing the temptation cards from a bowl. Ask each other what you would do if you were tempted in that way.

TRY THIS

Make a storm in a jar. Fill a jar three-fourths full with water. Add a drop of dishwashing liquid and one-half teaspoon of salt. Put the lid on the jar and shake it around in a circular motion as if you were stirring something in a large pot. Then hold the jar still. A funnel will form and whirl around inside the jar. What could you say or do that might encourage someone before or during a storm? What could you say or do that might encourage someone whose house has been damaged by a storm?

DAY 6

READ

2 Chronicles 32:1-19 ("Trying to Scare God's People," page 355 in the *Day By Day Kid's Bible*)

Assyria planned to fight Jerusalem...Hezekiah chose army leaders. He told them, "Be strong. Be brave. Don't be afraid... We have God to help us fight." So the people felt brave and sure of themselves... Assyria's army leader said, "Our king asks why you're so sure of yourself... You might say you are trusting in your God... But Hezekiah is just lying to you... Don't let him talk you into trusting God." ...But the people kept quiet. King Hezekiah had told them, 'Don't answer."

THINK AND TALK

Who tried to discourage the people? How? Who tried to encourage the people? How? If you had been one of the people listening to Hezekiah and the enemy leader, how would you have known who to believe? Do you ever get discouraged? What can you remember to help encourage yourself? What can you do to encourage others?

PRACTICE

Challenge someone to practice fighting temptation. You can take turns drawing the temptation cards from a bowl. Ask each other what you would do if you were tempted in that way.

TRY THIS

Blow up 15 balloons, any size. On each balloon, write one word from the memory verse for this week. One balloon should have the reference, Hebrews 10:24, on it. Get at least one other person to help you with this. Arrange the balloons in order so you can read the verse. Read it together. Ask the other person to pop any balloon he wants to pop. He can prick it with a pin or sit on it. Now read the verse again, saying the missing word when you get to it. If you have other people playing with you, choose someone else to pop another balloon, or if you have only one other person, it's your turn to pop a balloon. Read the verse again, saying both missing words. One by one, pop each balloon until at last there are no balloons and you are saying the verse by memory. When each balloon pops, remember "outbursts" of love and good deeds. What does that mean?

DAY 7

READ

2 Samuel 19 ("King David Goes Back Home," page 180 in the *Day By Day Kid's Bible*)

The army had been glad they won. Then they heard that King David was crying for Absalom. So they became sad. The army went into the town quietly. They were like men who felt bad because they lost... Joab went to see King David. "You've made your whole army feel bad," said Joab. "We just saved your life today!... Now go out and see your men. Cheer them up." ...So King David got up. He went out and sat at the gate of the city. The men heard that David was sitting at the gate. So they all went to see him there.

THINK AND TALK

The men in the army were discouraged. Why? Who else was discouraged? Who encouraged King David? Who encouraged the men in the army? What are some things that might keep us from encouraging someone? When is it hardest for you to encourage someone? Do you know someone who is discouraged right now? What can you do to encourage that person?

PRACTICE

Challenge someone to practice fighting temptation. You can take turns drawing the temptation cards from a bowl. Ask each other what you would do if you were tempted in that way.

TRY THIS

Sometimes a snack encourages someone who is working hard. Make a pinwheel snack. Spread cream cheese over some flour tortillas. Sprinkle the cream cheese with bacon bits, or spread salsa over it. You may also place thin slices of cherry tomato, avocado or other veggies on it. You can think of other yummy things to put in it also. Ask for adult help when using a sharp knife. Roll the tortilla up and slice it into circles as if you were slicing a banana or carrot. These will be pinwheel shaped. Serve them to family or friends.

Being Friendly

Your sword of the Spirit for this week is:

A friend loves at all times. PROVERBS 17:17

With the above sword you can fight back when you face this temptation:

You are tempted to be unfriendly.

DAY 1

READ

2 Kings 4:8-17 ("A Room on the Roof Top," page 296 in the *Day By Day Kid's Bible*)

One day Elisha went to a town called Shunem. A rich woman lived there. She asked Elisha to come for dinner. Every time Elisha went through Shunem, he ate there. The woman told her husband,… "Let's make a little room on our roof... Elisha can stay there when he comes."

THINK AND TALK

Friends like each other and enjoy spending time together. Being *friendly* is treating someone the way you would treat a friend. What did the woman from Shunem do to be friendly to Elisha? Name some of your friends. What do you like about each one? What do you like to do together?

PRACTICE

Read the verse. Try to repeat it several times without looking. Cut a sword shape from paper or cardboard. Write the verse on it. You'll want to hang it up in your house where it will remind you of the Spirit's sword from Proverbs 17:17. You can use it to fight against the temptation to be unfriendly.

DAY 2

READ

Proverbs 12:26; 13:20; 18:24; 27:9-10 ("Friends," page 253 in the *Day By Day Kid's Bible*)

People who do right say helpful things to their friends. But sinful people lead their friends to do wrong. Being around wise people makes you wise. Being around fools hurts you... Some people think they have many friends, but the real friend is the one who stays closer than a brother... Sweet smelling perfume makes you feel happy. Friends make you happy too. They tell you what's right. Don't forget your friends.

THINK AND TALK

Why is it important to choose the right kind of people to be your friends? What kind of person makes a good friend? What kind of person makes a bad friend? Does God want us to be friendly? Why or why not? Are there times when we should not be friendly?

PRACTICE

Challenge a friend or family member (or yourself) to a sword-fight. One person says, "What will you do if you are tempted to be unfriendly?" The other person says, "I will not be unfriendly because it is written, 'A friend loves at all times.'"

DAY 3

READ

John 15:1-16 ("The Vine," page 612 in the *Day By Day Kid's Bible*)

"This is my rule. Love each other like I love you. There is one thing that shows the greatest love. It's giving up your life for your friends. You're my friends if you do what I say. I'm not calling you servants anymore," said Jesus. "I'm calling you friends... I chose you. You didn't choose me. I chose you to go out and be like a tree that grows fruit. Grow fruit for God by doing things for him that will last."

THINK AND TALK

Describe the kind of friend Jesus was to his followers. Jesus has chosen you to be his friend too. Have you said yes to Jesus? Describe the kind of friend Jesus is to you. What was the rule Jesus gave to his friends? How can you follow this rule (to love each other) with your friends?

PRACTICE

Challenge someone to a sword-fight with your sword for this week. Write on an index card: "You are tempted to be unfriendly." Add this temptation card to the other cards you've collected. Place these cards in a bowl. The first person draws a card and challenges the second person with that temptation. The second person repeats the sword of the Spirit that she can use to fight the temptation. Then it's her turn to draw a card and challenge the first person.

DAY 4

READ

Ecclesiastes 4 ("Two Are Better than One," page 263 in the *Day By Day Kid's Bible*)

Two are better than one. They can get a lot more for their work. When one falls down, the other picks him up. But it's sad if there's nobody to help him up. Two can lie down together and stay warm. But how can one stay warm by himself? An enemy can win over one. But two can fight back. It's like tying three strings together. Three together is not easy to break.

THINK AND TALK

Why do we need friends? What are some things you can't do alone? What are some things you can do alone, but they're more fun to do with someone else? Tell about a time when someone was friendly to you. Tell about a time when you were friendly to someone.

PRACTICE

You and another person can challenge each other to practice fighting temptation. Do this by taking turns drawing the temptation cards from a bowl. Ask each other what you would do if you were tempted in that way, and answer by saying the appropriate verse.

TRY THIS

Place one of your hands on top of a piece of white paper. Your little finger should touch one of the short edges, and your other fingers spread out. Trace around your hand. Ask a friend to place one of his or her hands on the paper beside your handprint. The thumb of your friend's hand should touch the thumb of your handprint. And the little finger of your friend's hand should touch the opposite short edge of the paper. Trace around your friend's hand. Now tape several other pieces of white paper together short end to short end. Tape one of the short ends to the paper with the handprints on it. Keeping the handprint paper on top, fold the papers like an accordion so that they are stacked one on top of the other. Cut around the handprints through all the layers of paper, but don't cut around the tips of the thumbs or little fingers. Unfold the papers to see a chain of handprints from you and your friend.

DAY 5

READ

Acts 9:1-31 ("A Bright Light and a Voice," page 644 in the *Day By Day Kid's Bible*)

The Jews made plans to kill Saul. Every day and night, they watched the city gates... So one night, Saul's friends took him to the city wall. Saul got into a big basket. His friends put the basket through an open place in the wall. Then they let it down to the ground. Saul went back to Jerusalem. There he tried to meet with Jesus' followers. But they were afraid of him. They didn't believe he had really become a follower of Jesus. But Barnabas took Saul to the apostles... He told them how Saul taught people about Jesus. So they let Saul stay with them.

THINK AND TALK

Some people wanted to be Saul's friends, and some people didn't. Why were people tempted to be unfriendly to Saul? How did his friends help him? How did Barnabas show his friendship to Saul? How do you show friendship to your friends? Do you have any friends who live far away? Are you able to keep being friends with them? If so, how?

PRACTICE

Challenge someone to practice fighting temptation. You can take turns drawing the temptation cards from a bowl. Ask each other what you would do if you were tempted in that way.

TRY THIS

Get some white paper and a soft-lead pencil or a crayon. Go around your house or a friend's house and find different baskets. Place the paper on the side of the basket and rub over it with the pencil or crayon to see the design of the basket transfer to the paper. If you are doing this as a group, each person could bring a basket so you could have lots of baskets to use in making your designs. If the basket Saul's friends used was big enough to put Saul in, what do you think the basket was supposed to hold?

DAY 6

READ

Luke 6:12-19 ("Friends and Helpers," page 529 in the *Day By Day Kid's Bible*)

In the morning Jesus called his friends. He picked 12 of them to be his special friends and helpers. He chose Peter and his brother Andrew. He chose James and his brother John. He chose Philip and Nathanael. He chose Matthew, Thomas, and Simon. He chose another James... He chose Judas whose father's name was James. Then Jesus chose another Judas, called Judas Iscariot. He turned out to be an enemy.

THINK AND TALK

If you can get a concordance, use it to find other places in the Bible that tell about these men. Which men does the Bible tell most about? What can you find out about the men? They didn't always agree with each other. Sometimes they disagreed. Is it possible to disagree with a friend and still be friends? Why or why not? What are some ways to keep on loving your friends even when you disagree?

PRACTICE

Challenge someone to practice fighting temptation. You can take turns drawing the temptation cards from a bowl. Ask each other what you would do if you were tempted in that way.

TRY THIS

Get some dry cereal shaped like the letters of the alphabet. Find letters that spell out the memory verse. Glue them in order to a paper plate or piece of cardboard. Lay this on top of some old newspaper and spray over it with spray paint, any color, to make a plaque. Hang up your plaque. And every time you look at it, think about a way to be friendly to one of your friends.

DAY 7

READ

Acts 8:26-40 ("A Chariot Ride," page 643 in the *Day By Day Kid's Bible*) One of God's angels came to Philip. "Go to the road south of here," he said... Philip found the road. He started traveling down it... The Spirit said to Philip, "Go up to that chariot. Stay close to it." So Philip ran up to the chariot. He heard the man reading the book Isaiah wrote. "Do you understand what you're reading?" Philip asked.

THINK AND TALK

How did Philip make friends with the man in the chariot? Sometimes we can be friendly by asking a question, or by offering to help someone. Is it always easy to be friendly? Do you think it was easy for Philip? What are some things that might cause us to be unfriendly? Who is the friendliest person you know? What does that person do to make friends? What can you do to make friends?

PRACTICE

Challenge someone to practice fighting temptation. You can take turns drawing the temptation cards from a bowl. Ask each other what you would do if you were tempted in that way.

TRY THIS

Make a model chariot by using a plastic scoop from a box of laundry detergent, or by cutting a paper cup in half from top to bottom and turning it on its rounded side. This is the body of your chariot. Cut out two large wheels from the paper cup that will fit your chariot. Attach them with paper fasteners (brads).

Showing Respect

Your sword of the Spirit for this week is:

In everything, do to others what you would have them do to you. MATTHEW 7:12

With the above sword you can fight back when you face this temptation:

You are tempted to be disrespectful.

DAY 1

READ

Romans 13 ("Wake Up!" page 713 in the *Day By Day Kid's Bible*) People should obey the leaders of their country. Leaders were put in charge by God... So obey the people in charge. Do it not just because you'll get in trouble if you don't. Do it because it's what God wants. You'll feel better when you do what's right... Are you supposed to treat them as important people? Then treat them as important people... If you love people, you've done what God wants.

THINK AND TALK

To *respect* someone is to treat him or her as someone who is important to you, someone who is worth your time and attention. *Disrespect* is treating someone as if he or she is not important to you, and not worth your time and attention. Does God want us to respect everyone? Why or why not?

PRACTICE

Read the verse. Try to repeat it several times without looking. Cut a sword shape from paper or cardboard. Write the verse on it. You'll want to hang it up in your house where it will remind you of the Spirit's sword from Matthew 7:12. You can use it to fight against the temptation to be disrespectful.

DAY 2

READ

1 Peter 2 ("Living Stones," page 770 in the *Day By Day Kid's Bible*) Show people that they're important. Love God's people. Treat God as the most important one. Say good things about the king. If you're a servant, obey your master. Don't just obey masters who are good and kind. Obey masters who are hard on you too.

THINK AND TALK

How does a person show respect? How does a person show disrespect? How should you treat people who are disrespectful toward you? Why does God want us to show respect?

PRACTICE

Challenge a friend or family member (or yourself) to a sword-fight. One person says, "What will you do if you are tempted to be disrespectful?" The other person answers, "I will not be disrespectful, because it is written, 'In everything, do to others what you would have them do to you.'"

DAY 3

READ

Leviticus 19:1-18 ("Rules for Treating People Right," page 93 in the *Day By Day Kid's Bible*) Be kind to your father and mother... Stand up when an old person is with you. Be kind to old people. Be kind to women whose husbands have died. Be kind to children whose mother and father have died. Someone from another land may choose to live with you... Treat him like one of your own people... Don't say bad things about people who can't hear. Don't put something in the way of someone who can't see... Love your neighbor as you love yourself.

THINK AND TALK

Why did God give his people all of these rules? How can you treat your father and mother with respect? How can you treat old people with respect? How can you show respect to people from other countries? How can you show respect to people who are deaf or blind? Can you think of other people we should treat with respect?

PRACTICE

Challenge someone to a sword-fight with your sword for this week. Write on an index card: "You are tempted to be disrespectful." Add this temptation card to the other cards you've collected. Place the cards in a bowl. The first person draws a card and challenges the second person with that temptation. The second person repeats the sword of the Spirit that he can use to fight the temptation. Then it's his turn to draw a card and challenge the first person.

DAY 4

READ

2 Chronicles 30 ("A Holiday," page 348 in the *Day By Day Kid's Bible*)
Then King Hezekiah wrote letters to all the people of Judah... He asked everybody to come for the Pass Over holiday... So the king's helpers took the letters all over the land... Many people laughed at the letters. They laughed at the people bringing the letters. But some people came to Jerusalem.

THINK AND TALK

Has anyone ever laughed at you or made fun of you? How did it feel? Did it feel as though the other person respected you? Have you ever laughed at someone or made fun of someone? Why is it wrong to make fun of other people?

PRACTICE

You and another person can challenge each other to practice fighting temptation. Do this by taking turns drawing the temptation cards from a bowl. Ask each other what you would do if you were tempted in that way, and answer by saying the appropriate verse.

TRY THIS

Do you wish that someone would invite you to their house? Invite the person to your house. You could have other friends come too. You may even ask a friend to help you plan your party. Send invitations and have a party. You could make some of the snacks suggested in this book, and you could play the game from tomorrow's reading.

DAY 5

READ

Ruth 3 ("A Night in the Barn," page 113 in the *Day By Day Kid's Bible*) That night Ruth went to the barn. She did just what Naomi had told her to do... Late in the night, Boaz woke up... He saw someone lying by his feet... "Who are you?" he asked. "I'm Ruth," she answered. "You are from my husband's family. Would you take care of me?" "God will bring good things to you,'" said Boaz. "This is the kindest thing you could do for me... But there is another man from your husband's family. By law, he gets to marry you first if he wants... But if he won't, then God knows that I will... Now hold out your coat." Ruth held her coat out. Boaz filled it with grain.... Then she went back to Naomi's.

THINK AND TALK

How did Ruth show respect for Naomi? How did Boaz show respect for the law? How did Boaz show respect for Ruth and Naomi? Tell about someone you know who respects other people. What does that person do to show respect?

PRACTICE

Challenge someone to practice fighting temptation. You can take turns drawing the temptation cards from a bowl. Ask each other what you would do if you were tempted in that way.

TRY THIS

Play Barnyard Peanuts. Get some bags of peanuts in shells. Ask someone to hide the peanuts in the yard or around a room. Make teams of three people each. Each team chooses a leader to hold a grocery bag. Each team also chooses an animal that might be found in a barn. Someone starts the game by calling, "Go." Then all players except the leaders hunt for the peanuts. A player who finds a peanut cannot pick it up. Instead, that player must make the sound of his team's chosen barn animal. The leader hears the sound and goes to pick up that person's peanut. The leaders collect the peanuts that their team members find. When all peanuts have been found, count to see which team has the most peanuts. What did Boaz store in his barn?

DAY 6

READ

1 Samuel 26 ("In Saul's Camp at Night," page 153 in the *Day By Day Kid's Bible*)
David was in the desert. He found out that Saul had followed him there... "Who will go with me into the camp?" asked David. "I will," said one of David's men. So that night, David and the other man went quietly into Saul's camp. They went up to Saul. He was sleeping... "This is the day!" said the man with David.... "I can kill him with one blow".... "No," said David. "He is the one God chose to be king."... So David took Saul's spear and jug of water. Then the two men left. Nobody saw them.

THINK AND TALK

David knew that King Saul was chasing him in order to kill him. What choices did David have in Saul's camp that night? Why did David show respect to King Saul? Do you think David was tempted not to respect Saul? When is it hardest for you to be respectful? How can you show respect for the rulers of your land?

PRACTICE

Challenge someone to practice fighting temptation. You can take turns drawing the temptation cards from a bowl. Ask each other what you would do if you were tempted in that way.

TRY THIS

Make salt dough by mixing one and one-half cups of flour, one-half cup of salt, and one-half cup of water. If the dough is too sticky, add flour. If it's too thick, add a little water at a time until it's just right. Make a jug out of this flour dough. Let it dry. You can put dried flowers or pencils or paper clips in this jug. Why did David take Saul's spear and water jug?

DAY 7

READ
James 2 ("Rich Man, Poor Man," page 763 in the *Day By Day Kid's Bible*) Let's say someone comes to your meeting place. This person wears a gold ring and has very nice clothes. Then someone who is poor comes in. This person wears worn-out clothes. Let's say you're very nice to the rich person. You say, "Here's a good place for you to sit." But you tell the poor person to stand. Or you let that person sit on the floor next to your feet. Haven't you treated one better than the other? That's a sinful way to treat people.

THINK AND TALK
What does James say about how to treat people respectfully? Is it always easy to be respectful? What are some things that can tempt us to be disrespectful? What would you suggest to a friend who was tempted to be disrespectful?

PRACTICE
Challenge someone to practice fighting temptation. You can take turns drawing the temptation cards from a bowl. Ask each other what you would do if you were tempted in that way.

TRY THIS
On a piece of paper, draw very lightly the letters *D T O*. These stand for three words in this week's verse: "Do To Others." Now go back and make these letters into people. For example, the straight line in the letter *D* can be a tall thin person standing with his arms straight down by his side. The curve on the letter *D* can be a person with feet touching the feet of the straight person, legs and body curving around, head halfway up the curve, and arms stretched over his head to form the top of the curve. His fingers touch the top of the head of the straight person. Make the other letters the same way. Keep this poster to remind you of the verse.

Using Wisdom

Your sword of the Spirit for this week is:

Wisdom is more precious than rubies, and nothing you desire can compare with her.
PROVERBS 8:11

With the above sword you can fight back when you face this temptation:

You are tempted not to do or say the wise thing.

DAY 1

READ

Proverbs 4 ("Early Morning Light," page 231 in the *Day By Day Kid's Bible*)

Take my words into your heart. Obey me, and you'll live. Wise thinking will keep you safe. So love it. Get understanding, even if it costs a lot. Know that being wise is important... More than anything, be careful of what you let into your mind. Look ahead. Think about what you should do. Follow the ways that are sure and right.

THINK AND TALK

What does it mean to be wise? What is the difference between wisdom and knowledge? Can someone know a lot and still not be wise? How? Can someone be wise and not know a lot? How? Why is it important to be careful of what you let into your mind?

PRACTICE

Read the verse. Try to repeat it several times without looking. Cut a sword shape from paper or cardboard and write the verse on it. You'll want to hang it up in your house where it will remind you of the Spirit's sword from Proverbs 8:11. You can use it to fight against the temptation not to do or say the wise thing.

DAY 2

READ

Proverbs 17:12; 24:7, 13–14 ("Wise People and Fools," page 233 in the *Day By Day Kid's Bible*)

It's better to meet an angry bear than a person acting foolish. Wise thinking is too much for a fool. When he is with leaders, he has nothing to say. Honey is sweet to your taste. Wise thinking is sweet to your soul. You have hope if you think wisely.

THINK AND TALK

How can you tell if a person is wise? How can you tell if a person is foolish? Which would you rather have as a friend? Why would it be better to meet an angry bear than a person acting foolish?

PRACTICE

Challenge a friend or family member (or yourself) to a sword-fight. One person says, "What will you do if you are tempted not to do or say what's wise?" The other person answers, "I will say and do what's wise because it is written, 'Wisdom is more precious than rubies, and nothing you desire can compare with her.'"

DAY 3

READ

Proverbs 14:8, 15; 15:14 ("Understanding and Knowing," page 233 in the *Day By Day Kid's Bible*)

Wise people think about what they should do. Fools lie. Foolish people believe anything... A wise person looks for good things to know. But a fool takes in foolish things like he takes in food.

THINK AND TALK

What are some good things to know and look for? How does it feel when you know you've done or said something wise? How does it feel when you know you've done or said something foolish? Can realizing we've done or said something foolish be a way of becoming wise? How?

PRACTICE
Challenge someone to a sword-fight with your sword for this week. Write on an index card: "You are tempted not to do or say the wise thing." Add this temptation card to the other cards you've collected. Place the cards in a bowl. The first person draws a card and challenges the second person with that temptation. The second person repeats the sword of the Spirit that he can use to fight the temptation. Then it's his turn to draw a card and challenge the first person.

DAY 4
READ
Proverbs 8 ("What is Wise Thinking?" page 230 in the *Day By Day Kid's Bible*)
Wise thinking calls out to everybody. "Listen. Choose to learn from what I say. Choose wise thinking instead of silver. Knowing is better than having gold. Nothing you want can be better than being wise... If you find wise thinking, you find life and make God happy. But if you don't find wise thinking, you get hurt."

THINK AND TALK
Why is wisdom better than anything else you could want? Is it always easy to be wise? When is it hardest for you to do and say the wise thing?   Tell about someone you know who is wise. Tell about a time when you did or said something wise.

PRACTICE
You and another person can challenge each other to practice fighting temptation. Do this by taking turns drawing the temptation cards from a bow. Ask each other what you would do if you were tempted in that way, and answer by saying the appropriate verse.

TRY THIS
Fill a clear glass halfway with water. Place a index card or piece of cardboard over the top of the glass and hold it there with your hand.

Hold the glass over a sink. Now turn the glass upside down, still holding the card over the opening. Gently remove your hand. The card will stay in place, holding the water in the upside down glass. Why? Air pressure pushes up on the card, keeping it from falling off. We can learn many things by watching the world around us. If we know many things about our world, does that mean we are wise? Why or why not?

DAY 5

READ

Matthew 13:53-58 ("Sheep with No Shepherd," page 553 in the *Day By Day Kid's Bible*)
Jesus went back to the town where he grew up... Many people heard him there. They were surprised. "How can he say all these things?" they asked. "How can he be so wise? He even does wonders. Didn't he work in the wood shop when he was growing up? Isn't he Mary's son? He is the brother of James, Joseph, Judas, and Simon. All his sisters live here!"

THINK AND TALK

Why were the people surprised that Jesus was so wise? Why was Jesus so wise? What are some things that Jesus did or said that show you his wisdom? What are some things you can do to help yourself become wise?

PRACTICE

Challenge someone to practice fighting temptation. You can take turns drawing the temptation cards from a bowl. Ask each other what you would do if you were tempted in that way.

TRY THIS

Make a treasure wall hanging. Cut gem shapes that are about five inches wide. Cut them from diferent colors of construction paper: green for emeralds, red for rubies, yellow for topaz, blue for sapphires, purple for amethysts, white for pearls. You can use waxed paper for diamonds. On each gem write one word or phrase from James 3:17 that describes heavenly wisdom (pure, peace-loving, considerate, submissive, full of mercy, impartial, sincere).

Cut a long strip of ribbon or fabric and glue each gem onto the ribbon. You may want to hang one end of the ribbon on your wall or the door of your room. The gems will hang one below the other on the ribbon.

DAY 6

READ

Matthew 25:1-13 ("Ten Lamps," page 604 in the *Day By Day Kid's Bible*)

Jesus told a story. It was about the time when he would come back. "The kingdom of heaven will be like 10 young people... going to a wedding party... All the young people brought their lamps with them. Five of these young people were foolish. They didn't being any oil to keep their lamps lit up. Five of them were wise. They brought oil in jars... In the middle of the night, a voice called out. 'Here comes the groom! Come and meet him!'...They lit their lamps. But the foolish ones had run out of oil."

THINK AND TALK

Why do you think five of the young people did not bring extra oil? Why do you think Jesus told this story about the young people? How can you be like the wise young people while you are waiting for Jesus to come back? What are some things that might distract us and cause us to be foolish?

PRACTICE

Challenge someone to practice fighting temptation. You can take turns drawing the temptation cards from a bowl. Ask each other what you would do if you were tempted in that way.

TRY THIS

Make lanterns by folding construction paper in half lengthwise. Cut the paper every one-half inch through both sides. Start at the fold and go toward the other edge, stopping about one-half inch before you reach the edge. Now unfold the paper and roll it into a cylinder, overlapping and taping or stapling each end together. Cut a yellow or orange flame about three inches by two inches. Punch a hole through the top of the flame and two holes in the top of the lantern on opposite sides. Tie one end of a string through one of the holes in the lantern. Thread the string through the hole in the flame and then through the other hole in the lantern. Tie the string there. Cut a one-inch by ten-inch strip of construction paper for a handle and staple it to the top of the lantern. (This lantern is not for use around a real flame.) Your lantern will remind you to be wise as you wait for Jesus to come back.

DAY 7

READ
Genesis 41 ("The King's Dream," page 36 in the *Day By Day Kid's Bible*)
"I had a dream," said the king.... "I heard that you can tell what dreams mean." "I can't," said Joseph. "But God can." So the king told Joseph about the fat and thin cows... [Joseph said,] "There will be seven years of no food... Find a wise man. Put him in charge of Egypt. Save food that grows in the good years." ...The king liked Joseph's idea. He said, "God has told this to you. You are the wisest of all... You'll be in charge of all the land of Egypt."

THINK AND TALK
Why was Joseph wise? Was the king wise? Are all rulers wise? Why or why not? Is it possible for foolish people, even rulers, to become wise? How? How do you feel around wise people? How do you feel around foolish people? What would you suggest to a friend who wanted to become wise?

PRACTICE
Challenge someone to practice fighting temptation. You can take turns drawing the temptation cards from a bowl. Ask each other what you would do if you were tempted in that way.

TRY THIS
Collect soap pieces from your soap dish when they get too small to use, or break off small chunks from a bar of soap. Put these pieces in a bowl and pour water in the bowl so that it covers the soap. Let this soak until the soap gets very soft and begins to mix with the water. Stir it and put it into a pump bottle. Use it as soft liquid soap. This is a way to recycle soap that might get thrown away. Is recycling a wise thing to do? Why or why not?

Having Peace

Your sword of the Spirit for this week is:

**Do not worry about tomorrow,
for tomorrow will worry about itself.**
MATTHEW 6:34

With the above sword you can fight back when you face this temptation:

You are tempted to worry.

DAY 1

READ
Matthew 6:22-34 ("Birds' Food and Flowers' Clothes," page 534 in the *Day By Day Kid's Bible*)
"Don't worry. Don't say, 'What will we eat? What will we drink? What will we wear?' People who don't believe in God worry about those things. But your Father in heaven knows what you need. Put God first in your life. Then he will make sure you have everything you need."

THINK AND TALK
What is worry? Is it possible to feel worried and peaceful at the same time? Why or why not? Why would God want us not to worry? What does the word *stress* mean? What kinds of things cause people to feel stress? How do you think God wants us to handle stress?

PRACTICE
Read the verse. Try to repeat it several times without looking.

169

Cut a sword shape from paper or cardboard and write the verse on it. You'll want to hang it up in your house where it will remind you of the Spirit's sword from Matthew 6:34. You can use it to fight against the temptation to worry.

DAY 2

READ
John 14:23-27 ("Where Are You Going?" page 610 in the *Day By Day Kid's Bible*)
"Know my rules. Obey me," said Jesus. "Then I'll know you love me. The Father will love whoever loves me. I'll love them too... I'm giving you my peace," said Jesus. "Don't worry. Don't be afraid."

THINK AND TALK
Did Jesus worry? Why or why not? How can you tell if a person feels peaceful? How can you tell if a person is worried? There's an old saying that goes, "Worry is like a rocking chair. It gives you something to do, but it doesn't take you anywhere." Do you think that's true? Why or why not?

PRACTICE
Challenge a friend or family member (or yourself) to a sword-fight. One person says, "What will you do if you are tempted to worry?" The other person answers, "I will say, 'I will not worry, because it is written, 'Do not worry about tomorrow, for tomorrow will worry about itself.'"

DAY 3

READ
Hebrews 4:1-4, 9-16 ("Rest," page 781 in the *Day By Day Kid's Bible*)
God plans for us to have his peace. Let's be careful so we can have this peace. God's people in the desert didn't believe God. But we believe. So we have that peace from God... There is a special rest for God's people. They can rest from their work. They can rest like God rested from his work. So let's try to get that special rest. Don't turn away from God by not obeying him.

THINK AND TALK
What is it that will give us peace? Why do you think God rested

after he created the earth? Why does God want us to rest from our work? How does it feel to be peaceful? How does it feel to be worried? Is it always easy to feel peaceful? When is it hardest for you to feel peaceful? When is it easiest for you to feel peaceful?

PRACTICE

Challenge someone to a sword-fight with your sword for this week. Write on an index card: "You are tempted to worry." Add this temptation card to the other cards you've collected. Place the cards in a bowl. The first person draws a card and challenges the second person with that temptation. The second person repeats the sword of the Spirit that he can use to fight the temptation. Then it's his turn to draw a card and challenge the first person.

DAY 4

READ

1 Peter 5 ("The Chief Shepherd," page 774 in the *Day By Day Kid's Bible*) Tell God about all your worries. Then trust him to take care of those worries. God cares about you... God is the God of kind love... You may have trouble for a while. But he will make up for it. He will make you strong. He will keep you on track.

THINK AND TALK

Why should we tell God about our worries? What worries do you need to tell God about today? In Isaiah 9, Jesus is called "the Prince of Peace." When Jesus was born, the angels who appeared to the shepherds said, "Peace on earth." Why do you think Jesus is called the Prince of Peace? And why do you think the angels called, "Peace on earth?"

PRACTICE

You and another person can challenge each other to practice fighting temptation. Do this by taking turns drawing the temptation cards from a bowl. Ask each other what you would do if you were tempted in that way, and answer by saying the appropriate verse.

TRY THIS

Draw a straight line across a piece of drawing paper a little over halfway up. This is the horizon line of your drawing. Make a dot on the center of the horizon line. At the bottom of the page, make a dot somewhere on the right-hand side. Make a dot on the opposite side at about the same place. Using a ruler, draw a line from each of the bottom dots to the center dot. These are the tracks of a railroad. Make straight lines across the page between the tracks to make the railroad ties. Across the top of the page write, "God will keep me on track." You can draw trees or buildings or other objects around the track in this landscape.

DAY 5

READ

Psalm 131 ("Like a Well-Fed Baby," page 218 in the *Day By Day Kid's Bible*)
I don't worry about things that are too big for me to understand. I don't worry about things that are too wonderful for me. My soul is still and quiet like a well-fed baby with its mama. Put your hope in God now and forever.

THINK AND TALK

David wrote Psalm 131. How did he describe the peace that he felt? If you were writing a psalm, how would describe peace? Tell about someone you know who is peaceful. Tell about a time when you felt very peaceful. What are some things you can do to keep yourself from worrying?

PRACTICE

Challenge someone to practice fighting temptation. You can take turns drawing the temptation cards from a bowl. Ask each other what you would do if you were tempted in that way.

TRY THIS

Get two jars. Place ice and water in one jar. Boil some water and pour it into the other jar. If the ice has not melted in the first jar, take it out. Now drip two drops of food coloring into each jar. What happens? Which looks more peaceful? The molecules in hot water move faster. The molecules in cold water move slower. Have you ever heard someone say they were boiling mad? Have you ever felt like your feelings were swirling around inside you? When that happens, how can you start feeling peaceful again?

DAY 6

READ

Isaiah 48:17-22 ("Peace As Wide As a River," page 365 in the *Day By Day Kid's Bible*)

"I'm the Lord, your God. I teach you what's best for you. I show you the way you should go. I wish you had listened to my rules. Then peace as wide as a river would be yours. People who do wrong don't have peace," says God.

THINK AND TALK

How can we have peace "as wide as a river"? Who are the people who don't have peace? What are some things that might distract us from peace and cause us to worry? What would you suggest to a friend who wants to stop worrying and feel peaceful?

PRACTICE

Challenge someone to practice fighting temptation. You can take turns drawing the temptation cards from a bowl. Ask each other what you would do if you were tempted in that way.

TRY THIS

Take a walk with a friend to a park or on a nature trail. Or find another peaceful spot to sit and talk. Close your eyes and listen to the sounds around you. What makes this spot peaceful? Are there times when this place would not be peaceful? If so, when and why?

DAY 7

READ

Matthew 13:1-23 ("Seeds and Dirt," page 546 in the *Day By Day Kid's Bible*)

Then there was the seed that fell around weeds. It's like the person who hears God's words. But he has lots of things to worry about.

His riches make him worry too. That pushes God's words away.

THINK AND TALK
In Jesus' story, worry is like weeds that take over a garden. Why?
How can worry push God's words away, out of our thoughts? How
can riches make a person worry? How do you feel around worried
people? How do you feel around peaceful people? Which person
would you rather have as a friend?

PRACTICE
Challenge someone to practice fighting temptation. You can take
turns drawing the temptation cards from a bowl. Ask each other
what you would do if you were tempted in that way.

TRY THIS
Find a spot outside to pull some weeds. You could pull weeds from
your garden, out of your yard, from between cracks in a sidewalk
or driveway. As you pull these weeds, think about how worry is like
a weed.

Being Persistent

**Let us not become weary in doing good, for...
we will reap a harvest if we do not give up.**
GALATIANS 6:9

With the above sword you can fight back when you face this temptation:

**You are tempted to give up when you're
doing something that's good, but hard.**

DAY 1

READ

Jeremiah 36 ("The King in the Winter House," page 393 in the *Day By Day Kid's Bible*)

God told Jeremiah, "Get a roll of paper. Write on it everything I told you." ...So Jeremiah called his helper, Baruch. Jeremiah told his helper what to write. Baruch wrote it on the roll of paper... Now the king was in his winter house. Fire was burning in a pot in front of him. His helper would read part of the paper roll. Then the king would cut that part off with a knife. He'd throw it into the fire pot... Then God spoke to Jeremiah again. "The king burned up the first roll of paper," said God. "So get another roll of paper. Write the same things you wrote on the first paper.

THINK AND TALK

To be *persistent* means to continue or keep on going, even when it's hard, or there's something that's in your way to stop you.

What did the king do that might have stopped God's words from getting to the people? What did God tell Jeremiah to do after the first roll of paper was burned up? Did Jeremiah and Baruch choose to be persistent? When do you need to be persistent?

PRACTICE
Read the verse. Try to repeat it several times without looking. Cut a sword shape from paper or cardboard and write the verse on it. You'll want to hang it up in your house in a place where it will remind you of the Spirit's sword from Galatians 6:9. You can use it to fight against the temptation to give up.

DAY 2
READ
Nehemiah 4 ("Tools in One Hand, Swords in the Other," page 491 in the *Day By Day Kid's Bible*)
Sanballat and his friends... heard that the holes in the wall were being fixed... They planned to make trouble for us... Our people said, "The workers are getting tired. There are so many piles of sticks and stones! We can't build the wall." Our enemies said,... "We'll kill them. Then their work will end."...I told the people, "There's lots of work to do." ...So we kept working. We started every morning when the sky first got light. We worked until the stars came out.

THINK AND TALK
What choice did Nehemiah have? What was Nehemiah trying to do? What was getting in his way? How would you have felt if you were Nehemiah? Was Nehemiah persistent? How can you tell if a person is persistent? How can you tell if a person is not persistent?

PRACTICE
Challenge a friend or family member (or yourself) to a sword-fight. One person says, "What will you do if you are tempted to give up?" The other person answers, "I will not give up because it is written, 'Let us not become weary in doing good, for...we will reap a harvest if we do not give up.'"

DAY 3

READ

Luke 18:1-8 ("The Judge," page 587 in the *Day By Day Kid's Bible*)
"Once there was a judge," said Jesus... "There was a lady who lived in his town... The lady kept coming to see the judge. 'My enemies aren't treating me right,' she would say. 'Help me, please.' Time after time she came.... At last the judge thought,... 'This lady keeps bothering me. So I'll make sure she is treated fairly. Then she won't wear me out by coming so much.' Listen," said Jesus. 'Won't God help his people? They call him night and day... He will make sure they are treated right."

THINK AND TALK

What choice did the lady have? Why might she have been tempted to give up? Why was she persistent? Are there times when a person should not be persistent? Explain. When would God want us to be persistent? Why would God want us to be persistent? What happens when other people are counting on us to do something, but we give up?

PRACTICE

Challenge someone to sword-fight with your sword for this week. Write on an index card: "You are tempted to give up." Add this temptation card to the other cards you've collected. Place the cards in a bowl. The first person draws a card and challenges the second person with that temptation. The second person repeats the sword of the Spirit that he can use to fight the temptation. Then it's his turn to draw a card and challenge the first person.

DAY 4

READ

Genesis 18:16-33 ("Sodom," in the *Day By Day Kid's Bible*)
God said, "There is very bad sin in Sodom."... Abraham could tell that God was going to get rid of the bad people.... "Won't you save the city if 50 good people live there?" "I'll look for 50 good people here," said God. "If I find 50, I'll save the city."... "But what if you find only 40 good people?" asked Abraham.... "I'll save the city,"

said God... "But what if you find only 30?" "I'll save the city for 30 good people," said God... "What if you find only 20?"... "I'll save the city," said God.... "But what if you find only 10?" "If I find 10, I'll save the city," said God.

THINK AND TALK

Abraham kept on asking God to save the city of Sodom. Abraham was persistent. Did it make God angry for Abraham to ask again and again? Tell about someone you know who was persistent. Or tell about someone who gave up too soon. Tell about a time when you were persistent.

PRACTICE

You and another person can challenge each other to practice fighting temptation. Do this by taking turns drawing the temptation cards from a bowl. Ask each other what you would do if you were tempted in that way, and answer by saying the appropriate verse.

TRY THIS

Make pudding without using a mix. In a large pan, stir together three-fourths cup of sugar, one-fourth cup of flour, and one-fourth teaspoon of salt. Add two cups of milk and stir. Heat this over medium heat, stirring it constantly. Ask an adult to help you with this. When it gets thick and bubbly, take it off the stove. In a bowl, beat two eggs well. Stir a spoonful of hot pudding into the eggs. Then stir the eggs into the pudding. Put the pudding back on the stove and cook and stir it for two more minutes. Then take it off the stove again and add two tablespoons of margarine and one teaspoon of vanilla. Making pudding like this takes persistence!

DAY 5

READ

Exodus 8 ("Frogs, Bugs, and Flies," page 53 in the *Day By Day Kid's Bible*)

God told Moses,..."Go to the king. Tell him to let my people go." God said to tell the king, "If you don't, I'll send frogs... Frogs will get in all the houses." ...[The king] wouldn't listen to Moses and Aaron... So God talked with Moses again... "The dust will turn into tiny biting bugs that fly." ...But the king didn't care. He wouldn't listen to Moses... These were God's words for the king. "Let my people go... If you don't...I'll send flies." ...That's just what happened... But the king didn't think God was important. He didn't let God's people go.

THINK AND TALK
What choices did Moses have? What did Moses have to do over and over again? How would you have felt if you had been Moses going to see the great king? What might have tempted you to give up? What would have happened if Moses had given up? When is it hardest for you to be persistent?

PRACTICE
Challenge someone to practice fighting temptation. You can take turns drawing the temptation cards from a bowl. Ask each other what you would do if you were tempted in that way.

TRY THIS
Make a paperweight. Find a medium-sized rock that would hold down papers on a desk. Paint it with water-based acrylic paint and make it look like a frog or a bug. Think about Moses' persistence with the king whenever you look at your paperweight.

DAY 6

READ
Isaiah 41:8-16 ("Don't Give Up," page 361 in the *Day By Day Kid's Bible*)
I chose you. So don't be afraid. I'm with you. Don't feel so helpless that you give up. I'm your God. I'll make you strong. I'll help you... I'm the Lord. I'm your God. I hold your right hand. I tell you not to be scared, my little people. I will help you myself," says God.

THINK AND TALK
Is it always easy to be persistent? What are some things that might tempt us to give up? Why does God say we should not give up? What are some things you can do to help yourself become persistent? What are some things you can do to help other people be persistent?

PRACTICE

Challenge someone to practice fighting temptation. You can take turns drawing the temptation cards from a bowl. Ask each other what you would do if you were tempted in that way.

TRY THIS

Get 16 index cards. Using only the first part of the memory verse ("Let us not grow weary in doing good"), write each word on *two* index cards. Ask a friend to play this game with you. Mix the cards up. Lay the cards out face down in front of you in four rows. Let your friend turn over two cards. If they match, your friend keeps the cards and tries two more cards. If they don't match, your friend turns the cards face down again. Now it's your turn to turn over two cards. Try to find and collect the matching pairs. If you're persistent, you won't give up until you match all the cards. What are some other times when you should be persistent?

DAY 7

READ

Hebrews 12:1-13 ("Keep On Running," page 789 in the *Day By Day Kid's Bible*)

Let's get rid of sin. It's so easy to get mixed up in sin. Life is like a race. So let's run the race that God has made for us. Let's keep on running no matter what. Let's keep looking at Jesus. Our faith started with him. He will help us keep our faith all the way. Jesus saw the joy that was waiting for him. So he kept on going, even to the cross... When it was over, he sat down beside God. He is sitting at the King's right side. Think about Jesus. Many sinful people were against him. Think about him so you won't get tired. Think about him so you won't give up.

THINK AND TALK

Who are we supposed to think about so we won't give up? Why does thinking about Jesus help us be persistent? How was Jesus persistent? Galatians 6:9 says, "We will reap a harvest if we do not give up." What does it mean for us to "reap a harvest"? Tell what a farmer must do to be persistent so he can reap a harvest of crops. Tell something you must be persistent in doing. What will the harvest be if you don't give up?

PRACTICE
Challenge someone to practice fighting temptation. You can take turns drawing the temptation cards from a bowl. Ask each other what you would do if you were tempted in that way.

TRY THIS
Plant a seed in a small pot and water it. Get a clean Popsicle stick or craft stick. Write on it: "Stick To It." Place this stick into the soil near the seed to help you remember that just as seeds take time to grow, so other things in life take time too.

Having
Courage

Your sword of the Spirit for this week is:

In God I trust; I will not be afraid. PSALM 56:11

With the above sword you can fight back when you face this temptation:

You are tempted to be afraid.

DAY 1

READ

1 Samuel 17 ("The Giant," page 138 in the *Day By Day Kid's Bible*)
A winning fighter was in the enemy camp. His name was Goliath. He was more than nine feet tall! ... He shouted at God's people... Then God's people ran from Goliath. They were very scared... "Nobody should be scared of Goliath," said David. "I'll go fight him... God is alive and well. He saved me from the lion and the bear. He will save me from Goliath."

THINK AND TALK

The word *courage* comes from the French word *coeur,* which means "heart." So courage is having the strength in your heart to keep doing what's right when it's hard or dangerous. In our reading, what choices did David make? What happened because of his choices? Why did God's people not have courage? Why did David have courage? Can a person show courage and be afraid at the same time? Explain.

PRACTICE

Read the verse. Try to repeat it several times without looking. Cut a sword shape from paper or cardboard and write the verse on it. You'll want to hang it up in your house in a place where it will remind you of the Spirit's sword from Psalm 56:11. You can use it to fight against the temptation to be afraid.

DAY 2

READ

Judges 7 ("A Night Fight," page 109 in the *Day By Day Kid's Bible*) Gideon told his men to go home if they were scared. So 22,000 (twenty-two thousand) of them went home... God said,... "I'll save my people with 300 men." ...Gideon and his servant... went to the edge of the enemy camp...They heard a man talking to his friend. "I dreamed about bread," said the man. "A big round loaf rolled into our camp. It hit our tent so hard, the tent fell down." "That dream is about Gideon!" said the other man. "God is going to let Gideon win!" Gideon heard all this. Then he went back to his camp. He called to everyone, "Get up! God is going to let us win!"

THINK AND TALK

In our reading, what choices did Gideon's men have to make? What choices did Gideon make? What happened because of their choices? How can you tell if a person has courage? How can you tell if a person does not have courage? Which would you rather have as a friend in hard or dangerous times?

PRACTICE

Challenge a friend or family member (or yourself) to a sword-fight. One person says, "What will you do if you are tempted to be afraid?" The other person answers, "I will not be afraid because it is written, 'In God I trust; I will not be afraid.'"

DAY 3

READ

1 Samuel 10 ("Long Live Our King!" page 131 in the *Day By Day Kid's Bible*)

Samuel took out a small jar of oil. He put some on Saul's head... He said, "God has made you king of his people... I'll come to see you next week. Then I'll tell you what to do." ...Samuel called God's people together. He told them that God said,..."You have asked for a king to rule you. So now you must come and stand in front of me."...God picked Saul's family... But no one could find Saul. They asked God, "Is Saul here yet?" "Yes," said God. "Saul is hiding behind the boxes and bags."

THINK AND TALK

What choices did Saul make? Why do you think he was hiding behind the boxes and bags? Why might someone be afraid of becoming a king or other leader? Were you ever afraid of being a leader? Why or why not? Why does God want us to have courage? What happens when we don't have courage?

PRACTICE

Challenge someone to sword-fight with your sword for this week. Write on an index card: "You are tempted to be afraid." Add this temptation card to the other cards you've collected. Place the cards in a bowl. The first person draws a card and challenges the second person with that temptation. The second person repeats the sword of the Spirit that he can use to fight the temptatiion. Then it's his turn to draw a card and challenge the first person.

DAY 4

READ

Genesis 6-9 ("A World Under Water," page 6 in the *Day By Day Kid's Bible*)

God told Noah, "I'm going to get rid of people. They are mean and hateful. So make a big boat, an ark." ...Noah did everything God told him to do... Noah and his wife went into the ark. His sons and their wives went into the ark. The animals also went into the ark, two by two. A week passed. Then the flood water came... Rain kept falling for 40 days and 40 nights... Soon the water covered all the mountains.

THINK AND TALK

What choices did Noah make? Give some reasons for why Noah could have been afraid at times. Why do you think Noah had courage? How does it feel to be afraid? How does it feel to have courage? When is it hardest for you to have courage?

PRACTICE

You and another person can challenge each other to practice fighting temptation. Do this by taking turns drawing the temptation cards from a bowl. Ask each other what you would do if you were tempted in that way, and answer by saying the appropriate verse.

TRY THIS

Find materials that would make a small model ship that really floats. Try cardboard boxes, foil, clay or play dough, wood, plasticfoam, or even soap that floats. Try making a paper sail to go on your boat. Does a sailor need to have courage? Why or why not?

DAY 5

READ Genesis 28:10-22 ("A Ladder up to Heaven," page 25 in the *Day By Day Kid's Bible*)
Jacob left his home and began his trip to Laban's. The sun went down before he got there. So Jacob... lay down for the night. That night Jacob had a dream. He saw a ladder that went all the way up to heaven... God stood at the top of the ladder. God said, "I am the Lord... I'll be with you. I will watch over you everywhere you go. I won't leave you. I will keep all my promises to you."

THINK AND TALK

Give some reasons for why Jacob could have been afraid on his trip. Why could Jacob have courage? Is it always easy to have courage? Why or why not? Have you ever been afraid at night? Have you ever been afraid on a trip? Why can you have courage at night or on a trip?

PRACTICE

Challenge someone to practice fighting temptation. You can take urns drawing the temptation cards from a bowl. Ask each other what you would do if you were tempted in that way.

TRY THIS

Make a paper angel. First, make a cone out of a square piece of white paper. Do this by overlapping two of the opposite corners as you bring a third corner together to form a point with a small opening. Tape or staple this cone in place. Stick the handle of a white plastic spoon down into the small hole at the point of the cone. This is the head of the angel. With a permanent marker, draw a face on the bottom of the bowl of the spoon. Glue yarn hair on if you want. Fold a coffee filter in half and tape or staple it to the back of the angel to make wings. When some people in the Bible saw angels, they lost their courage and became afraid. Do you think seeing the angels made Jacob afraid or gave him courage? Explain.

DAY 6

READ

Matthew 8:23-27 ("The Storm," page 550 in the *Day By Day Kid's Bible*)

"Let's go across the lake," Jesus told his friends. So they got into a boat... But a roaring storm blew in. Waves crashed over the boat... All this time, Jesus was in the back of the boat. He was sleeping on a pillow. Jesus' special friends woke him up. "We're about to die in this water!" ...Jesus got up... He spoke firmly to the waves. He said, "Be quiet. Be still."... Everything became still. Jesus looked at his friends. "Why are you so scared?" he asked. "Could it be that your faith is still very small?"

THINK AND TALK

What choice did Jesus' friends make? What happened because of their choice? What would you have done? What was the reason that Jesus gave for why his friends might have been afraid? Tell about someone you know who has courage. Tell about a time when you had courage. Why did you have courage? Do you need courage for something that's happening in your life right now? If so, talk to God about it.

PRACTICE

Challenge someone to practice fighting temptation. You can take turns drawing the temptation cards from a bowl. Ask each other what you would do if you were tempted in that way.

TRY THIS

Get an empty egg carton and put plastic Easter eggs or Ping-Pong balls in it. Write one word of the memory verse on each egg. You will have a few eggs left over. Mix the order of the eggs up. ("Scramble" the eggs!) Now see how long it takes you to put them in order again. Challenge a friend or family member to beat your time.

DAY 7

READ

Exodus 2 ("The Princess and the Basket," page 47 in the *Day By Day Kid's Bible*)

One Jewish mother hid her baby boy....for three months. Then he was too big to hide anymore. So...the mother put the baby in the basket. She put the basket at the edge of the Nile River....The baby's sister stayed a little way off... to see what would happen. The princess went down to the Nile River that day... The princess saw the basket among the water plants... When the princess opened the basket, she saw the baby... Then the baby's sister spoke to the princess. "Shall I go find a Jewish woman? She could take care of the baby for you." "Yes," said the princess.

THINK AND TALK

What choices did the baby's sister make? What happened because of the choices she made? Why might she have been afraid? What are some things that might tempt you to be afraid? What are some things you can do to help yourself have courage? What would you suggest to a friend who needs courage?

PRACTICE

Challenge someone to practice fighting temptation. You can take turns drawing the temptation cards from a bowl. Ask each other what you would do if you were tempted in that way.

TRY THIS

Some objects float because of their shape. Moses' basket was the right shape to float, and his mother had made it waterproof by coating it with tar. But other objects might float for a different reason. Put an uncooked egg, still in the shell, into a tall jar or glass. Does it float? Take the egg out. Add two tablespoons of salt to the water and stir it well. Put the egg back in. If it sinks, take it back out and add two more tablespoons of salt. Put the egg back in. Keep adding salt, a little at a time, until the egg floats when you put it into the water. Why does it float now? Salt water is heavier than fresh water, so it pushes up on the egg. The egg does not go as far down. Whenever you see an object float, think about Miriam. She trusted God and was not afraid as she watched her baby brother float in his basket.

Being Honest

Your sword of the Spirit for this week is:

Do not lie to each other. COLOSSIANS 3:9

With the above sword you can fight back when you face this temptation:

You are tempted to lie.

DAY 1

READ
Proverbs 17:23; 19:9; 20:10 ("Telling the Truth," page 247 in the *Day By Day Kid's Bible*)
God doesn't like it when people lie about how big something is. He doesn't like it when people lie about how much it weighs... Sinful people will take money to keep quiet. They'll keep quiet instead of saying what's true... A person who lies about what happened will get into trouble.

THINK AND TALK
Being *honest* means that you refuse to lie or steal or cause someone to believe something that's not true. *Lying* is saying something that is not true. Could a person lie by not saying anything at all? If so, how? Causing or allowing someone to believe something that's not true is called *deceit*. Sometimes ads on TV or in magazines are deceitful. Can you think of some? What's wrong with deceit?

PRACTICE
Read the verse. Try to repeat it several times without looking.

191

Cut a sword shape from paper or cardboard and write the verse on it. You'll want to hang it up in your house in a place where it will remind you of the Spirit's sword from Colossians 3:9. You can use it to fight against the temptation to lie.

DAY 2

READ

Genesis 20 ("Abraham Lies Again," page 15 in the *Day By Day Kid's Bible*)

Abraham moved to Gerar for a while. He told people there that his wife, Sarah, was his sister. So the king brought Sarah to his palace. He planned to make her his wife. But God came to the king one night in a dream. God said to the king, "You are in big trouble. Sarah is already married." ...Then the king called for Abraham. "Why did you do this to me?" asked the king. "I thought you would kill me," said Abraham. "That way, you could have Sarah to be your wife."

THINK AND TALK

What choice did Abraham make? What happened because of his choice? Why does God want us to be honest? What happens when we are not honest? Think and talk about the old saying, "What a tangled web we weave when first we practice to deceive." Is that true? Why or why not?

PRACTICE

Challenge a friend or family member (or yourself) to a sword fight. One person says, "What will you do if you are tempted to lie?" The other person answers, "I will not lie, because it is written, 'Do not lie to each other.'"

DAY 3

READ

Genesis 27–28:9 ("Jacob Tricks Isaac," page 23 in the *Day By Day Kid's Bible*)

Isaac grew old. He could not see anymore. One day he called Esau to come to him. "I'm old now," said Isaac.... "Go to the field and get some meat for me... Let me eat it. Then I will pray for

God's best to come to you." Rebekah... put Esau's best clothes on Jacob.... Jacob went to Isaac. "Father," he said. "Who is it?" asked Isaac. "I'm Esau," said Jacob... Jacob kissed Isaac. Isaac smelled Esau's clothes on Jacob. So Isaac prayed for God's riches to come to Jacob... From then on, Esau was angry with Jacob.

THINK AND TALK

What choices did Rebekah make? What choices did Jacob make? What happened because of their choices? How does it feel to lie or deceive someone? How does it feel to be honest? When is it hardest for you to be honest? If you could choose, would you rather have a friend who lies or a friend who is honest? Why?

PRACTICE

Challenge someone to sword-fight with your sword for this week. Write on an index card: "You are tempted to lie." Add this temptation card to the other cards you've collected. Place the cards in a bowl. The first person draws a card and challenges the second person with that temptation. The second person repeats the sword of the Spirit that he can use to fight the temptation. Then it's his turn to draw a card and challenge the first person.

DAY 4

READ

Acts 5:1-11 ("A Locked Jail," page 637 in the *Day By Day Kid's Bible*)

Ananias and his wife, Sapphira, sold some of their land. They kept part of the money for themselves. But they didn't tell anyone else... They gave the rest of the money to the apostles. "Ananias," said Peter... "Why did you need to lie? You haven't lied to people. You have lied to God." Then Ananias fell down and died... Three hours passed. Then Sapphira came in... "Tell me something," said Peter. "Is this how much money you got for your land?" "Yes," said Sapphira. "That's how much we got." "How could you and your husband plan this lie together?"...asked Peter. Then Sapphira fell down at Peter's feet. She died.

THINK AND TALK

What choices did Ananias make? What choices did Sapphira make? They helped each other lie. How can friends help each other be honest? Have you ever heard of "a little white lie"? What does that mean? Is it all right to tell "a little white lie"? Why or why not?

PRACTICE

You and another person can challenge each other to practice fighting temptation. Take turns drawing the temptation cards from a bowl. Ask each other what you would do if you were tempted in that way.

TRY THIS

On a piece of paper, write Proverbs 23:15–16. But when you come to a word that can be drawn as a picture, draw it instead of writing the word. For example: Draw a heart instead of writing the word *heart*. And write a *W* plus a pair of eyes makes the word *wise*.

DAY 5

READ

1 Kings 22 ("The Prophet Who Told the Truth," page 289 in the *Day By Day Kid's Bible*)

King Jehoshaphat from Judah was visiting King Ahab. So King Ahab asked him, "Would you fight with us?"..."Yes," said King Jehoshaphat.... "But first, you'll have to ask God about it." So King Ahab got his prophets together... "Go and fight," they said. "God will help you win."..."Don't you have any prophets from God?" asked Jehoshaphat... So King Ahab called for... Micaiah... Micaiah told the truth. "I saw your army in my mind," he said. "They were running here and there... God plans terrible trouble for you, Ahab."..."Take Micaiah away," said King Ahab. "Throw him in jail."

THINK AND TALK

What choice did Ahab's prophets make? What choice did Micaiah make? What happened to Micaiah because of his choice? Should Micaiah have lied? Why or why not? Is it always easy to be honest? What are some things you can do to help yourself be honest?

PRACTICE

Challenge someone to practice fighting temptation. You can take turns drawing the temptation cards from a bowl. Ask each other what you would do if you were tempted in that way.

TRY THIS

Get friends to help you with this game. On a piece of paper, each person writes three things about himself (his favorite food, his talents, his shirt or shoe size, etc.). But one of these things has to be untrue. In other words, one "fact" out of the three on his paper is a lie. Now each person takes a turn telling these three facts about himself. The others must guess which are the true facts and which one is the lie.

DAY 6

READ

Numbers 23-24 ("From These Mountains of Rock," and "Balaam Tries Again," pages 87 and 88 in the *Day By Day Kid's Bible*)

The next day the king of Moab took Balaam with him. They went to a high place... They could see part of the camp of God's people... Balaam said,... "You asked me to say that bad things will come to these people. But I can't. God has not planned bad things for them... I have to say what God says," said Balaam... Then the king of Moab was very angry at Balaam... "God has kept you from getting your pay." "Didn't I tell your men?" asked Balaam. "You could give me a palace full of silver and gold. But I can say only what God tells me to say."

THINK AND TALK

What choice did Balaam make when he was on the mountain with the king of Moab? What happened because of his choice? What are some things that might tempt a person to lie? Is there a difference between tricking someone and lying or deceiving? Explain. Is there a difference between teasing someone and lying or deceiving? Explain.

PRACTICE

Challenge someone to practice fighting temptation. You can take turns drawing the temptation cards from a bowl. Ask each other what you would do if you were tempted in that way.

Look at advertisements in newspapers and magazines. Think of ads on TV. Think about whether each statement is true or not. Is it an exaggeration? Is there a difference between an exaggeration and a lie? If so, what's the difference?

DAY 7

READ
Matthew 28:1-15 ("Angels," page 625 and "The Guards' Story," page 626 in the *Day By Day Kid's Bible*)
Guards went to the grave...The next day... an angel came down from heaven...The guards... were so afraid that they shook. Then they fell down... Some of the guards went back to the city. They told some leaders... what happened. The leaders... paid the guards lots of money to tell a lie. "Say that Jesus' friends came while it was night and you were sleeping. Say that Jesus' friends took his body away."...They told their story to many of the Jewish people. And these people still tell that story, even today.

THINK AND TALK
What choice did the leaders and guards make? What happened because of their choice? Tell about someone you know who is honest. Tell about a time when you could have lied, but you chose to be honest. Why is it important to be honest?

PRACTICE
Challenge someone to practice fighting temptation. You can take turns drawing the temptation cards from a bowl. Ask each other what you would do if you were tempted in that way.

TRY THIS
Do a coin trick. Lay a piece of paper on a table. Place a coin on top. Tell it to stay. Then quickly pull the paper straight out from under the coin. If you pull the paper straight and pull it quickly enough, the coin will stay right where it is. Now place another coin on top of the first one on the piece of paper. Use the same kind of coin, so both coins are nickels or dimes or pennies. Tell the coins to stay and pull the paper out again. Keep stacking the same kind of coins and see how many coins will stay. Is there a difference between tricks and lies? Is there a difference between teasing and lies?

Forgiving Others

Your sword of the Spirit for this week is:

Forgive as the Lord forgave you. COLOSSIANS 3:13

With the above sword you can fight back when you face this temptation:

You are tempted not to forgive someone.

DAY 1

READ

Genesis 50 ("A Trip to the Cave," page 44 in the *Day By Day Kid's Bible*)

Now Joseph's brothers were afraid. They said, "Joseph might still be angry with us. It's all because we sold him many years ago." So they sent Joseph a message. "Before our father died ... he said we should tell you to forgive us." ...Joseph was kind to them and said, "Don't be afraid. You meant to hurt me. But God planned for good things to come from it."

THINK AND TALK

To forgive is to stop feeling angry or resentful toward someone who has hurt you or done wrong to you. What did Joseph's brothers do to him? What choices did Joseph have in his attitude toward his brothers? Why did Joseph choose to forgive them? How can you tell when someone is a forgiving person? How can you tell when someone is not a forgiving person?

PRACTICE

Read the verse. Try to repeat it several times without looking. Cut a sword shape from paper or cardboard and write the verse on it. You'll want to hang it up in your house where it will remind you of the Spirit's sword from Colossians 3:13. You can use it to fight when you are tempted not to forgive others.

DAY 2

READ

Luke 15:11-32 ("Pig Food," page 583 in the *Day By Day Kid's Bible*) "A man had two sons," said Jesus. "Someday, the father's money would belong to his sons. But his younger son came to him one day. 'Father, give me my share of the money now,' he said. So the man gave the younger son his part of the money... Soon after that, the younger son... moved to a land far away. He lived a wild life there. He used up all his money... He went back home... The son said,... 'I've sinned against you. I'm not good enough to be called your son.' But the father called his servants. 'Hurry!' he said. 'Let's have a party! I thought I would never see my son again! It's like he was lost. But now he is found!'"

THINK AND TALK

What choices did the son make? What choices did the father make? Why did the father forgive his son? What happened because of the father's choice to forgive his son? Why does God want us to forgive others? What happens when we don't forgive people?

PRACTICE

Challenge a friend or family member (or yourself) to a sword fight. One person says, "What will you do if you are tempted not to forgive someone?" The other person answers, "I will forgive because it is written, 'Forgive as the Lord forgave you.'"

DAY 3

READ

Colossians 3 ("A New Self," page 735 in the *Day By Day Kid's Bible*) God chose you to be his people... Treat other people with care...

Work with each other. Forgive each other. Forgive like Jesus forgave you. And more than all this, love each other. Love will help us do all these good things together... God wants you to live together in peace. So let Jesus' peace control your hearts.

THINK AND TALK

How did Jesus forgive us? Why did Jesus forgive us? How can you forgive someone else like Jesus forgave you? How does it feel when you choose not to forgive someone? Sometimes the unforgiving feeling we have is called *bitterness*. How do people look when they are bitter? How do people act and talk when they are bitter? When is it the hardest for you to forgive someone?

PRACTICE

Challenge someone to sword-fight with your sword for this week. Write on an index card: "You are tempted not to forgive." Add this temptation card to the other cards you've collected. Place them in a bowl. The first person draws a card, opens it and challenges the second person with that temptation. The second person repeats the sword of the Spirit that she can use to fight that temptation. Then it's her turn to draw a card and challenge the first person.

DAY 4

READ

Matthew 18:21-35 ("The Servant Who Would Not Forgive," page 568 in the *Day By Day Kid's Bible*)

"This king wanted his servants to pay what they owed him. One man owed him millions. But he couldn't pay the money back... The king felt sorry for the man. So he told the man not to worry about what he owed. The king wouldn't make him pay it back... But the servant met a man who owed him just a little money. 'Pay me back what you owe me!' he said... He had the man put in jail... The king called the servant. 'You are a sinful servant!' he said.... 'I was kind to you. So shouldn't you have been kind to this other man?'... Forgive other people from your heart," said Jesus.

THINK AND TALK

What choices did the king's servant make? What happened because of the choices he made? Jesus told this story. Which person in the story represents God? Which person represents us? What has God forgiven you for doing? Who else sins in the same way you do? Has God forgiven them? Since God has forgiven us, how does he want us to treat other people when they sin against us?

PRACTICE

You and another person can challenge each other to practice fighting temptation. Do this by taking turns drawing the temptation cards from a bowl. Ask each other what you would do if you were tempted in that way.

TRY THIS

Wet a piece of paper and lay it on your counter. Put a dry piece of paper on top of it and write the verse for this week on the paper. Now take the dry paper off. You will see where the writing has been pressed onto the wet paper. Lift the wet paper carefully off of the counter and let it dry. The words disappear. But if you want to see the words again, just wet the paper. The disappearing words are like our guilt that disappears when we are forgiven.

DAY 5

READ

Matthew 18:21-22 (Read again the first two paragraphs of "The Servant Who Would Not Forgive," page 568 in the *Day By Day Kid's Bible*)

Peter came to Jesus. "How many times should I forgive somebody for doing wrong? Seven times?" asked Peter. "Not just seven times," said Jesus. "Seventy-seven times. Someone may do something wrong to you. Then tell him what he did. If he is sorry, forgive him. He may sin against you seven times in one day. He may come back seven times saying, 'I'm sorry.' So forgive him."

THINK AND TALK

What did Jesus mean when he told Peter to forgive someone

seventy-seven times? Why do you think Jesus said this? Should you forgive a person even if they never come to you and say, 'I'm sorry'? Why or why not? When you refuse to forgive someone, who does it hurt more, you or the other person? Why?

PRACTICE

Challenge someone to practice fighting temptation. You can take turns drawing the temptation cards from a bowl. Ask each other what you would do if you were tempted in that way.

TRY THIS

With a yellow pencil, write the word *anger* on a piece of paper. Now place a piece of red cellophane or a see-through, red plastic report cover over the writing. The words disappear. When we forgive people, we let our anger against them disappear.

DAY 6

READ

Luke 23:26-34 ("Skull Hill," page 621 in the *Day By Day Kid's Bible*) The guards made fun of Jesus... Then they took him out to kill him on a cross... They all came to Skull Hill. There they nailed Jesus and the two other men to crosses... "Father, forgive the people who are doing this," said Jesus. "They don't know what they're doing."

THINK AND TALK

Why did Jesus ask God to forgive the people who made fun of him and nailed him to the cross? Did these people say they were sorry? Who else was Jesus forgiving by dying on the cross? Why do we need to be forgiven by God? What happens because of God's choice to forgive us and our choice to receive his forgiveness? Why does God want us to forgive other people?

PRACTICE

Challenge someone to practice fighting temptation. You can take turns drawing the temptation cards from a bowl. Ask each other what you would do if you were tempted in that way.

TRY THIS

Glue two Popsicle sticks or craft sticks together to make a cross. Write the word *FORGIVE* on it.

DAY 7

READ

Acts 6:8–7:5; 7:48-60 ("Stephen Sees Jesus," page 640 in the *Day By Day Kid's Bible*)

Stephen was very wise... The leaders could not win against him by talking. So the leaders got together in secret. They told some men to say that Stephen was against God... The leaders were so angry, they couldn't stand it... They started throwing rocks at him. The rocks were hitting Stephen. But he prayed, "Lord Jesus, take my spirit... Don't blame them for this sin." After he said that, he died.

THINK AND TALK

What choices did Stephen make? What happened because of his choices? Why did Stephen forgive the men who were killing him? Is it always easy to forgive people? What are some things that might keep us from forgiving someone? What can you do to help yourself become a forgiving person?

PRACTICE

Challenge someone to practice fighting temptation. You can take turns drawing the temptation cards from a bowl. Ask each other what you would do if you were tempted in that way.

TRY THIS

Put about one inch of water in a pie pan. Sprinkle pepper on top of the water. The pepper represents our sins. Then drip one drop of liquid dishwashing detergent into the center of the pan. What happens to the pepper? The dishwashing liquid breaks the surface tension of the water so that it can't hold the pepper. Forgiving breaks the tension of sin in our lives. When we forgive others, we don't hold onto our anger toward them. When they forgive us, they don't hold onto their anger toward us.

Feeling Joyful

Your sword of the Spirit for this week is:

The joy of the Lord is your strength. NEHEMIAH 8:10

With the above sword you can fight back when you face this temptation:

You are tempted to stay sad.

DAY 1

READ

1 Samuel 21; Psalm 34:1-10 ("Goliath's Sword" and "Taste and See," page 145 in the *Day By Day Kid's Bible*)

The king of Gath sent David away. Then David wrote this song. "I will always tell how wonderful God is... People shine with joy when they love God. Their faces never look like they feel bad. I called God, and he heard me. God saved me from all my troubles... Taste and see. God is good. Good things come to people who trust him. People who love him have all they need."

THINK AND TALK

Is it wrong to be sad? We have feelings that just come up inside us. They aren't wrong or right, they're just feelings. But then we have to decide what to do with those feelings. What we do can be wrong or right. Many times when David was afraid, he prayed to God. (One of those prayers is in Psalm 56.) Was that the right thing to do? Why or why not? God saved David, but that didn't mean that everything in David's life was perfect. Did David choose to be sad about the other troubles in his life? After God had saved David, David wrote the psalm in our reading. What are the reasons David gives for why people who trust God can be full of joy? What are some other reasons for us to be joyful?

PRACTICE
Read the verse. Try to repeat it several times without looking. Cut a sword shape from paper or cardboard and write the verse on it. You'll want to hang it up in your house at a place where it will remind you of the Spirit's sword from Nehemiah 8:10. You can use it to fight when you are tempted to stay sad.

DAY 2

READ
2 Samuel 12; Psalm 51 ("The Poor Man's Sheep," page 168 in the *Day By Day Kid's Bible*)
Nathan told David what God said...."Why have you done this terrible wrong? You killed Uriah. You took his wife to be your wife." ..."I've sinned against God," said David. David wrote, "Be kind to me, God... Wash away all my sin, and clean my heart... Let my sad bones know joy again."..."God has taken away your sin," said Nathan.... "But...your baby boy will die."...David begged God to make the baby well. David wouldn't eat any food. He stayed in his palace... Seven days later, the baby died... David got up... He worshiped God... He asked for some food, and he ate.

THINK AND TALK
What were the choices that David had made? What happened because of his choices? What reason did David have for being sad? Why didn't David choose to stay sad? David found out that there is a time when God wants us to feel sad. When is it? Why would God want us to feel this kind of sadness? When we feel sad because we've done wrong, how can we get our feeling of joy back?

PRACTICE
Challenge a friend or family member (or yourself) to a sword fight. One person says, "What will you do when you are tempted to stay

sad?" The other person answers, "I will not stay sad because it is written, 'The joy of the Lord is your strength.'"

DAY 3

READ

Proverbs 15:13, 30; 17:22; 29:6 ("Happy and Sad," page 254 in the *Day By Day Kid's Bible*)

When you're happy, your face shows it. But a sad heart makes your spirit feel unhappy. A happy heart can make you feel well. But a sad heart makes your bones feel dried up... People who do wrong are trapped by their own sin. But people who do right can sing and be happy. Looking happy gives people joy. Good news gives people good health.

THINK AND TALK

Joy is the feeling that everything is all right or is going to be all right. Is it possible to feel joy even when you're sad? Why or why not? Has anyone every tried to cheer you up when you were sad? If so, what did the person do? When is it the hardest for you to cheer up?

PRACTICE

Challenge someone to sword-fight with your sword for this week. Write on an index card: "You are tempted to stay sad." Add this temptation card to the other cards you've collected. Place them in a bowl. The first person draws a card and challenges the second person with that temptation. The second person repeats the sword of the Spirit that she can use to fight the temptation. Then it's her turn to draw a card and challenge the first person.

DAY 4

READ

Ecclesiastes 2 ("Chasing the Wind," page 261 in the *Day By Day Kid's Bible*)

I said, "I'll look for things that make me feel good." But that ended up being good for nothing... I wanted to find out what's really good to do. So I started doing things... I got whatever I wanted... When it was done, I looked at it all. I had worked hard to get it. But it was not good for anything. It was like chasing the wind... The best thing to do is eat and drink. Be happy in your work. This comes from God. If you don't have God, how can you enjoy anything?

THINK AND TALK
What are some things that people try to *do* or to *get* as they try to bring themselves joy? King Solomon wrote the words in today's reading. What was the one thing he found out that people need in order to enjoy what they have and what they do? How can you tell when people enjoy what they have and what they do? How can you tell when people don't enjoy what they have and what they do? Does God want us to enjoy what we have and what we do? Why or why not?

PRACTICE
You and another person can challenge each other to practice fighting temptation. Do this by taking turns drawing the temptation cards from a bowl. Ask each other what you would do if you were tempted in that way, and answer by saying the appropriate verse.

TRY THIS
Fill three coffee cups one-third full with rubbing alcohol. Drip red food coloring into one cup, yellow into another, and blue into another. Get several coffee filters and fold them any way you like. Dip parts of each one into each color as though you were tie-dying. Lay them on old newspapers to dry. Then poke a hole in the center of each coffee filter. Cut a 36-inch piece of string. Tie one end onto a button. Then put the string through the hole in the coffee filter, pushing it all the way down until it touches the button. Now tie another button onto the string six or more inches away from the first. Slide another coffee filter onto the string up to the second button. Do the same with more buttons and coffee filters. Then tie the end of the string to a porch post or railing, or tie it to a dowel. Let these flags blow in the wind. What did Solomon mean when he talked about "chasing the wind"?

DAY 5

READ

Psalm 126 ("Laughing and Joy," page 471 in the *Day By Day Kid's Bible*)

Enemies had taken us away. But God brought us back to Jerusalem. It was like a dream. We were full of laughing and joy. God has done great things for us. We are full of joy.

THINK AND TALK

What are some of the things God has done for you and your family that fill you with joy? What are some other words that would describe the feeling of joy? Is it always easy to be joyful? Tell about someone you know who is joyful, even though they may have hard times. Tell about a time when you were joyful, even though what you were doing was hard work.

PRACTICE

Challenge someone to practice fighting temptation. You can take turns drawing the temptation cards from a bowl. Ask each other what you would do if you were tempted in that way.

TRY THIS

Scatter several paper clips across a paper plate. Then drag a magnet along the bottom of the plate, gathering the clips above. See if you can get them to line up into a long trail of clips. A long line of God's people returned home after being in enemy country for many years. Why were they joyful?

DAY 6

READ

1 Thessalonians 5 ("People Will Be Surprised," page 670 in the *Day By Day Kid's Bible*)

God didn't choose us so he could be angry at us. He chose us to be saved by Jesus. Jesus died for us. That way, if we die, we live with him. And if we live, we live with him. So help each other. Cheer each other up... Always show your joy. Always pray. Always thank God. This is what God wants you to do.

THINK AND TALK
Paul wrote today's reading. What reason did Paul give for helping each other and cheering each other up? Why do you think God wants us to always show our joy? What are some things that might tempt us not to show our joy?

PRACTICE
Challenge someone to practice fighting temptation. You can take turns drawing the temptation cards from a bowl. Ask each other what you would do if you were tempted in that way.

TRY THIS
With a crayon, write *JOY* in large, bold letters on a piece of paper. Press down hard with the crayon. Drip a drop of watercolor paint, any color, onto the paper below the word *JOY*. Blow through a straw at this drop of color to make it branch out and up and cross the word. Continue to drip different colors of paint onto the paper and blow them to make a design.

DAY 7

READ
1 Peter 1 ("Richer than Gold," page 769 in the *Day By Day Kid's Bible*)
You haven't seen Jesus, but you love him anyway. You believe in him. You are full of joy. It's better than words can tell. It shines in you. That's because your souls are being saved. You are getting what you wanted from your faith... It's like you've been born again... You've been born again into a family that never dies.

THINK AND TALK
Peter wrote today's reading. What are some things he tells about that bring us joy? What is the choice that people make that brings them this kind of joy? What would you suggest to a friend who wants to have this kind of joy that lasts forever?

PRACTICE

Challenge someone to practice fighting temptation. You can take turns drawing the temptation cards from a bowl. Ask each other what you would do if you were tempted in that way.

TRY THIS

Staple a stack of five index cards together at one of the short ends. On the top card, close to the end without the staples, draw a frowning face. On the next card, exactly under the frowning face, draw the same face with the mouth frowning, but not as much. On the next card, draw the same face with its mouth straight across, not frowning or smiling. On the next card, make the mouth starting to smile. On the last card, make the face smiling. Flip through the pages of this little book to see how the face turns from a frown to a smile. What can you do to turn a frown into a smile?

Speaking
Kind Words

Your sword of the Spirit for this week is:

A gentle answer turns away wrath, but a harsh word stirs up anger. PROVERBS 15:1

With the above sword you can fight back when you face this temptation:

You are tempted to speak unkind words.

DAY 1

READ

Proverbs 15:23, 28; 16:23-24, 27-28 ("The Words We Say," page 244 in the *Day By Day Kid's Bible*)

A wise person's mind tells his mouth what to say... People who please God think about what they're going to say. But sinful people rush to say bad things... A word said at the right time is good... Kind words are like honey. They are sweet to the soul... A person who talks about others turns friends into enemies.... Bad people look for bad things to say. Their words burn like fire.

THINK AND TALK

Wrath is another word for anger. Have you ever seen a gentle word turn away wrath or a harsh word stir up anger? If so, tell about it. Why is that verse true? What kinds of words are "gentle" words? What does the reading for today mean when it says, "A person who talks about others turns friends into enemies"?

PRACTICE

Read the verse. Try to repeat it several times without looking. Cut a sword shape from paper or cardboard. Write the verse on it. You'll want to hang it up in your house at a place where it will remind you of the Spirit's sword from Proverbs 15:1. You can use it to fight when you are tempted to speak unkind words.

DAY 2

READ

Titus 2:1-14 ("Teaching Us to Say No," page 755 in the *Day By Day Kid's Bible*)

Do good things. Teach truth. Mean what you say, and say what you mean. Then nobody can blame you for what you say. Teach servants... not to talk back to their masters... God's kind love... teaches us to say no to bad things. It teaches us to say no to things the world loves.

THINK AND TALK

Paul wrote today's reading. What kinds of words is he writing about? Is it possible "to say no to bad things" and be kind at the same time? If so, how? Why does God want us to use kind words? What happens when we don't? What should we do when someone else speaks to us unkindly?

PRACTICE

Challenge a friend or family member (or yourself) to a sword-fight. One person says, "What will you do when you are tempted to speak unkind words?" The other person answers, "I will not speak unkindly, because it is written, 'A gentle answer turns away wrath, but a harsh word stirs up anger.'"

DAY 3

READ

James 3 ("A Small Fire in a Big Forest," page 764 in the *Day By Day Kid's Bible*)

Your mouth is a small part of your body. But it talks big! ... Think of all the parts of your body. Your mouth can bring the most pain. It can make you sin... We praise God with our mouths. Then we turn around and say bad things about people... Good words and bad words come from the same mouth. It shouldn't be this way.

THINK AND TALK

How can your mouth bring pain? How can your mouth make you sin? Has someone else's mouth ever brought you pain? How does it feel when you know you've said something that hurt someone else? Is there anything you can do to take that feeling away? How can you tell someone the truth if you know it will make them feel sad or afraid or worried?

PRACTICE

Challenge someone to sword-fight with your sword for this week. Write on an index card: "You are tempted to say unkind words." Add this temptation card to the other cards you've collected. Place them in a bowl. The first person draws a card, opens it and challenges the second person with that temptation. The second person repeats the sword of the Spirit that he can use to fight the temptation. Then it's his turn to draw a card and challenge the first person.

DAY 4

READ

Luke 6:43-49 ("Good Fruit and Bad Fruit," page 536 in the *Day By Day Kid's Bible*)

"Good things happen when good people are around," said Jesus. "That's because they have good stored up in their hearts. But bad things happen when bad people are around. That's because they have sin stored up in their hearts. People's words come from their hearts first. Then the words come out of their mouths."

THINK AND TALK

When people say bad words or speak unkindly, what does that tell us about their heart? How can you store up good in your heart? Tell about someone you know who always seems to say kind things. Tell about a time when you were tempted to say something unkind, but you didn't.

PRACTICE

You and another person can challenge each other to practice fighting temptation. Do this by taking turns drawing the temptation cards from a bowl. Ask each other what you would do if you were tempted in that way, and answer by saying the appropriate verse.

TRY THIS

Cut out a six-inch square of aluminum foil. Place it over your lips and gently press it around your lips, molding it as if making a sculpture. Then gently remove the foil and see a model of your lips. Think about how important it is to have kind words coming from your mouth.

DAY 5

READ

Ecclesiastes 10 ("A Sharp Ax," page 267 in the *Day By Day Kid's Bible*)

A wise person says kind, loving words. But the words of fools get them into trouble. At first their words are foolish. The words end up being crazy. The fool talks and talks and talks... Don't say bad things about the king. Don't even think bad things about him. A little bird might tell what you said.

THINK AND TALK

Who are your leaders? How does God want us to speak about our leaders? Why? Is it always easy to say kind words to people? When is it hardest for you to speak kindly? What are some things you can do to help yourself use kind words?

PRACTICE

Challenge someone to practice fighting temptation. You can take turns drawing the temptation cards from a bowl. Ask each other what you would do if you were tempted in that way.

TRY THIS

Hunt for bird feathers around a yard or a park. When you find some, take them home and use them to paint designs on paper as if they were paintbrushes. What did Solomon mean when he said, "A little bird might tell what you said"?

DAY 6

READ

Ecclesiastes 7:19-25 ("Good and Bad Days," page 264 in the *Day By Day Kid's Bible*)

There's nobody on earth who always does right. There's not one person who never sins. Don't listen to everything people say. You might hear your helper say bad things about you. You know you've said bad things about others.

THINK AND TALK

Have you ever heard someone say something bad about you? If so, how did it make you feel? How does it make people feel to hear you say something bad about them? Telling something bad about somebody else is called *gossip*. Why does God want us not to gossip? When is it hardest for you not to gossip? How can you keep from listening to gossip?

PRACTICE

Challenge someone to practice fighting temptation. You can take turns drawing the temptation cards from a bowl. Ask each other what you would do if you were tempted in that way.

TRY THIS

Roll a piece of paper into a cone shape by overlapping two opposite corners. Leave a two-inch opening in the pointed end. Now sit someplace where you can hear things going on around you. Put a hand over one ear. Listen. Keeping your hand over one ear, place the small end of the cone up to your other ear. Can you hear better or worse or just the same? What is *eavesdropping*? Sometimes people gossip about things they were never supposed to hear in the first place. Why would a person be tempted to eavesdrop?

DAY 7

READ

2 Chronicles 10 ("One Nation Turns into Two Nations," page 271 in the *Day By Day Kid's Bible*)

Jeroboam and many other people went to see King Rehoboam. "When Solomon was the king, he was very hard on us," they said. "Make things easier for us."..."Come back in three days," said the king... Three days passed. Jeroboam and the people came back. King Rehoboam had an answer for them that was not kind... "My father was hard on you. But I'll be harder... " "Then we won't be your people!" everyone said... After that day, Israel and Judah were two different nations.

THINK AND TALK

What choice did King Rehoboam make? What happened because of the choice he made? What might have happened if he had spoken kindly to the people? What are some things that might tempt us to speak unkindly? What would you suggest to a friend who wanted to stop speaking unkind words?

PRACTICE

Challenge someone to practice fighting temptation. You can take turns drawing the temptation cards from a bowl. Ask each other what you would do if you were tempted in that way.

TRY THIS

You will need two mugs. Fill one halfway with water. Add about one tablespoon of dirt and stir it up. Take a paper towel and fold it lengthwise. Set the mug with dirt in it up on a short can (like tuna comes in). Set the second mug down lower, beside the can. Put one end of the folded paper towel into the muddy water of the first mug. Put the other end of the paper into the empty mug. Leave them overnight and check them the next morning. What happened? The mud and water separated. God's people separated into two different nations because of the unkind words that Rehoboam spoke.

Seeking God
and His Ways

Your sword of the Spirit for this week is:

**You will...find me when you seek me
with all your heart.** JEREMIAH 29:13

*With the above sword you can fight back when you face this
temptation:*

**You are tempted to stop learning all you can
about God and his ways.**

DAY 1

READ

John 3:1-21 ("A Night Visit," page 516 in the *Day By Day Kid's
Bible*)

There was once a Jew named Nicodemus. He was one of the
leaders. One night he came to see Jesus. "We know you are a
teacher from God," he said. "Nobody can do the wonders you do
unless God is with him." "Here's the truth," said Jesus. "Nobody
can even see God's kingdom without being born again." "Born
again?" asked Nicodemus.

THINK AND TALK

Seeking means asking and trying to find out. What do you think
Nicodemus was seeking? Why do you think God wants us to
seek him? Is there a time when we will know everything there is
to know about God? When can we stop seeking God? Is there
a difference between knowing about God and knowing God? If
so, what's the difference?

PRACTICE

Read the verse. Try to repeat it several times without looking. Write the verse on a paper or cardboard sword. You'll want to hang it up in your house where it will remind you of the Spirit's sword from Jeremiah 29:13. Use it to fight when you are tempted to stop learning about God and his ways.

DAY 2

READ

2 Chronicles 34 ("Finding a Book," page 386 in the *Day By Day Kid's Bible*)

Now Josiah was still Judah's king. He sent some men to God's worship house to fix it... While all of this was going on, the priest found something. It was the book of laws God gave Moses... The king's helper read part of the book to King Josiah. The king... told the leaders, "Go ask God about this book."...Then King Josiah called all the leaders together. He led them to the worship house. All the other people went too. There Josiah read all the words of the Law Book.

THINK AND TALK

Did Josiah want to know what the Law Book said or not? When he heard the words, what did he choose to do? Second Chronicles 34:3 says, "While he was still young, [Josiah] began to seek the God of... David." How can a person today seek God? How can you tell if a person seeks God? How can you tell if a person does not seek God?

PRACTICE

Challenge a friend or family member (or yourself) to a sword-fight. One person says, "What will you do when you are tempted not to seek God?" The other person answers, "I will keep seeking God, because it is written, 'You will... find me when you seek me with all your heart.'"

DAY 3

READ

Psalm 42 ("Like a Deer," page 216 in the *Day By Day Kid's Bible*)
My soul is like a deer that is thirsty for water. My soul is thirsty for the living God. When can I meet with God?... I will trust in God. I will praise him, because he saves me

THINK AND TALK

What are some reasons for why people seek God? Why did the person who wrote Psalm 42 seek God? What does it feel like when you are thirsty for something to drink? What do you think the writer of this psalm meant when he said his soul was thirsty for God? Have you ever been thirsty for God? When you are thirsty for God, what can you do?

PRACTICE

Challenge someone to sword-fight with your sword for this week. Write on an index card: "You are tempted to stop seeking God." Add this temptation card to the other cards you've collected. Place them in a bowl. The first person draws a card and challenges the second person with that temptation. The second person repeats the sword of the Spirit that he can use to fight the temptation. Then it's his turn to draw a card and challenge the first person.

DAY 4

READ

Amos 5 ("Look for Good; Look for God," page 328 in the *Day By Day Kid's Bible*)
Here's what God says. "Look for me. Then you'll live. Don't look for other people to save you."... Look for what's good, not for what's bad. Then God will be with you. Hate wrong. Love right. Be fair when you judge.

THINK AND TALK

Only God can satisfy us. Only he can fill our spirit so we don't feel empty in our heart. When people do not seek God, how do they try to fill their empty heart? Does it work? Why or why not? What are you tempted to fill your heart with? When is it hardest for you to seek God?

PRACTICE
You and another person can challenge each other to practice fighting temptation. Do this by taking turns drawing the temptation cards from a bowl. Ask each other what you would do if you were tempted in that way, and answer by saying the appropriate verse.

TRY THIS
Play "Flashlight Tag" outside at night with friends or family. Choose one person to hold the flashlight and tag the others. Also choose a home base. A player is tagged "out" if the flashlight shines on him. But if he can get to home base before the light shines on him, he's safe. The players hide. The person with the flashlight tries to find the others and tag them. Take turns holding the flashlight and tagging others. Flashlights help us find things. What helps us find God?

DAY 5

READ
2 Chronicles 15 ("Good King Asa," page 276 in the *Day By Day Kid's Bible*)
Asa was a good king. He did what was right... So his kingdom had peace... Now God's Spirit came upon a man who went to see Asa. He said,... "When you are with God, he is with you. Look for him. Then you will find him."...King Asa called the people of Judah together... They all said they'd love God with their whole heart... They looked for God, and they found him. So God gave them peace.

THINK AND TALK
What did King Asa choose to do? What choice did the people of Judah make? What happened because of their choice? How can we find out about God? Why do you think God doesn't let us find out everything about him?

PRACTICE
Challenge someone to practice fighting temptation. You can take turns drawing the temptation cards from a bowl. Ask each other what you would do if you were tempted in that way.

TRY THIS
Make a yellow cake from a cake mix. Before you put the batter in the oven, put one chocolate chip down into the batter. When you serve the cake, you can look to see who gets the piece with the chip. How do we look for God and seek him?

DAY 6

READ
Matthew 5:1-12 ("Up the Mountain," page 530 in the *Day By Day Kid's Bible*)
Jesus saw how many people were coming to hear him. So he went up on the side of a mountain. There he sat down... Then he began to teach them. "God will bring good to people who know they need him. The kingdom of heaven belongs to them," said Jesus... "God will bring good to people who are hungry for what's right. They're thirsty for what's right. They'll be filled up."

THINK AND TALK
What does it mean to be hungry and thirsty for what's right? How can people who are hungry and thirsty for what's right be filled up? Tell about someone you know who seeks God. What do you most want to know about God? Do you think God will teach you more about himself if you ask him? How does God teach us about himself?

PRACTICE
Challenge someone to practice fighting temptation. You can take turns drawing the temptation cards from a bowl. Ask each other what you would do if you were tempted in that way.

TRY THIS
Invent a drink by mixing different fruit juices. You can blend in

vanilla yogurt or fruit pieces chopped in a blender. Taste your juice after you add each ingredient, and think about what else it needs to taste just right. You are seeking the best blend of flavors. God is the best blend of love, joy, peace, patience, kindness, goodness, faithfulness, gentleness, and self-control. Should we ever stop seeking God? Why or why not?

DAY 7

READ
John 1:29-51 ("The Lamb of God," page 514 in the *Day By Day Kid's Bible*)
John saw Jesus going by. So John said, "Look! It's the Lamb of God!" Andrew and his friend heard what John said. So they followed Jesus. Jesus turned around and saw them. "What do you want?" he asked. "Teacher, we want to know where you're staying," they said. "Come and see," said Jesus... It was about four o'clock in the afternoon. They spent the rest of the day with Jesus.

THINK AND TALK
Why do you think Andrew and his friend followed Jesus and spent the rest of the day with him? What were they seeking? If you could have been Andrew or one of Jesus' other special friends, what is one question you would have asked Jesus? What are some things that take our thoughts away from seeking Jesus? What would you suggest to a friend who wanted to know Jesus better?

PRACTICE
Challenge someone to practice fighting temptation. You can take turns drawing the temptation cards from a bowl. Ask each other what you would do if you were tempted in that way.

TRY THIS
Get a friend to stand in front of you, face to face. Now you begin to move one arm slowly. Your friend must copy your movements at the same time, as if your friend were your reflection in a mirror. Your friend must follow exactly what you do. After a few minutes, let your friend lead, and you can be the mirror image. How can we "follow" Jesus?

Helping and
Serving

Your sword of the Spirit for this week is:

Serve one another in love. GALATIANS 5:13

With the above sword you can fight back when you face this temptation:

You are tempted not to help others.

DAY 1

READ

Genesis 2 ("Adam's Helper," page 4 in the *Day By Day Kid's Bible*)

God said, "It's not good for Adam to be alone. I'll make a helper for him." Now God had made all the animals. So he showed them to Adam... But God didn't find any animal that was able to help Adam. So God made Adam go to sleep....Then God took one rib from Adam. He made a woman from it. God showed the woman to Adam. Adam said, "I will call her 'woman' because she came from a man."

THINK AND TALK

How can animals be helpful to people? Why did God make a woman to be Adam's helper? Another word for helping is *serving*. Serving is helping wherever help is needed. It shows the people you're helping that you think they are important. How can you tell if someone is a serving, helping person? How can you tell if someone is not a serving, helping person?

PRACTICE

Read the verse. Try to repeat it several times without looking. Cut a sword shape from paper or cardboard and write the verse on it. You'll want to hang it up in your house where it will remind you of the Spirit's sword from Galatians 5:13. You can use it to fight when you are tempted not to help or serve.

DAY 2

READ

Exodus 17 ("Water from a Rock," page 64 in the *Day By Day Kid's Bible*)

An enemy army came out to fight against God's people... So Joshua took some men out to fight. Moses and Aaron and Hur went up the hill. They watched from the top. When Moses held his hands up, God's people would win. When he put his hands down, the enemy would win. Moses' hands got tired. So Aaron and Hur... held Moses' hands up until the sun set. So Joshua and his men won the fight.

THINK AND TALK

Why did Moses need help? What choice did Aaron and Hur make? What happened because of their choice? Why does God want us to help and serve others? What happens when we don't? Moses was a leader. Aaron and Hur helped him. Name one of your leaders at home or school or on a team. How can you help this leader?

PRACTICE

Challenge a friend or family member (or yourself) to a sword-fight. One person says, "What will you do when you are tempted not to help or serve others?" The other person answers, "I will help and serve because it is written, 'Serve one another in love.'"

DAY 3

READ

Proverbs 11:17; 12:10; 25:21-22 ("Love, Hate, and Caring," page 239 in the *Day By Day Kid's Bible*.)

Give food to your enemy if he is hungry. Give water to your enemy if he is thirsty. God will bring good things to you for doing this. Good things come to kind people. But trouble comes to mean people. People who do what's right take care of their animals.

THINK AND TALK
Are we supposed to help and serve only the people who are our friends? Why or why not? Is it always easy to serve others? When is it hardest for you to help and serve?

PRACTICE
Challenge someone to sword-fight with your sword for this week. Write on an index card: "You are tempted not to help or serve." Add this temptation card to the other cards you've collected. Place them in a bowl. The first person draws a card and challenges the second person with the temptation. The second person repeats the sword of the Spirit that she can use to fight that temptation. Then it's her turn to draw a card and challenge the first person.

DAY 4

READ
Jeremiah 38:1-13 ("A Muddy Well," page 421 in the *Day By Day Kid's Bible*)
Some of the king's men... took Jeremiah. They put him in a well in the guards' yard... There was just mud at the bottom. Jeremiah sank down into the mud. But a leader at the palace heard about it... He got some old rags and clothes. He tied ropes to them. He let them down into the well... Jeremiah put the old rags under his arms. Then he put the ropes under his arms. The men pulled him up out of the well.

Talk and Think
Why did Jeremiah need help? Who chose to help him? How does it feel to help someone who really needs your help? Tell about someone who has helped you. Tell about a time when you helped someone who really needed your help.

PRACTICE

You and another person can challenge each other to practice fighting temptation by taking turns drawing the temptation cards from a bowl. Ask each other what you would do if you were tempted in that way, and answer by saying the appropriate verse.

TRY THIS

You will need two friends, two brooms, and a rope. Ask your friends to face each other, and have each one hold a broom sideways in front of himself. The brooms should be about two feet apart as your friends hold them. Tie one end of the rope to one of the brooms. Then loop the rope around both broom handles three times. You stand beside one friend as you hold the end of the rope. When you say go, all of you should pull. Your friends should pull on the broom handles, trying to keep them apart. You should pull on the rope, trying to pull them together. What happens? The rope around the brooms acts like a pulley and helps you to pull with greater strength. Do you think it would have been hard or easy to pull Jeremiah out of the muddy at the bottom of the well? Why?

DAY 5

READ

John 19:17-27 ("Close to the Cross," page 622 in the *Day By Day Kid's Bible*)

One of the men being killed made fun of Jesus.... The other man being killed...said, "Jesus! Remember me when you get to your kingdom." "You'll get to be with me in heaven today," said Jesus. Jesus' mother stood close to the cross. His aunt was there too... Jesus looked out. He saw his mother. He saw his friend John there too. "Dear woman!" Jesus said to his mother. "John will be like your son now. Take care of her," he told John. "Care for her like you'd care for your own mother." After that, John let Jesus' mother stay at his house. He took care of her.

THINK AND TALK

What did Jesus choose to do when he saw John and his mother standing nearby? What choice did John make? Name the people

226

in your family who need your help. How do you help them? How do they help you? What would a family be like if none of the family members helped each other?

PRACTICE
Challenge someone to practice fighting temptation. You can take turns drawing the temptation cards from a bowl. Ask each other what you would do if you were tempted in that way.

TRY THIS
Bake cookies that are the favorite of someone in your family. Serve the cookies to that person—and to your whole family. You can also serve your family by cleaning the kitchen after you've baked the cookies.

DAY 6

READ
Nehemiah 5:14-19 ("Money for Grain," page 493 in *Day By Day Kid's Bible*)

Now the king chose me to be the leader of Judah. The leaders before me had made the people pay a big tax. Their helpers had bossed the people around. But I loved God too much to do that. Instead, I kept working hard on the wall. All of my men worked. We didn't take land from anyone. Every day I fed 150 Jews and Jewish leaders at my table. I could have asked for food like leaders do. But I never asked for food. That's because I saw that these people worked hard.

THINK AND TALK
Nehemiah was the boss. What choices did he make? Why didn't Nehemiah make the people serve him? What are some things that might tempt us not to serve someone? Is there ever a time when we should not help someone? If so, when?

PRACTICE
Challenge someone to practice fighting temptation. You can take turns drawing the temptation cards from a bowl. Ask each other what you would do if you were tempted in that way.

TRY THIS

Make a napkin holder for your family's dinner table. Get an empty cake-mix box (or another box about that size–rice, granola, or instant potato box). Set the box on one of its narrow sides. Cut off the side that is now on top. Cover the rest of the box with Con-Tact paper. You can add designs made with stickers or permanent markers. Place the napkins in the box and put it on your kitchen counter or table. What are some other ways you can serve your family?

DAY 7

READ

Matthew 20:20-28 ("To Sit at Your Right Hand," page 592 in the *Day By Day Kid's Bible*)

[Jesus] said, "You know, the world's rulers boss everyone around. They tell everyone what to do. But you're not supposed to act like that. Instead, if you want to be great, you'll serve people," said Jesus. "Anybody wanting to be first has to be a servant. Even I didn't come to earth to be served. I came to serve."

THINK AND TALK

Tell about a leader you know who serves others. What are some jobs or careers that are built around serving other people? Give several reasons for why people might serve others. What are some reasons that God wants us to serve others? Name some ways in which you can serve and help people this week.

PRACTICE

Challenge someone to practice fighting temptation. You can take turns drawing the temptation cards from a bowl. Ask each other what you would do if you were tempted in that way.

TRY THIS

Be a serving spy for a day. Look around your house to see what needs to be cleaned or picked up. Do it without being asked. Don't tell anyone you did it unless they ask.

Having Purpose

Your sword of the Spirit for this week is:

The Lord will fulfill his purpose for me.
PSALM 138:8

With the above sword you can fight back when you face this temptation:

**You are tempted to think you are
not important to God.**

DAY 1

READ

Exodus 3 ("Fire!" page 49 in the *Day By Day Kid's Bible*)
Moses took care of Jethro's sheep. One day he took them far across the desert. He came to Horeb Mountain... God came to Moses there. He showed himself as fire that was burning on a bush... I've seen how unhappy my people are," said God... "I'm sending you to the king. You'll bring my people out of Egypt."

THINK AND TALK

What purpose and plan did God have for Moses? How did God prepare Moses for that plan? (God let Moses grow up in the palace, so he knew the ways of the rulers, he knew many of the people, he knew his way around. God let Moses lead sheep. God let Moses spend time in the desert, learning how to live in desert places and how to get around in the desert.) Did Moses know that God was preparing him? Does God still have purposes and plans for people? Does we always know the purpose God has for our lives? Why or why not?

PRACTICE

Read the verse. Try to repeat it several times without looking. Cut a sword shape from paper or cardboard and write the verse on it. You'll want to hang it up in your house where it will remind you of the Spirit's sword from Psalm 138:8. You can use it to fight when you are tempted to think that you are not important to God.

DAY 2

READ

1 Samuel 7 ("Fighting with Thunder," page 128 in the *Day By Day Kid's Bible*)

As long as Samuel lived, God worked against their enemies. Samuel was a judge for God's people all his life. When people would disagree, he'd say who was right. Samuel traveled around to judge the people. He was a judge in the city where his home was, too. He built an altar there to God.

THINK AND TALK

If you remember the beginning of Samuel's life, tell about it. If you don't remember, read 1 Samuel 1-3 (pages 121–124 in the *Day By Day Kid's Bible*). What was God's purpose and plan for Samuel's life? How did he prepare Samuel to be a judge and prophet? Why do you think God has a plan for every person? What happens when people don't follow God's plan for them?

PRACTICE

Challenge a friend or family member (or yourself) to a sword-fight. One person says, "What will you do when you are tempted to think you are not important to God?" The other person answers, "I will say that I am important to God because it is written, 'The Lord will fulfill his purpose for me.'"

DAY 3

READ

2 Samuel 2:1-11 and 5:1-5 ("A Marching Sound in the Tree Tops," page 160 in the *Day By Day Kid's Bible*)

There was lots of fighting between Saul's men and David's men...

David and his men got stronger. Saul's army got weaker... Now all the people who followed Saul's son turned to David. They chose David to be their king... Then David lived in Jerusalem. Everyone called it David's City... He became great because God was with him.

THINK AND TALK

Do you remember what David did when he was a boy? Do you know what happened to him when he was still just a young man? If you do, tell about it. If you don't, read 1 Samuel 16–17 (pages 137–140 in the *Day By Day Kid's Bible*). What was God's purpose and plan for David's life? How did God prepare David to be a brave leader and a good king? Why do you think God wanted to make David the king of his people? How do people know what God's plan for them is?

PRACTICE

Challenge someone to sword-fight with your sword for this week. Write on an index card: "You are tempted to think that you're not important to God." Add this temptation card to the other cards you've collected. Place them in a bowl. The first person draws a card and challenges the second person with that temptation. The second person repeats the sword of the Spirit that she can use to fight the temptation. Then it's her turn to draw a card and challenge the first person.

DAY 4

READ

Daniel 2 ("A Figure in a Dream," page 396 in the *Day By Day Kid's Bible*)

Then the king bowed to Daniel... He said, "I'm sure your God is the God of gods. He's the Lord of kings... I know that's true, because you were able to tell my dream!" The king gave Daniel many gifts. He put Daniel in charge of all Babylon. He put Daniel in charge of all the wise men.

THINK AND TALK

If you remember how Daniel came to Babylon and what first happened to him there, tell about it. If you don't, read Daniel 1 (page 395 in the *Day By Day Kid's Bible*). What was God's plan for Daniel's life? How did God prepare Daniel to be in charge of all the wise men of Babylon? Why do you think God wanted to put Daniel in that place? Tell about some of the people you know now who are living out God's purpose and plan for their lives. What makes you think they are fulfilling God's purposes for them?

PRACTICE

You and another person can challenge each other to practice fighting temptation. Do this by taking turns drawing the temptation cards from a bowl. Ask each other what you would do if you were tempted in that way.

TRY THIS

Use as many three-inch by five-inch index cards as there are letters in your first name. For example, if your name is Jon, you'll need three cards. If your name is Elizabeth, you'll need nine. Write one letter of your name on each card. Now use a hole puncher to punch holes about one-half inch to one inch apart along the lines of each letter. Pull yarn up from underneath the first hole in the first letter, and pull the yarn back through the second hole. Come up through the third, down through the fourth, and so on, sewing the yarn through the holes. You can use a blunt-tipped yarn needle for this if you want. You can sew all letters with the same color of yarn, or change colors of yarn from letter to letter. If you are doing this with a friend and know what your names mean, tell each other. If you don't know the meanings, tell each other what you would like your name to mean. Tell God you're glad he has a purpose for you.

DAY 5

READ

Acts 22 ("Tossing Dust into the Air," page 721 in the *Day By Day Kid's Bible*)

"Listen to me," said Paul... "I'm a Jew... I grew up in this city. I went

to school here. Gamaliel was my teacher. He taught me the Law...
I was hard on the followers of Jesus... I took men and women to
jail. I even went to Damascus to catch more of them. I was on my
way to Damascus... About noon, a bright light shone down on me
from heaven. I fell down, and I heard a voice. 'Saul! Saul! Why
are you hurting me?' said the voice." Paul told the crowd his story...
"The Lord talked to me again. 'Go. I'm sending you far away to
people who aren't Jewish.'"

THINK AND TALK

What was God's purpose for Paul's life? How did Paul know? How
had God prepared Paul to be a missionary to people who weren't
Jewish and to write letters that we still read today? What are some
of the letters that Paul wrote? Is it always easy for people to know
what God's plan for them is? What are some things you can do to
find out what God's plan is for you?

PRACTICE

Challenge someone to practice fighting temptation. You can take
turns drawing the temptation cards from a bowl. Ask each other
what you would do if you were tempted in that way.

TRY THIS

You will need someone to help you with this. Shine a bright light
onto a blank wall. Ask a friend to hold a piece of paper up to the
wall in the light. Now you stand between the light and the paper,
so that your shadow is on the paper. Turn sideways and move
close to the paper so that your silhouette–your profile–is shadowed
on the paper. Your friend can draw around the outline of your
profile. Then you can do the same for your friend on another piece
of paper. You can color these profiles. Or you may want to cut
them out and glue them to a different color of paper. Think about
what God's plan and purpose might be for your life.

DAY 6

READ

Esther 2–4 ("The New Queen," "A Letter with Bad News," and "If I Die," pages 477–479 in the *Day By Day Kid's Bible*)

Everyone who saw Esther liked her... The king... made her the new queen... Haman had the king's helpers write a letter in every language... The letter said to kill all the Jewish people... Now Mordecai heard about the law... Mordecai wanted [Esther] to talk to the king. Then Esther sent [a] message to Mordecai. "I can't go see the king about this. Everyone knows that you can't choose when to see the king." ...Mordecai sent a message back to Esther. "Don't think you're safe just because you live at the palace... Maybe the reason you became queen is so you can help our people now."

THINK AND TALK

What was God's purpose for Esther's life? How did he prepare Esther to help save the Jewish people? Why are people tempted to think that they are not important to God? What might tempt you to think that God does not have a plan for you? Does God have a plan and purpose for you?

PRACTICE

Challenge someone to practice fighting temptation. You can take turns drawing the temptation cards from a bowl. Ask each other what you would do if you were tempted in that way.

TRY THIS

Sit down in front of a mirror with a piece of paper and pen or pencil. Be sure you can see the paper in the mirror. Watching your paper in the mirror, write your name on the paper. This is tricky. Mirrors reflect things straight across. When others look at you from the front, your right side is on their left and your left side is on their right. But in a mirror, you don't see yourself as they do. Your right side is on your right, and your left side is on your left. Try to write your name so that it looks right from the mirror. Then look down and see what it really looks like on paper. In what way are God's plans for each of us alike? In what way are his plans for each of us different?

DAY 7

READ

Psalm 139 ("In the Secret Place," page 212 in the *Day By Day Kid's Bible*)

God, you know me. You know when I sit down and when I get up. You know what I'm thinking... Even before I say a word, you know it all, God... You made every part of me. You put me together inside my mother. I praise you, because the way you made me is wonderful... You saw my body before it had a shape. You planned all my days. You wrote them in your book, even before I had lived one of them... Look into me, God... Lead me in the way that lasts forever.

THINK AND TALK

David wrote the words of our reading today. What was God's plan for David? Name some other people the Bible tells us about, and tell what God's plan was for them. (Abraham, Joseph, Ruth, Samson, Gideon, Deborah, Ezra, Nehemiah, Mary, Peter, etc.) God loves you just as much as he loved anyone you read about in the Bible. God has a plan and purpose for you, too. What is God's plan for you? You may not know all of the plan, but you know part of it. Part of it is to know and follow God's ways, to seek God, and to do the very best at what he has given you to do today. He will show you more of his plan for you as you take care of what he's given you already.

PRACTICE

Challenge someone to practice fighting temptation. You can take turns drawing the temptation cards from a bowl. Ask each other what you would do if you were tempted in that way.

TRY THIS

Make a name shadow. Fold a large piece of construction paper in half lengthwise. Draw a one-half inch border across the folded side. This is the base line. Write your name (cursive or printed) on the base line in large letters. Then cut through both thicknesses of paper around the outline of each letter, leaving the letters attached to the folded baseline. Do not cut on the fold. Cut out the center areas of the letters that have openings (like *B* and *D*). Set the name on the table. With the name that's folded under serving as the stand, gently bring up the top name. Whenever you look at your name, thank God for the plans he has for you.

Showing Love

Your sword of the Spirit for this week is:

**All people will know that you are my followers
if you love each another.** JOHN 13:35

*With the above sword you can fight back when you
face this temptation:*

You are tempted not to love someone.

DAY 1

READ

1 Corinthians 13 ("Love," page 687 in the *Day By Day Kid's Bible*)
Love waits quietly. Love is kind. It doesn't want what others
have. It doesn't brag. It isn't proud. It has good manners. It
doesn't think of itself ahead of others. It doesn't get angry very
fast. It doesn't try to remember who was wrong. Love isn't happy
with sin. Instead, it's happy to know the truth. Love always takes
care of people. It always trusts. It always hopes. It always keeps
going. Love never fails.

THINK AND TALK

A *disciple* is a follower of Jesus. Jesus had twelve special friends
who were his disciples. But they weren't his only disciples. Many
people followed Jesus. Are you a disciple—a follower of Jesus?
How will people know that you are one of Jesus' followers? Why
will your love show them that you are a follower of Jesus?

PRACTICE

Read the verse. Try to repeat it several times without looking.
Cut a sword shape from paper or cardboard and write the verse
on it. You'll want to hang it up in your house where it will remind

you of the Spirit's sword rom John 13:35. You can use it to fight when you are tempted not to love someone.

DAY 2

READ
Genesis 37 ("The Dreamer," page 32 in the *Day By Day Kid's Bible*)
Jacob was also called Israel. He loved Joseph more than his other sons. He made a beautiful, long coat for Joseph. Now Joseph's brothers saw that Jacob loved Joseph best. They hated Joseph for that. In fact, they could hardly say anything kind to him.

THINK AND TALK
Jacob loved his other sons less than he loved Joseph. What choice did Jacob make because he loved Joseph more? What happened because of his choice to show his love to Joseph more than to Joseph's brothers? Joseph's brothers were tempted to hate Joseph. Did they fall for that temptation? What happened because of their choice? Why does God want us to love others, even when we have a reason to hate them? What happens when we don't love others?

PRACTICE
Challenge a friend or family member (or yourself) to a sword fight. One person says, "What will you do when you are tempted not to love someone?" The other person answers, "I will love because it is written, 'All people will know that you are my followers if you love each another.'"

DAY 3

READ
1 Samuel 19 ("Michal's Trick," page 142 in the *Day By Day Kid's Bible*)
King Saul told Jonathan and his servants to kill David. But Jonathan loved David. So he told David, "Be careful... You should go hide."...Saul sent some men to David's house... They were going to kill David the next morning. But David's wife, Michal, told him about it... Michal helped David climb out a window. So David got away.

THINK AND TALK

Why did King Saul hate David? (If you don't remember, read 1 Samuel 18, page 140 in the *Day By Day Kid's Bible*.) Could King Saul have chosen to love David? Why or why not? What happened because of King Saul's hatred? What choice did Jonathan make? What choice did Michal make? What happened because of Jonathan's choice and Michal's choice? Who are some of the people you love? How do you show your love for them?

PRACTICE

Challenge someone to sword-fight with your sword for this week. Write on an index card: "You are tempted not to love someone." Add this temptation card to the other cards you've collected. Place them in a bowl. The first person draws a card and challenges the second person with that temptation. The second person repeats the sword of the Spirit that he can use to fight the temptation. Then it's his turn to draw a card and challenge the first person.

DAY 4

READ

Song of Songs 8:6–7 ("Solomon's Song," page 258 in the *Day By Day Kid's Bible*)

"You are beautiful," said the king. "When you come, it's like the sun coming up. You are as pretty as the moon. You are as bright as the sun. You are as wonderful as the stars." "Love is strong," said his bride. "It's like a fire that burns. Water can't put it out. Rivers can't wash it away. No one can buy it."

THINK AND TALK

The Greek people had three words for love. One was *agape*. This love was the kind that made someone want to be unselfish, kind, and good toward people. Another kind of love was *phileo*. This love was like the love you feel for a close friend. It was liking someone and wanting what's best for that person. The third kind of love was *eros*. This love was the love that happens between a husband and wife. Which kind of love is in "Solomon's Song"? Why is it important to save this kind of love for the person that you marry? Name someone that you have *phileo* love for? Name other people that you have *agape* love for?

PRACTICE

You and another person can challenge each other to practice fighting temptation. Do this by taking turns drawing the temptation cards from a bowl. Ask each other what you would do if you were tempted in that way, and answer by saying the appropriate verse.

TRY THIS

Cut a sponge into one or more heart shapes. Spread a little water-based washable paint onto paper plates, using one plate for each color of paint. Moisten your sponge or sponges and press a sponge onto the first color you want to use. Then press the sponge onto paper. Continue printing hearts of different colors to make a design on your paper. You can make gift wrap paper this way by printing onto blank newsprint, butcher paper, or even brown grocery bags turned inside out. How does a gift show your love?

DAY 5

READ

1 Peter 4 ("In Trouble for Following Jesus," page 773 in the *Day By Day Kid's Bible*)

Time is coming to an end. So have a clear mind and control yourself. Then you can pray. Most of all, have a deep love for each other. Love can make up for lots of sins. Welcome each other into your homes. Don't fuss about it. God has given each of you a gift in your spirit. Use your gift to help people. Show God's kindness in different ways.

THINK AND TALK

How can love make up for lots of sins? How did Jesus' love make up for your sins? Peter wrote the words of our reading. What are some of the things he says to do that can show love? Is it always easy to show love? When is it hardest for you to show love to someone?

PRACTICE

Challenge someone to practice fighting temptation. You can take turns drawing the temptation cards from a bowl. Ask each other what you would do if you were tempted in that way.

TRY THIS

Make heart candle holders. You will need disposable aluminum cookie sheets and disposable aluminum soufflé cups. Draw several hearts of different sizes, three to four inches wide, on the cookie sheet. Then cut these hearts out. Ask an adult to supervise with the next part. Punch several holes in each heart with a nail or ice pick. If the aluminum gets wrinkled, you can smooth it out by rubbing a spoon over it. Bend one or two hearts around each soufflé cup. Staple them on. Then place a votive candle in the soufflé cup. You can show love to one of Jesus' followers by giving the person this candle holder. If you are going to burn the candle yourself, have an adult with you.

DAY 6

READ

1 John 2 ("Living in the Light," page 792 in the *Day By Day Kid's Bible*)

Someone might say, "I'm living in God's light." But if he hates somebody else, he is still in the dark. If you love, it's like living in God's light... But if you hate, it's like living in the dark. You don't know where you're going. You can't see... God chose you. He cleaned sin out of you. He has told you that you're his. So stay with him. God is sinless. He does what's right. So everybody who does what's right belongs to him. They're his children.

THINK AND TALK

Most people know someone who is hard to love. Are there people that are hard for you to love? If so, why is it hard for you to love them? Is it possible for us to love everyone? If so, how?

PRACTICE

Challenge someone to practice fighting temptation. You can take turns drawing the temptation cards from a bowl. Ask each other what you would do if you were tempted in that way.

TRY THIS

Slice a pound cake. Cut each slice into a heart shape using heart shaped cookie cutters. Serve these with berries and whipped cream. Can making and serving food show love? If so, how?

DAY 7

READ

1 John 3 ("God's Children," page 793 in the *Day By Day Kid's Bible*)
Here's the message. You heard it from the start. Love each other...
Here's how we know what love is. Jesus gave up his life for us. We
should give up our lives for God's people too... Let's show love not
just by what we say. Let's show love by what we do. That's how we
know we belong to God.

THINK AND TALK

How can you tell if a person is loving? How can you tell if a person
is unloving? Which would you rather have as a friend? How do
you feel around people who love you? Tell about the most loving
person you know. Tell about a time when you chose to show love
to a person, even though it was hard. What are some practical
ways in which you can show Jesus' love to others?

PRACTICE

Challenge someone to practice fighting temptation. You can take
turns drawing the temptation cards from a bowl. Ask each other
what you would do if you were tempted in that way.

TRY THIS

Make "heartwiches." For each sandwich, cut four slices of
sandwich bread into heart shapes using heart shaped cookie
cutters. For each sandwich, put about one tablespoon of soft
cream cheese into each of three coffee cups. Drip a drop of red
food coloring into one, yellow into one, and blue into one. Stir these
to mix the color in. Spread one heart with red cream cheese. Place
a bread heart on top. Spread that heart with yellow cream cheese.
Place a bread heart on top. Spread that heart with blue cream
cheese. Place the last heart on top. Show Jesus' love to someone
by sharing a "heartwich."

Repenting

Your sword of the Spirit for this week is:

If we confess our sins, he is faithful and just and will forgive us our sins. 1 JOHN 1:9

With the above sword you can fight back when you face this temptation:

You are tempted not to repent after you've done wrong.

DAY 1

READ

Jonah 1–3 ("The Storm," "Deep Water and Sea Weeds," and "The King's Order," pages 319–320 in the *Day By Day Kid's Bible*)
God told Jonah, "Go to the big city of Nineveh. I see very sinful people here. Tell them they're in trouble." But Jonah ran away. He went down to the sea. There he saw a ship... So he paid for a ride... The ship sailed out to sea. Then God sent... a storm... "How can we make the sea quiet again?" asked the sailors. "Throw me into the sea," said Jonah... Then they threw Jonah into the sea... Now God sent a big fish to swallow Jonah... Jonah prayed... "I will keep my promise." ...Then God told the fish to spit Jonah out on dry ground... This time Jonah obeyed God. He went to Nineveh.

THINK AND TALK

What were some of the choices Jonah made? What happened because of his choices? To repent is to be sorry for the wrong you did and to change your life so you will make the right choices next time. It's not just being sorry you got caught doing something wrong. It's not just making up for what you did wrong. It's changing your mind so you'll trust God and do what's right. How did Jonah show that he repented?

243

PRACTICE

Read the verse. Try to repeat it several times without looking. Cut a sword shape from paper or cardboard and write the verse on it. You'll want to hang it up in your house where it will remind you of the Spirit's sword from 1 John 1:9. You can use it to fight when you are tempted not to repent.

DAY 2

READ

Ezekiel 18 ("Sour Grapes," page 410 in the *Day By Day Kid's Bible*)
God said,... "Let's say a sinful man changes.... He starts doing what is right and good. Then he will live. I won't remember any of the wrong things he has done.... Am I glad to see sinful people die? No. But I'm glad to see them stop doing wrong. I'm glad to see them live.... So change! Get rid of your sin. Get a new heart. Get a new spirit... Start doing right, and live!"

THINK AND TALK

How can you tell when a person repents? How can you tell when a person does not repent? Why does God want us to repent when we've done wrong? What happens when we don't repent?

PRACTICE

Challenge a friend or family member (or yourself) to a sword-fight. One person says, "What will you do when you are tempted not to repent and say you're sorry?" The other person answers, "I will repent and say I'm sorry because it is written, 'If we confess our sins, he is faithful and just and will forgive us our sins.'"

DAY 3

READ

Matthew 3:1-10 ("The Man Who Wore Camel's Hair," page 511 in the *Day By Day Kid's Bible*)
John went to the land around the Jordan River. He told all the people to be sorry for their sins... Crowds of people came out to hear John... Many of the people said they had sinned. They were sorry. So John put them under the water and brought them up again. He baptized them, and God forgave them... John had this

message for some of the Jewish leaders.... "Do things that will show you are sorry for your sins."

THINK AND TALK
When John told people to be sorry for their sins, what did many of them choose to do? Why? Why was it important for the people to do things that would show they were sorry for their sins? When you know you've done something wrong, how does your heart feel? When you repent and say you're sorry, and when you've been forgiven, how does your heart feel?

PRACTICE
Challenge someone to sword-fight with your sword for this week. Write on an index card: "You are tempted not to repent." Add this temptation card to the other cards you've collected. Place them in a bowl. The first person draws a card and challenges the second person with that temptation. The second person repeats the sword of the Spirit that he can use to fight the temptation. Then it's his turn to draw a card and challenge the first person.

DAY 4

READ
Matthew 26:57-75 ("The Rooster Crows," page 616 in the *Day By Day Kid's Bible*)

The guards tied Jesus up. They took him to the high priest's house. Peter and John followed... A servant girl saw Peter sitting in the fire light... She said, "This man was with Jesus." "I don't even know him," said Peter... An hour passed. People were standing around Peter... "We're sure you're one of Jesus' followers!" they said... "I don't know the man," said Peter... This servant looked at Peter. "Didn't I see you with Jesus in the olive garden?" "Man, I don't know what you're talking about," said Peter. Right then... the rooster crowed. Jesus turned and looked at Peter... Then Peter went outside and cried hard.

THINK AND TALK
What choice did Peter make? Did he know he was doing something wrong? If he knew, why did he do it? Have you ever done something

wrong and you know it's wrong while you're doing it? Why do we do wrong things? Peter lied. Did Jesus stop loving Peter? Did Jesus kick Peter out of his group of friends? Was Peter sorry he had lied? What did Peter do? Read John 21:13-24 ("Do You Love Me?" page 630 in the *Day By Day Kid's Bible*) to hear what Jesus and Peter later talked about. Does Jesus stop loving you when you do wrong? What does Jesus want you to do about sin?

PRACTICE
You and another person can challenge each other to practice fighting temptation. Do this by taking turns drawing the temptation cards from a bowl. Ask each other what you would do if you were tempted in that way, and answer by saying the appropriate verse.

TRY THIS
Use wax paper to make crowing sounds like a rooster. Cut a six-inch wax paper square. Holding this square by the sides, place it against your lips and crow like a rooster. Do you know why it tickles your lips? It's because sound travels in waves and causes things to vibrate. What does a crowing rooster mean to most people? What did it mean to Peter?

DAY 5

READ
Acts 3 ("The Man at Beautiful Gate," page 635 in the *Day By Day Kid's Bible*) "You didn't know what you were doing when you killed Jesus. Your leaders didn't know what they were doing," said Peter. "So be sorry. Come back to God. Then your sins can be cleaned out of your hearts. God can make you feel like new."

THINK AND TALK
How did Peter know that the sins of these people could be cleaned out of their hearts? How did he know that God could make them feel like new? Is it always easy to repent and say you're sorry? When is it hardest to repent and say you're sorry?

PRACTICE

Challenge someone to practice fighting temptation. You can take turns drawing the temptation cards from a bowl. Ask each other what you would do if you were tempted in that way.

TRY THIS

Cut a piece of tissue paper, any color, into a rectangle about five inches long and two inches wide. Wrap this rectangle lengthwise around a pencil. Now slide the tissue paper off, starting at the top of the pencil, pulling the paper down and off as if you were taking off a sock. The paper should be crumpled up as it comes off the pencil. Lay the paper onto a plate and drip a couple of drops of water onto it. What happens? Drip another couple of drops on. It begins to straighten out, although it won't straighten out all the way. Repenting means straightening our lives out, leaving behind the way we were so we can do things differently from now on. Jesus can straighten our lives out all the way.

DAY 6

READ

Acts 19:1-22 ("Seven Sons and Lots of Magic Books," page 674 in the *Day By Day Kid's Bible*)

Paul went to Ephesus... Paul went to the town's worship house... He told people about God's kingdom... God did surprising wonders through Paul... People in Ephesus heard about this. It made them very scared. They wondered about Jesus' name. Lots of believers came and told what they'd done wrong. Many of them had done magic by the power of bad spirits. So they brought their magic books and burned them... God's Word went out all over the place. Its power grew.

THINK AND TALK

Why did the believers repent? How did they show that they repented? What are some things that might tempt us not to say we're sorry? Tell about a time when you said you were sorry. Did you do anything else to show you were going to choose to do right? If so, tell about what you did.

247

PRACTICE
Challenge someone to practice fighting temptation. You can take turns drawing the temptation cards from a bowl. Ask each other what you would do if you were tempted in that way.

TRY THIS
Gather some old dirty quarters, nickels, and dimes. Place your coins In a small bowl. Add 1 teaspoon of salt, 1 teaspoon of baking soda, and enough water to cover the coins. Then fill a glass pot or heat-safe glass dish with water and add some aluminum foil torn into pieces. Bring this water to a boil, and then let it cool. When it's cool, take the coins out of the salt mixture and rinse them in the aluminum water. What happens? When some people repent, they say they're going to "clean their lives up." What do they mean?

DAY 7

READ
James 4 ("Like a Fog," page 765 in the *Day By Day Kid's Bible*)
Let God lead you. Turn away from Satan. Then he will run away from you. Come close to God. Then he will come close to you. You people who sin, clean up your hearts. Be sorry. Cry. Stop laughing about it. Stop being glad for what you've done. Let God know he is the most important to you. Then he will make you important to him.

THINK AND TALK
Why might someone not be sorry for what they did wrong? What's a good reason to be sorry for doing wrong? Sometimes people have problems because they've been doing wrong, but they don't know what to do about it. What would you suggest to someone who needed to know how to be free from sin and guilt?

PRACTICE
Challenge someone to practice fighting temptation. You can take turns drawing the temptation cards from a bowl. Ask each other what you would do if you were tempted in that way.

TRY THIS

You may want a friend to help you with this. Put a penny in the middle of an empty bowl. Fill a pitcher with water. Now move your head down just until you can't see the penny over the side of the bowl anymore. Keep your head here and slowly pour water into the bowl. Keep watching until you see the penny again. You have not moved. The penny has not moved. What happened? The penny reflects light, and the water bends that reflected light so that you can see the penny again. When we are doing wrong, we do not reflect God's goodness. God wants us to repent so that we reflect his light again.

Being Careful

Your sword of the Spirit for this week is:

Give careful thought to your ways. HAGGAI 1:5

With the above sword you can fight back when you face this temptation:

You are tempted to be careless.

DAY 1

READ

Leviticus 11; 13:1-8 ("Rules about Sickness and Food," page 92 in the *Day By Day Kid's Bible*)

A person might get a sickness that others could catch. Then that person should live by himself... You may eat the ox, sheep, goat, deer and gazelle.... But don't eat camels or rock badgers or rabbits or pigs. You may eat sea animals that have fins and scales. But if they don't have fins and scales, don't eat them.

THINK AND TALK

Why do you think God gave his people laws like this? He was teaching his people to be careful. Why? Being *careful* means paying attention so you can make wise choices. It means watching out for things that might cause trouble so you can stay away from them. How are you careful so you won't get sick? How are you careful about foods you eat?

PRACTICE

Read the verse. Try to repeat it several times without looking. Cut a sword shape from paper or cardboard and write the verse on it. You'll want to hang it up in your house where it will remind you of the Spirit's sword Haggai 1:5. You can use it to fight when you are tempted to be careless.

DAY 2

READ

Exodus 21:33-36; 22:5-6 ("Other Rules," page 91 in the *Day By Day Kid's Bible*)

Let's say someone digs a pit and doesn't cover it. What if an ox or a donkey falls into it? Then he has to pay for the animal that died. Let's say someone starts a fire. It may get out of control and burn somebody's wheat. What if it burns the whole field? Then the person who started it pays for what burned. What if somebody lets his animals eat from another person's field? He has to pay for what they ate.

THINK AND TALK

Sometimes accidents happen because someone was not careful. Someone was careless. Tell about a time when an accident happened because someone you know was careless. How can you tell if a person is being careful? How can you tell if a person is being careless? Can a careless person learn to be careful? If so, how?

PRACTICE

Challenge a friend or family member (or yourself) to a sword-fight. One person says, "What will you do when you are tempted to be careless?" The other person answers, "I will not be careless because it is written, 'Give careful thought to your ways.'"

DAY 3

READ

Psalm 101 ("Proud Eyes," page 217 in the *Day By Day Kid's Bible*)

I will sing about your love, God. I will sing about how fair you are. I will be careful to live a life without sin. I will walk in my house with a sinless heart. I won't let my eyes see anything bad.

THINK AND TALK

David wrote the reading for today. What does he say he'll be careful to do? How can he do that? Can you be careful to live a life without sin? How? Being *careful* means caring about the choices you make and caring about what happens because of your choices. Why do you think David wanted to be careful about the choices he made?

PRACTICE

Challenge someone to sword-fight with your sword for this week. Write on an index card: "You are tempted to be careless." Add this temptation card to the other cards you've collected. Place them in a bowl. The first person draws a card and challenges the second person with that temptation. The second person repeats the sword of the Spirit that she can use to fight the temptation. Then it's her turn to draw a card and challenge the first person.

DAY 4

READ

Proverbs 9:10-12; 10:27; 28:14 ("Looking Up to God," page 232 in the *Day By Day Kid's Bible*)

You can begin to be wise by looking up to God. If you're wise, good things will come to you. If you make fun of wise thinking, you'll be in trouble. Caring about God will make your life long. But being sinful will make your life short.... Good things come to people who always look up to God. But some people won't let themselves care about God. They are headed for trouble.

THINK AND TALK

What does "caring about God" mean? What kind of trouble might come to a person who doesn't care about God? Tell about someone you know who cares about God and God's ways. This is a more important kind of carefulness than just being careful not to spill your milk. How are these two kinds of carefulness different?

PRACTICE

You and another person can challenge each other to practice fighting temptation. Do this by taking turns drawing the temptation cards from a bowl. Ask each other what he would do if he were tempted in that way, and answer by saying the appropriate verse.

Get seven plastic foam cups. Turn them upside down and line them up. On each one, write one word from the verse for this week. Now mix up the order of the cups and time yourself to see how long it takes you to put them in order again.

DAY 5

READ

Matthew 16:5-12 ("Yeast," page 563 in the *Day By Day Kid's Bible*) Jesus' friends had only one loaf of bread... "Be careful about the leaders' yeast," said Jesus. His friends looked at each other. "Is it because we're running out of bread?" they whispered. Jesus knew what they were saying... "Don't you understand?" asked Jesus. "I wasn't talking to you about bread. Be careful about the leaders' yeast." Then they understood... He meant, "Be careful about what the leaders teach."

THINK AND TALK

Why did Jesus want his friends to be careful about what the leaders taught? Do you need to be careful about what your leaders and teachers teach? Why or why not? How do you know if someone is teaching you something wrong or not? What can you do if you know a teacher is teaching you something wrong?

PRACTICE

Challenge someone to practice fighting temptation. You can take turns drawing the temptation cards from a bowl. Ask each other what you would do if you were tempted in that way.

TRY THIS

Make a Mexican pizza. Spread canned refried beans on top of a flour tortilla. Put grated cheese on top. Put salsa on if you want. Then put it under the broiler and heat it until the cheese gets bubbly and melts. Remember to be careful when you are cooking. Ask an adult to help.

DAY 6

1 Corinthians 8 ("Food for Idols," page 681 in the *Day By Day Kid's Bible*)

Some people are still used to idols. They think food given to idols is bad for you. But food doesn't make us closer to God. It's not bad if we don't eat this food. It's not better if we do eat it. Be careful. We might think we are free to do something. But we don't want others to do something they think is wrong... What if the food I eat makes someone sin? Then I'll never eat that food again. That way, I won't make anyone lose his faith.

THINK AND TALK

Paul wrote the reading for today. What did Paul want to be careful about? Why did Paul care about what someone else thought? Paul was being respectful about someone else's feelings. What if someone wanted you to do something wrong? Why would you need not to care too much about what that person thought? What are some things that you care about?

PRACTICE

Challenge someone to practice fighting temptation. You can take turns drawing the temptation cards from a bowl. Ask each other what you would do if you were tempted in that way.

TRY THIS

With a toothpick, dip grapes into vanilla yogurt. Then roll them in shelled sunflower seeds and eat them. Do we need to be careful about what we eat? Why or why not?

DAY 7

READ

2 Samuel 4:4 ("The Day the Enemy Won," page 158 in the *Day By Day Kid's Bible*)

Saul's son Jonathan had a son who was five years old. His name was Mephibosheth. The news came that Jonathan and Saul had been killed. So the woman who took care of the boy picked him up and ran. She was in such a hurry that she dropped the boy. He fell and hurt his feet very badly. From then on, he couldn't walk.

THINK AND TALK
Is it always easy to be careful? When we are hurrying too fast, it's hard to be careful. Is it always easy to slow down? When is it hardest for you to slow down? When are you tempted to go too fast? Why does God want us to be careful? What are some things other than hurrying that might tempt us to be careless? What would you suggest to a friend who wanted to start being more careful?

PRACTICE
Challenge someone to practice fighting temptation. You can take turns drawing the temptation cards from a bowl. Ask each other what you would do if you were tempted in that way.

TRY THIS
Have a three-legged race. Ask at least three friends to help you with this, and do it in a gym or outdoors. Decide where the starting point and the finish line will be. Form two teams. You and another friend stand next to each other. With bandannas, tie your right leg to your friend's left leg. Your other two friends should do the same. Stand at the starting line. Ask someone to say "Go." Then both teams should run for the finish line to see who can get there first. What are some things to remember that will help you be careful when playing active games and sports?

Being Cooperative

Your sword of the Spirit for this week is:

Love is what binds us all together in perfect harmony. COLOSSIANS 3:14

With the above sword you can fight back when you face this temptation:

You are tempted to fuss and argue.

DAY 1

READ

Genesis 45 ("Telling the Secret," page 41 in the *Day By Day Kid's Bible*)

The king soon heard that Joseph's brothers were in Egypt. So he told Joseph, "Bring your brothers' families here to live." ...So Joseph gave his brothers some carts. He gave them food for their trip... As his brothers were leaving, Joseph called out to them. "Don't fuss and fight on the way!" he said.

THINK AND TALK

Why did Joseph tell his brothers not to fuss and fight on the way? To cooperate means to work together. Is it easy to cooperate with everyone in your family when you take a long trip? Why or why not? Why is it important to cooperate? Another way to say that we're cooperating is to say that we are working together in harmony. *Harmony* is what happens in music when the notes are working together to make a song. Working together in harmony means working peacefully.

PRACTICE

Read the verse. Try to repeat it several times without looking.

257

Cut a sword shape from paper or cardboard write the verse on it. You'll want to hang it up in your house where it will remind you of the Spirit's sword from Colossians 3:14. You can use it to fight when you are tempted to fuss and argue.

DAY 2

READ

Numbers 16 ("A Crack in the Ground," page 81 in the *Day By Day Kid's Bible*)

Now a man named Korah got mad at Moses. Two of Korah's friends got mad at Moses. They got about 250 other men mad at Moses, too... They said,... "Why are you so special? Why do you think you can lead us?" Moses...said to the men, "Tomorrow morning God will show which man he chooses." ...So the next morning Korah and all his followers came together... Right away a big crack opened in the ground. Korah and his two friends fell in... Then fire came from God. It burned up the 250 men who were mad at Moses.

THINK AND TALK

What choices did Korah and his followers make? What happened because of their choices? What might have happened if Korah had not been stopped? Why was it important for people to cooperate with Moses? Why does God want us to cooperate with godly leaders? What happens when we don't cooperate with godly leaders?

PRACTICE

Challenge a friend or family member (or yourself) to a sword-fight. One person says, "What will you do when you are tempted to fuss and argue?" The other person answers, "I will not fuss and argue because it is written, 'Love is what binds us all together in perfect harmony.'"

DAY 3

READ

I Kings 5 ("King Hiram Helps," page 224 in the *Day By Day Kid's Bible*)

Solomon told men to start building a worship house... Solomon sent a message back to [King] Hiram... "Please send some cedar logs for building a worship house... Send someone who can work with gold and silver." ...King Hiram wrote back,... "I'm sending a good worker to you... We'll cut the logs you want." ...Every year Hiram sent wood to Solomon. Solomon sent wheat, barley, oil, and wine to Hiram. Solomon got 30,000 (thirty thousand) men... They would work on Hiram's land for a month. Then they would work at home for two months.

THINK AND TALK

How did King Solomon and King Hiram and their men cooperate? Tell about a time when you cooperated with someone else to make something. When you are working with someone and you disagree about something, how can you settle your disagreements so you can keep cooperating? How does it feel to fuss and argue and have to stop working together? How does it feel to cooperate with people?

PRACTICE

Challenge someone to sword-fight with your sword for this week. Write on an index card: "You are tempted to fuss and argue." Add this temptation card to the other cards you've collected. Place them in a bowl. The first person draws a card and challenges the second person with that temptation. The second person repeats the sword of the Spirit that he can use to fight the temptation. Then t's his turn to draw a card and challenge the first person.

DAY 4

READ

Luke 13:10-17 ("The Woman Who Couldn't Stand Up Tall," page 546 in the *Day By Day Kid's Bible*)

One worship day, Jesus was teaching... A woman there was all bent over... [Jesus] ...put his hands on her. Right away, she stood up tall. She praised God. The man in charge was mad... "There are six days for work," he said. "You can come and be made well any other day. But don't come... on the worship day." Then Jesus said, "Don't you take your ox or donkey outside on the worship day? Don't you lead it to water so it can drink? ...Shouldn't she be set free on this worship day?"

THINK AND TALK
Why didn't Jesus cooperate with the man in charge? When might it be a good idea *not* to cooperate? Exodus 23:2 says, "Do not follow the crowd in doing wrong." What does that tell us about cooperation? Tell about a time when you or someone you know did *not* cooperate with someone, because it would have been wrong.

PRACTICE
You and another person can challenge each other to practice fighting temptation. Do this by taking turns drawing the temptation cards from a bowl. Ask each other what he would do if he were tempted in that way, and answer by saying the appropriate verse.

TRY THIS
Try carrying different things on your head. Start with a pillow and walk across the room. Try a book. Try a basket. What kinds of things can you carry with your arms without help? What kinds of things need to be carried with the help of just one other person? What kinds of things need to be carried by lots of people? Why would these people need to cooperate?

DAY 5

READ
2 Corinthians 6:4-18 ("A Fair Trade," page 697 in the *Day By Day Kid's Bible*)
Don't get tied down with people who don't believe in God. Can right and wrong fit together? Can light and darkness be together? Do Jesus and Satan agree? Does a believer agree with someone who doesn't believe?... "Come away from other people. Be

different," says God. "Don't get near anything bad. Then I will welcome you. I will be your Father. You will be my sons and daughters."

THINK AND TALK

Paul wrote our reading for today. What did he mean by saying we shouldn't get tied down with people who don't believe in God? Who would it be harder for you to cooperate with: someone who believes in God or someone who doesn't believe in God? Why? Is it always easy to cooperate with someone who believes in God? Why or why not? When is it hardest for you to cooperate with someone?

PRACTICE

Challenge someone to practice fighting temptation. You can take turns drawing the temptation cards from a bowl. Ask each other what you would do if you were tempted in that way.

TRY THIS

At night, turn a flashlight on in a brightly lit room. Walk into a dimmer room. Keep your flashight on and walk into different rooms, trying to go into places that are darker and darker, until you come to a room that has no light in it. Go into this room with your flashlight and close the door. Does the darkness make your light go out? Can it be light and dark at the same time? What was Paul trying to say when he asked, "Can light and darkness be together?"

DAY 6

READ

Romans 15 ("One Heart," page 715 in the *Day By Day Kid's Bible*) We shouldn't try to make just ourselves happy. We should try to make others happy. We should try to do good for them and help them. Even Jesus didn't try to make himself happy... I pray that God will help you work together to follow Jesus. That way, it will seem like you have one heart. Together you can show God's greatness.

THINK AND TALK

What are some ways in which we can work together to follow Jesus? What is it about *love* that "binds us all together in perfect harmony"? Is there anything else that can help people cooperate? What are some things that might make it hard to cooperate with someone? Why does it show God's greatness when we cooperate?

PRACTICE

Challenge someone to practice fighting temptation. You can take turns drawing the temptation cards from a bowl. Ask each other what you would do if you were tempted in that way.

TRY THIS

You'll need one friend to help you. Kneel on the ground or the floor. Place your hands on the ground in front of you. Ask your friend to pick up your legs, holding your feet by the ankles. You walk around on your hands now as if you are the wheelbarrow. Trade places and let your friend be the wheelbarrow. Can you do this stunt without cooperating?

DAY 7

READ

Ephesians 4 ("We Won't Be Babies," page 741 in the *Day By Day Kid's Bible*)

Live the way God wants you to live. Live like others are better than you. Wait quietly when you need to. Put up with each other and love each other. Try to work together in God's Spirit. Be at peace with each other... There is one group of God's people, one "body." ...Jesus is like the head. We are like the body. Each part of the body helps the whole body. When each part does its work, the body grows. Its love gets stronger.

THINK AND TALK

What kinds of groups are you a member of? (A band, choir, drama group, home-school group, church group, family group, ball team?) Tell how the members of your group cooperate to help the group be the best that it can be. What is your part in the group? How do you all stay at peace with each other?

PRACTICE
Challenge someone to practice fighting temptation. You can take turns drawing the temptation cards from a bowl. Ask each other what you would do if you were tempted in that way.

TRY THIS
Lay one index card on your desk or table so that the short edges are on the right and left side. Place another index card just below it. Place a third index card just below that one. Draw a person's head on the top card, body on the middle card, and legs and feet on the card closest to you. Move these cards out of the way and do the same thing again, only this time, draw a very different person, animal or pretend creature. Make at least two more different characters this same way. If you have a friend or two working with you, you can all draw different characters. Then mix up all the head cards, all the body cards, and all the leg-feet cards. Turn them over face down in three decks. Pick up the top head card, the top body card and the top leg-feet card. Lay these on the table face up to make a new character. Go through all the decks this way and see what interesting characters you can make. All your body parts have to cooperate with each other to do anything. How can a family, a sports team, or children in a class at school cooperate to get things done?

Honoring Others

Your sword of the Spirit for this week is:

Love your neighbor as yourself. MATTHEW 22:39

With the above sword you can fight back when you face this temptation:

You are tempted to be jealous.

DAY 1

READ

I Samuel 22 ("Saul's Shepherd Tells," page 146 in the *Day By Day Kid's Bible*)

Saul was sitting under a tree on a hill. All his leaders stood around him. Saul said, "Listen! Will David give you fields? Will he make you leaders?" ...Then Saul sent for the priest... "Why did you make plans against me?" asked Saul. "You gave David bread and a sword. David has turned against me." "I don't know anything about this," said the priest. "I just know that David is your servant... Everyone says he is an important person." "You'll die!" said Saul. Then Saul told his guards, "Kill the priests." But they wouldn't.

THINK AND TALK

Why was Saul angry? Why was he chasing David? Remember that people sang, "Saul killed thousands, but David killed tens of thousands." When Saul heard this, what choices did he have in his feelings toward David? What choice did Saul make? What happened because of Saul's choice? *Honoring* people means respecting them and being glad that good things are happening to them. Being *jealous* means being upset that the other person is being honored. You're upset because you wish *you* had that honor. What honor did Saul want?

PRACTICE
Read the verse. Try to repeat it several times without looking. Cut a sword shape from paper or cardboard and write the verse on it. You'll want to hang it up in your house where it will remind you of the Spirit's sword from Matthew 22:39. You can use it to fight against the temptation to be jealous.

DAY 2

READ
Esther 6 ("The King's Book," page 480 in the *Day By Day Kid's Bible*)
"Bring Haman in," said the king. So Haman came in. "There's a man I want to thank," said the king. "What should I do to make him great?" Haman thought, "Who would the king want to thank? Me!" So Haman said,… "Put your robe on this man... Lead the man on your horse.… Shout... that the king gladlly makes this man great!" "Go right away," said the king.… "I want you to do this for Mordecai. He sits at my gate. Do everything you said."

THINK AND TALK
When Haman did what the king asked, did he feel a sense of honor toward Mordecai? Why was he jealous? Is it possible to act as though you are honoring someone, but feel jealous while you are doing it? Is there anything wrong with that? Why or why not? How does it feel to be jealous? Why is it important to be glad when God blesses someone? What does that have to do with loving your neighbor as yourself?

PRACTICE
Challenge a friend or family member (or yourself) to a sword-fight. One person says, "What will you do when you are tempted to be jealous?" The other person answers, "I will not be jealous because it is written, 'Love your neighbor as yourself.'"

DAY 3

READ

John 7:32-8:1 ("Streams of Living Water," page 571 in the *Day By Day Kid's Bible*)

The Jewish leaders heard people whisper about Jesus. So they sent the worship-house guards to catch him... but nobody even touched him. At last, the worship-house guards went back to the leaders... "Did he fool you, too?" the leaders asked. "Have any leaders believed in him? No! It's this foolish crowd! They don't know anything about the Law!"

THINK AND TALK

What reason did the Jewish leaders have for being jealous of Jesus? What other choice could they have made? What happened because of their choice? How can you tell when a person is jealous of someone? How can you tell when a person is truly honoring someone? When is it hardest for you to honor someone?

PRACTICE

Challenge someone to sword-fight with your sword for this week. Write on an index card: "You are tempted to be jealous." Add this temptation card to the other cards you've collected. Place them in a bowl. The first person draws a card and challenges the second person with that temptation. The second person repeats the sword of the Spirit that she can use to fight the temptation. Then it's her turn to draw a card and challenge the first person.

DAY 4

READ

2 Samuel 11 ("On the Palace Roof," page 166 in the *Day By Day Kid's Bible*)

One evening David couldn't sleep and took a walk on the palace roof. From his roof, he saw a beautiful woman. So David asked someone who she was. "It's Bathsheba," someone said. "She is Uriah's wife." Then David sent someone to get Bathsheba. She came, and David loved her. He slept with her as if she were his wife. Then she went home again.

THINK AND TALK

What choices did David have, and what choice did he make? *Coveting* is very much like being jealous. To covet means to want something someone else has. When you covet something, are you honoring the person belongs to? Why or why not? How did David show that he did not honor Uriah? Why does God want us not to covet? If we don't try to take the thing we covet, is it still wrong to covet that thing secretly in our hearts? Why or why not? What does this have to do with loving your neighbor as yourself?

PRACTICE

You and another person can challenge each other to practice fighting temptation. Do this by taking turns drawing the temptation cards from a bowl. Ask each other what you would do if you were tempted in that way, and answer by saying the appropriate verse.

TRY THIS

Get an ink pad. Or make a paint pad by pouring a bit of paint on a folded paper towel which you have set on a paper plate. Press your thumb onto this pad and then press it onto a piece of paper to make a thumbprint. You may have to press your thumb down in several spots to make a clear print. Ask friends and family to make their thumbprints too. Then get a magnifying glass and look carefully at each person's thumbprint to see how it is different. Different people like to be honored in different ways. How can you honor your mom? How can you honor your friend?

DAY 5

READ

Acts 8:1-25 ("Simon, the Magic Man," page 641 in the *Day By Day Kid's Bible*)

Simon had done magic for a long time... People said, "Simon has the power of the gods. He is called the Great Power." They followed him because they liked to watch his magic. But now people believed... in Jesus. They were baptized. Even Simon believed... Peter and John put their hands on people. Then the Holy Spirit came to the people. Simon watched... "Give me this power," he said. "I want to put my hands on people. Then I want them to get the Holy Spirit."

THINK AND TALK
What reason did Simon have for being jealous of Peter and John? What other choice could he have made? Is it always easy to honor others? Why does God want us not to be jealous? What happens when we become jealous of someone?

PRACTICE
Challenge someone to practice fighting temptation. You can take turns drawing the temptation cards from a bowl. Ask each other what you would do if you were tempted in that way.

TRY THIS
Make an "honored guest" place mat. Do this by coloring a design on a piece of poster board which you have cut to the size of a place mat. Fold a small piece of paper or index card to make a place card. Then invite a friend or grandparent over for dinner and let them sit at the place of honor.

DAY 6

READ
Galatians 5 ("A Good Tree Growing Good Fruit," page 661 in the *Day By Day Kid's Bible*)
It's easy to see what sin is: Using sex in the wrong way. Worshiping idols. Following witches. Hating. Fussing and fighting. Wanting what other people have. Showing great anger. Being selfish. Talking against each other. Getting drunk. Having wild parties. Things like that. So be careful. People who do these things won't be in God's kingdom... We live by God's Spirit. So let's follow the Spirit... Let's not want what other people have.

THINK AND TALK
Why would we want what someone else has? Why is it a sin to want what other people have? When is it hardest for you to keep from wanting what someone else has? Tell about someone you

know who honors others and is happy for blessings God has given those people. Tell about a time when you honored someone even though you were tempted to be jealous of the person instead.

PRACTICE
Challenge someone to practice fighting temptation. You can take turns drawing the temptation cards from a bowl. Ask each other what you would do if you were tempted in that way.

TRY THIS
Think about something you can do to honor a neighbor. Then do it. Bake something to take to him. Cut her grass. Wash his car windows. Sweep her porch.

DAY 7

READ
Proverbs 23:17-18 ("Being Brave and Full of Hope," page 254 in the *Day By Day Kid's Bible*)
Don't let yourself want what sinful people have. Always think about how wonderful God is. Then many good days will come to you. You will always have hope.

THINK AND TALK
Why should we not envy or be jealous of sinful people? Does that mean that we can envy or be jealous of good people? Why or why not? What is the difference between being jealous and wanting to be like a good person whose character you admire?

PRACTICE
Challenge someone to practice fighting temptation. You can take turns drawing the temptation cards from a bowl. Ask each other what you would do if you were tempted in that way.

TRY THIS
Write this week's memory verse on a piece of colored construction paper. Then glue dry, uncooked macaroni onto the lines of the letters.

Showing Mercy

Your sword of the Spirit for this week is:

Make sure that nobody pays back wrong for wrong, but always try to be kind to each other.
1 THESSALONIANS 5:15

With the above sword you can fight back when you face this temptation:

You are tempted to get back at someone who has done something wrong to you.

DAY 1

READ

2 Samuel 16 ("Throwing Rocks at the King," page 175 in the *Day By Day Kid's Bible*)

A man from Saul's family... yelled bad things about David. He threw rocks at David... "Get out of here," called the man. "You're a killer! You're good for nothing! ...One of David's army leaders spoke to David.... "Why let him talk to you like that? Let me go take off his head!" "You and I don't think alike," said David.... "...Leave him alone." ...The man from Saul's family... kept saying bad things and kept throwing rocks. He even threw dirt at them.

THINK AND TALK

Mercy is being kind to someone when they deserve to be punished. David was the king. What choices did he have when the man yelled and threw rocks at him? What choice did David make? Why? Has anyone ever had mercy on you? If so, how did you feel?

271

PRACTICE

Read the verse. Try to repeat it several times without looking. Cut a sword shape from paper or cardboard and write the verse on it. You'll want to hang it up in your house where it will remind you of the Spirit's sword from 1 Thessalonians 5:15. You can use it to fight against the temptation to get back at someone who has done something wrong to you.

DAY 2

READ

Jonah 4 ("The Vine," page 321 in the *Day By Day Kid's Bible*)

God didn't send trouble to Nineveh. This made Jonah upset. He got angry. "I knew this would happen," Jonah prayed. "That's why I ran away. I know you're a loving, kind God. You're not in a hurry to get angry. You have plenty of love for everyone. You change your mind about sending trouble. So just let me die. It's better for me to die than to live. "What right do you have to be angry?" asked God... "There are more than 120,000 (one hundred twenty thousand) people in Nineveh... Shouldn't I care about them?"

THINK AND TALK

Jonah had told the people in Nineveh that unless they changed their wrong way of living, God would punish them. So they changed. How did Jonah feel about that? Why? Have you ever felt disappointed when kids didn't get the punishment they deserved? Why do people show mercy on someone who deserves to be punished?

PRACTICE

Challenge a friend or family member (or yourself) to a sword-fight. One person says, "What will you do when you are tempted to get back at someone?" The other person answers, "I will not get back at someone, because it is written, 'Make sure that nobody pays back wrong for wrong, but always try to be kind to each other.'"

DAY 3

READ

Matthew 5:29-48 ("An Eye for an Eye," page 532 in the *Day By Day*

You've heard that if somebody hurts you, then you can hurt that person. But I tell you not to fight a sinful person," said Jesus... You've heard that you're to love your neighbor and hate your enemy," said Jesus. "I say, love your enemies. Pray for people who hurt you. Then you will be children of your Father in heaven... God is kind to people who are not even thankful. He is kind to sinful people. So be kind like your Father."

THINK AND TALK

Why do you think God is kind to sinful people? Why would God want us to have mercy on people who have done wrong to us? Is it easy to be merciful to someone who hurts you? Why or why not? When is it hardest for you to have mercy on someone?

PRACTICE

Challenge someone to sword-fight with your sword for this week. Write on an index card: "You are tempted to get back at someone." Add this temptation card to the other cards you've collected. Place them in a bowl. The first person draws a card and challenges the second person with that temptation. The second person repeats the sword of the Spirit that he can use to fight the temptation. Then it's his turn to draw a card and challenge the first person.

DAY 4

READ

Luke 7:36-50 ("Perfume," page 539 in the *Day By Day Kid's Bible*)
Now there was a sinful woman in town. She heard that Jesus was having dinner at Simon's house. So she went there. She took a beautiful stone jar with her... She stood close to Jesus, at his feet... She let perfume flow out of the jar onto his feet. Simon saw this. He said to himself, "Jesus can't really be a prophet. If he was, he would know this is a sinful woman."..."This woman has lots of love," said Jesus. "She had many sins. But they have been forgiven. Some people haven't been forgiven for very much. So they don't love very much."

THINK AND TALK

How did Simon show that he did not feel mercy toward the woman? How did Jesus show that he had mercy on her? What reason does Jesus give for why some people don't show love, or mercy? Tell about someone you know who shows mercy to people. Tell about a time when you showed mercy to someone.

PRACTICE

You and another person can challenge each other to practice fighting temptation. Do this by taking turns drawing the temptation cards from a bowl. Ask each other what you would do if you were tempted in that way, and answer by saying the appropriate verse.

TRY THIS

Gather several things that have very different scents. Examples: a jar of dill pickles, a lemon, a flower, a bottle of vanilla, a peppermint stick, chili powder, and perfume. Blindfold a friend. Then let him smell each item and guess what it is. Take turns retelling the story of the woman who put perfume on Jesus' feet.

DAY 5

READ

Luke 13:6-9 ("Clouds from the West," page 545 in the *Day By Day Kid's Bible*)

A man planted a fig tree... He was watching for fruit to grow on it. But there was no fruit. At last the man talked to his gardener about it. He said,... "I've been looking for fruit on this fig tree. But I haven't found any. So cut it down." ...But the gardener spoke up. "Sir, leave the fig tree alone one more year... I'll make the soil richer. Maybe it will give you fruit next year. If it doesn't, you can cut it down."

THINK AND TALK

Jesus told this story to tell a lesson about people. What do you think Jesus was trying to say about people? Has anyone ever given you a second chance? If so, tell about it. Have you ever given someone else a second chance? If so, tell about it. Giving someone a second chance is showing them mercy.

PRACTICE

Challenge someone to practice fighting temptation. You can take turns drawing the temptation cards from a bowl. Ask each other what you would do if you were tempted in that way.

TRY THIS

Put sand or dirt into a disposable pie plate. Cut the tops off of two or three carrots. Put the cut end into the soil. Give cut tops sunlight and water. Make sure the soil stays moist. You should see something happening in about a week. Instead of throwing these carrot tops away, you are giving them a second chance. They won't make carrots again, but they'll be a pretty house plant.

DAY 6

READ

1 Peter 3 ("What Makes You Beautiful," page 771 in the *Day By Day Kid's Bible*)

All of you, live peacefully with each other. Try to understand each other's feelings. Love each other as if you were family. Be kind. Don't act like you're the greatest. Don't do wrong to others because they did wrong to you. Instead, do good things for others. That's what God chose you to do.

THINK AND TALK

Does having mercy on someone mean you can't tell them what they've done wrong? How can you tell someone in a merciful way that they've done something wrong? What if that person doesn't admit that they've done wrong?

PRACTICE

Challenge someone to practice fighting temptation. You can take turns drawing the temptation cards from a bowl. Ask each other what you would do if you were tempted in that way.

TRY THIS

Write the alphabet down the left side of several sheets of writing paper, skipping two lines between each letter. Now go down the alphabet and try to think of a feeling that starts with each letter. You can ask family or friends for help if you get stuck. Then draw a face that looks like each feeling beside each word. If someone said, "I feel merciful today," what would that mean? Do you have to feel merciful to show mercy? Why or why not?

DAY 7

READ
Hebrews 10:19-39 ("Keep Following," page 785 in the *Day By Day Kid's Bible*)
Let's think about how to help each other love. Let's think about how to help each other do good... Think how bad it is to turn away from Jesus. He is God's Son. People who turn away from him... say bad things about God's kind Spirit. God says, "It's my job to pay people back for their sins."

THINK AND TALK
How do you feel around merciful people? How do you feel around people who have no mercy? What are some things that might tempt us to try to get back at someone who has done something wrong to us? Whose job is it to pay people back for what they did wrong? How can you help yourself remember to have mercy on people?

PRACTICE
Challenge someone to practice fighting temptation. You can take turns drawing the temptation cards from a bowl. Ask each other what you would do if you were tempted in that way.

TRY THIS
Make a fruit salad. Ask an adult to supervise cutting and chopping. Scoop out sections from a fresh orange into a bowl. Squeeze the fresh juice into the bowl too. Scoop the rest of the orange out so the half orange rind is empty. Save these to be cups for your fruit salad. Add more fruit to the bowl of orange sections and juice. You can add chopped apple, grapes, and sliced bananas. Mix this up and spoon it into the orange halves. Serve it to family or friends. They don't always deserve to be served, but you serve them anyway because of your kind love–your mercy.

Having Common Sense

Your sword of the Spirit for this week is:

Keep your head in all situations. 2 TIMOTHY 4:5

With the above sword you can fight back when you face this temptation:

You are tempted not to use common sense.

DAY 1

READ

Philippians 2:3-18 ("Shining like Stars," page 746 in the *Day By Day Kid's Bible*)

Keep looking up to God, because he is saving you. God is working in you to help you think and act right. He is helping you fit into his good plans. Do everything without fussing and fighting. Then you can be sinless and clean... You'll shine like stars in the sky. You'll shine because you show God's Word and talk about it.

THINK AND TALK

"Keep your head" is another way to say "Think." Who works in you to help you think and act right? Have you ever been in such a hurry that you did something without stopping to think? Why is it dangerous to choose to do something without thinking about it first?

PRACTICE

Read the verse. Try to repeat it several times without looking.

Cut a sword shape from paper or cardboard and write the verse on it. You'll want to hang it up in your house where it will remind you of the Spirit's sword from 2 Timothy 4:5. You can use it to fight against the temptation not to use common sense.

DAY 2

READ

Hebrews 5 ("Our Priest," page 782 in the *Day By Day Kid's Bible*) You should be teachers yourselves by now. But you still need somebody to teach you. You still need to learn the simple parts of God's Word. Grown-up teaching is for people who live what they're taught. They train themselves to tell right from wrong.

THINK AND TALK

Common sense means knowing what's right and what's wrong so that you make the right choices naturally. In the reading for today, what kind of people have trained themselves to tell right from wrong? How can we train ourselves to tell right from wrong?

PRACTICE

Challenge a friend or family member (or yourself) to a sword-fight. One person says, "What will you do when you are tempted not to use common sense?" The other person answers, "I will use common sense because it is written, 'Keep your head in all situations.'"

DAY 3

READ

Psalm 119:97-112 ("Sweet Words," page 210 in the *Day By Day Kid's Bible*) I love your law so much! I think about it all day. Your rules make me wiser than my enemies. I understand more than my teachers do....That's because I think about your rules. I stay away from sin... Your commands teach me to understand... Your word is like a lamp that shows my feet where to go. It is like a light for my path.

THINK AND TALK

What is it that trains our minds, helps us stay away from sin, and makes us understand more than our teachers? How can you tell if a person has common sense? How can you tell if a person doesn't have common sense? Which person would you rather have as a friend?

PRACTICE

Challenge someone to sword-fight with your sword for this week. Write on an index card: "You are tempted not to use common sense." Add this temptation card to the other cards you've collected. Place them in a bowl. The first person draws a card and challenges the second person with that temptation. The second person repeats the sword of the Spirit that he can use to fight the temptation. Then it's his turn to draw a card and challenge the first person.

DAY 4

READ

1 Samuel 28 ("The Witch," page 157 in the *Day By Day Kid's Bible*) King Saul called his servants. "Go find a witch," he said. "I want to ask what will happen in the fight." ...Now Saul had told all witches to leave the land. So he dressed up as another man... That night he went to see the witch... "Call up Samuel for me," said Saul. Now Samuel was dead. But he showed himself to the witch. She cried out loudly and said to the king, "You've tricked me! You're Saul!" "Why did you bother me?" asked Samuel... "God is your enemy now."

THINK AND TALK

Did Saul use common sense when he chose to go see the witch? Why or why not? Sometimes we are so scared that we panic. That means we don't stop to think about what's right and what's wrong. Why does God want us to stop and think and use our common sense? What happens when we don't?

PRACTICE

You and another person can challenge each other to practice fighting temptation. Do this by taking turns drawing the temptation cards from a bowl. Ask each other what you would do if you were tempted in that way, and answer by saying the appropriate verse.

TRY THIS
Draw a large stop sign on a sheet of red poster board or construction paper. Cut it out. Write STOP AND THINK on it. Post it on the back of your bedroom door.

DAY 5

READ
Proverbs 3:11-12; 10:17; 12:1; 20:18 ("Being Trained to Do What's Right," page 234 in the *Day By Day Kid's Bible*)
Your plans will work if you have helpers who tell you what's right... Don't be mad when God shows you you're wrong. God shows these things to people he loves. He is like a father showing his children what's right and wrong. Listen when someone shows you what's right. That shows you how to live. People who don't listen lead others to do wrong. Let's say you love to be shown what's right. Then you love knowing. But let's say you hate to be shown what's right. That's dumb!

THINK AND TALK
We are not born with common sense. How do we learn common sense? There's an old saying: "A wise man learns by experience. A wiser man learns by someone else's experience." How can you learn by someone else's experience? How have you learned right from wrong? Is it always easy to use common sense? Why or why not?

PRACTICE
Challenge someone to practice fighting temptation. You can take turns drawing the temptation cards from a bowl. Ask each other what you would do if you were tempted in that way.

TRY THIS
Put a clean, empty two-liter, soft drink bottle into the freezer. Be sure it is clean and made of plastic. Also put a quarter into a cup

f water. In five minutes, take the bottle out of the freezer and tand it up on a table. Then put the wet quarter over the mouth of he bottle so it completely covers the opening. What happens? Vhy? In the freezer, the air in the bottle got cold and closer ogether, letting more air into the bottle. As the air in the bottle varms up, it moves out again, pushing the extra air out the top. How can learning fill you up and make you wiser? Can learning nore about the world around you help you develop common ense?

DAY 6

READ Judges 14 ("Honey from a Lion," page 116 in the *Day By Day Kid's Bible*)

ike most grooms, Samson had a party. Thirty young men were here with him. "I have a riddle for you," Samson said. "I'll give you even days to find the answer... Food came out of the eater. The weet came out of the strong," said Samson... At last they went to Samson's wife. "Tell Samson to give you the answer," they said... So Samson's wife went to him, crying... "You didn't tell me the nswer to it." "I didn't even tell my father and mother," said Samson... [She] cried every day... So at last... Samson told her. Then she went and told the 30 men.

THINK AND TALK

What choices did Samson have? What choice did he make? Do ou think he used his common sense? Why did Samson choose o tell his wife the answer to the riddle? Sometimes we don't use ur common sense even when we know what's right and what's vrong. Why?

PRACTICE

Challenge someone to practice fighting temptation. You can take urns drawing the temptation cards from a bowl. Ask each other vhat you would do if you were tempted in that way.

TRY THIS

oast a whole-wheat English muffin. Spread honey on one side

and peanut butter on the other for a tasty snack. Can you think of a riddle you could make about honey?

DAY 7

READ
Acts 20:6-12 ("Falling Out the Window," page 718 in the *Day By Day Kid's Bible*)
Paul and his friends... met together for the Lord's Supper. Paul taught the people there... He kept talking until after midnight. They were in a room upstairs on the third floor... One young man sat in a window. His name was Eutychus. Now Paul talked and talked and talked. Eutychus went to sleep... All of a sudden, he fell out the window. He fell to the ground. When the people picked Eutychus up, he was dead. Paul went downstairs too. He hugged the young man. "Don't worry," Paul said. "He is alive!"...The people went home. So did the young man.

THINK AND TALK
Back in the days when Paul lived, windows did not have glass panes or screens in them. Did Eutychus use his common sense when he sat in the window on the third floor? Why or why not? Tell of a time when you used your common sense, or a time when you didn't use your common sense. How can you remember to use your common sense?

PRACTICE
Challenge someone to practice fighting temptation. You can take turns drawing the temptation cards from a bowl. Ask each other what you would do if you were tempted in that way.

TRY THIS
Make a balance beam with a narrow board and two bricks. Place each end of the board on top of one of the bricks. This puts it only a few inches off the floor, so if you fall you won't get hurt. Walk across the balance beam. Stand in the center of it on one foot. Turn around in the middle. What kinds of things does your common sense tell you *not* to try to balance on?

282

Thinking Pure Thoughts

Your sword of the Spirit for this week is:

Whatever is true, whatever is noble, whatever is right, whatever is pure, whatever is lovely, whatever is admirable—if anything is excellent or praiseworthy—think about such things. PHILIPPIANS 4:8

Hint: To make this easier to learn, remember the beginning letters of each word in the list. They are TNR PLA EP, which can be said in the words tenor play eep. Imagine a tenor saxophone playing eep.)

With the above sword you can fight back when you face this temptation:

You are tempted to think thoughts that are not pure.

DAY 1

READ

Proverbs 20:11, 27; 27:19 ("Plans of the Heart," page 237 in *Day By Day Kid's Bible*)

Even children show what they're like by how they act. You can tell they are good if what they do is right. God looks inside people to see their spirits. He sees what they are thinking. When you look into water, you can see your face. When you understand someone's heart, you see what that person is really like.

THINK AND TALK
Pure means "free from dirt, free from what doesn't belong." What does it mean when we say God wants us to have pure thoughts? What doesn't belong in our thoughts? What would make our thoughts "dirty"?

PRACTICE
Read the verse. Try to repeat it several times without looking. Cut a sword shape from paper or cardboard and write the verse on it. You'll want to hang it up in your house where it will remind you of the Spirit's sword from Philippians 4:8. You can use it to fight against the temptation to think thoughts that are not pure.

DAY 2

READ
Matthew 12:22-37 ("A Pack of Snakes," page 540 in the *Day By Day Kid's Bible*)
"The mouth says what comes from the heart. Good things come from good hearts," said Jesus. "Sin comes from sinful hearts. Someday God will judge the world. People will have to tell why they said words without thinking. You'll be made clean from sin because of your words. Or you'll be dirty with sin because of your words."

THINK AND TALK
In the Bible, when people talk about your heart, they are talking about your mind and your thoughts, and sometimes your feelings, too. How can you tell if a person has pure thoughts? How can you tell if a person has sinful thoughts? Is it possible for a person to hide their thoughts and act as though their thoughts are pure? If so, how? How would you know if someone were trying to fool you like this? Can these people fool God?

PRACTICE
Challenge a friend or family member (or yourself) to a sword-fight. One person says, "What will you do when you are tempted to think thoughts that are not pure?" The other person answers, "I will think

pure thoughts because it is written, 'Whatever is true, whatever is noble, whatever is right, whatever is pure, whatever is lovely, whatever is admirable–if anything is excellent or praiseworthy– think about such things.'"

DAY 3

READ

Matthew 15:1-20 ("The Leaders'Rules," page 559 in the *Day By Day Kid's Bible*)

The leaders went to Jesus. They asked, "Why don't your friends follow the leaders' rules? They don't wash their hands like we do."... "You're not obeying God's rules," said Jesus... "Nothing a person eats can make him dirty from sin... It's the words that come out of a person that make him dirty. Bad thoughts come from inside him, from his heart. Sinning with sex, stealing, and killing come from the heart.... Wanting what someone else has comes from the heart. Bragging and foolish thinking come from the heart.... That's what makes a person dirty," said Jesus.

THINK AND TALK

Have you ever felt the dirty feeling of guilt? *Guilt* is knowing that we've done something wrong. It's feeling that we are to blame. Guilt is the dirt in our hearts. Is the *thought* of doing the wrong thing sin, or is it only doing the wrong thing that is sin? Explain. Why does God want us to think pure thoughts? What happens when we don't?

PRACTICE

Challenge someone to sword-fight with your sword for this week. Write on an index card: "You are tempted to think thoughts that are not pure." Add this temptation card to the other cards you've collected. Place them in a bowl. The first person draws a card and challenges the second person with that temptation. The second person repeats the sword of the Spirit that she can use to fight the temptation. Then it's her turn to draw a card and challenge the first person.

DAY 4

READ

2 Corinthians 10 ("Face to Face," page 699 in the *Day By Day Kid's Bible*)

We may live in the world. But we don't fight the way the world does. What we fight with has power from God. It tears down the enemy's strong places. We fight anything that comes against knowing God. We catch every thought. We make those thoughts obey Jesus.

THINK AND TALK

Sometimes sinful thoughts just pop into our heads when we don't even mean to have them. That's temptation. The temptation is not sin. The temptation is daring you to keep thinking about it. When we have a temptation thought, what choice do we have? How can you catch that thought and make it obey Jesus? Why does God want us to throw those thoughts out of our minds? Some temptations are not very strong, and they are easy to throw out. But a strong temptation is something that we would really like to do. It looks like it would feel good or be fun or bring us some kind of pleasure. Does it hurt if we think of doing the wrong thing for just a little while?

PRACTICE

Challenge someone to practice fighting temptation. You can take turns drawing the temptation cards from a bowl. Ask each other what you would do if you were tempted in that way.

TRY THIS

Get an adult to help you grow some crystals. Place four charcoal briquets (the kind used for grilling outdoors) into a glass bowl or pie plate. Mix one tablespoon of ammonia, two tablespoons of water, one tablespoon of salt, and two tablespoons of laundry bluing. Pour this over the charcoal. Let this sit for a few days, and then watch what happens. Just as the mixture of ammonia and bluing changed the charcoal into something beautiful, so with God's help we can turn our life into something beautiful. This can happen only when we think pure thoughts instead of giving in to temptation.

DAY 5

READ

Matthew 26:36-46 ("Praying in the Garden," page 614 in the *Day By Day Kid's Bible*)

Jesus and his friends crossed the valley. There was an olive garden on the other side. That's where they went... Jesus took Peter, James, and John with him. "Stay here and watch," he told them... He walked just a little way from Peter, James, and John... He started praying... He went back to his friends. They were sleeping... "Couldn't you men watch for just one hour?" Jesus asked Peter. "Watch! Pray, so you won't think about doing wrong."

THINK AND TALK

Why do you think Peter, James and John fell asleep? Do you think it's easier to make wrong choices when you're tired? Why or why not? What did Jesus tell them to do so they wouldn't be tempted (think about doing wrong)? Will prayer help us keep temptation away? Why or why not?

PRACTICE

Challenge someone to practice fighting temptation. You can take turns drawing the temptation cards from a bowl. Ask each other what you would do if you were tempted in that way.

TRY THIS

Fill a bowl with water. Put a tablespoon of vegetable oil into a measuring cup. Add three drops of red food coloring, three drops of blue food coloring, and three drops of green food coloring to the cooking oil, and stir it well to mix the colors. Let's say that the bowl of clear water represents your clear, pure thoughts. Now pour the oil mixture into the water. This represents thoughts that are not pure coming into your mind. Keep watching. What happens? You can't separate the colors back out of the water. How can you get your thoughts to be pure again?

DAY 6

READ
Proverbs 2; 3:17-24 ("Hidden Riches," page 231 in the *Day By Day Kid's Bible*)
My child, listen to what's wise. Try to understand. Ask for help with all that you need to know. Then you'll understand how to look up to God....Your heart will be wise. It will feel good to know....Wise thinking will help you be safe.

THINK AND TALK
What kinds of thoughts are wise thoughts? Why is it wise to think thoughts that are true, noble, right, pure, lovely, admirable, excellent, and praiseworthy? One man says he thinks of temptation as if he stepped into the wrong room. If he steps into the wrong room, he doesn't stay there, he just turns around and walks back out. When he's tempted, he just shoves that thought back out. It's easier to shove a thought out if you replace the tempting thought with a pure thought. What are some pure thoughts that you can have ready to use when a tempting thought comes in?

PRACTICE
Challenge someone to practice fighting temptation. You can take turns drawing the temptation cards from a bowl. Ask each other what you would do if you were tempted in that way.

TRY THIS
Make hot cider. Ask an adult to supervise. Pour a quart of apple juice, a quart of cranberry juice, and two tablespoons of lemon juice into a large pot. Stir in three whole cloves, one-fourth teaspoon of allspice, one-fourth teaspoon of nutmeg, and one stick of cinnamon. Heat this to a boil on the stove. To serve this, you will have to strain out the spices. When bad thoughts come into our minds, we have to strain them out. How can we do that?

DAY 7

READ

I Corinthians 7:25-35 ("To Marry or Not to Marry," page 680 in the *Day By Day Kid's Bible*)

Time is short. Don't live just to make your wife or husband happy. Don't buy things just to have things. Don't use your time thinking about things of the world. The world is not going to last forever.

THINK AND TALK

What are the things of the world that we think about? Is it wrong to think about your schoolwork or about your chores at home or about your family or about the game you're playing? Is there a right way to think about these and a wrong way to think about these? Explain. What are some "things of the world" that it would be wrong to think about? How do some of these wrong thoughts come to us? What can we do to lessen our chances of being tempted to think as the world thinks?

PRACTICE

Challenge someone to practice fighting temptation. You can take turns drawing the temptation cards from a bowl. Ask each other what you would do if you were tempted in that way.

TRY THIS

Cut eight "thought clouds" out of white paper. On each cloud, write one of the kinds of thoughts that this week's verse talks about. Glue these to a blue poster board. Draw a face onto a paper plate and glue that below the thought clouds. This can help remind you of the kinds of things God wants you to think about.

Trying for Excellence

Your sword of the Spirit for this week is:

Work hard and cheerfully at whatever you do, as though you were working for the Lord rather than for people. COLOSSIANS 3:23

With the above sword you can fight back when you face this temptation:

You are tempted not to do your best.

DAY 1

READ

Matthew 5:13-20 ("Salt and Light," page 530 in the *Day By Day Kid's Bible*)

You're like a light to this world," said Jesus. "You're like a city high on a hill. It's up where everyone can see it. People don't put a lamp under a bowl," said Jesus. "Instead, they put it out where it will shine. It lights up the house. So let your light shine where people can see it. They'll see the good things you do. Then they'll cheer for God your Father."

THINK AND TALK

Working "hard and cheerfully" means doing the very best you can and being happy to do it. Why should we do the very best we can? What did Jesus mean when he told us to "let our lights shine"? What are some of the jobs—work and play—that God has given you to do? How can you do them the very best you can?

291

PRACTICE

Read the verse. Try to repeat it several times without looking. Cut a sword shape from paper or cardboard and write the verse on it. Hang it up as a reminder of the Spirit's sword from Colossians 3:23. You can use it to fight when you are tempted not to do your best.

DAY 2

READ

Philippians 2:19-30 ("Brothers and Workers," page 747 in the *Day By Day Kid's Bible*)

I hope I can send Timothy to you soon. I don't have anyone else like Timothy. He really cares about you. It seems like people look only for what they want. They don't care about what Jesus wants. But Timothy shows that he is a good man. He worked with me to tell the Good News. He worked like a son would work with his father... I think I should send Epaphroditus back to you... He is a worker and a fighter with me... Look up to people like him. He nearly died for Jesus' work.

THINK AND TALK

Paul wrote these words in a letter to the people in Philippi. How can you tell that Paul's helpers did excellent work? How did that make Paul feel? How does it make you feel to have an excellent worker do a job for you? How does it feel to work with an excellent worker?

PRACTICE

Challenge a friend or family member (or yourself) to a sword-fight. One person says, "What will you do when you are tempted not to do your best?" The other person answers, "I will do my best, because it is written 'Work hard and cheerfully at whatever you do, as though you were working for the Lord rather than for people.'"

DAY 3

READ

Malachi 1:1-13 ("A Gift of Sick Animals," page 484 in the *Day By Day Kid's Bible*)

"Where are the good things my servants should say about me?" asks God. "It's you priests who treat me like nothing... You offer me animals you don't want. You bring me the sheep that can't see. You bring me sick animals and animals that can't walk. Just try to give those animals to your rulers. Would they be happy with a gift like that?" asks God... You talk about the table in my worship house. You say, 'It's dirty.' You talk about the food there. 'It's bad,' you say. They you say that doing my work is too hard for you. You treat it as if it's not important," says God.

THINK AND TALK

Does it sound as though the priests were doing an excellent job? How can you tell? How did God feel about the kind of work they were doing? When people don't do their best, we might say their work is sloppy or shabby or careless. How does it feel when you know you've done work that is sloppy? How does it feel when you've done work that is excellent? Why does God want us to do excellent work?

PRACTICE

Challenge someone to sword-fight with your sword for this week. Write on an index card: "You are tempted not to do your best." Add this temptation card to the other cards you've collected. Place them in a bowl. The first person draws a card and challenges the second person with that temptation. The second person repeats the sword of the Spirit that he can use to fight the temptation. Then it's his turn to draw a card and challenge the first person.

DAY 4

READ

1 Corinthians 15:32-34; 50-58 ("Coming Back to Life," page 689 in the *Day By Day Kid's Bible*)

Some people say, "Let's eat and drink as much as we want. Tomorrow we'll just die." Don't believe a lie like that. "Bad friends mess up the good in you." Wake up and think! Stop sinning... Stay with Jesus. Don't let anything move you away. Always do your best work for the Lord. You know that none of the work you do for him is for nothing.

THINK AND TALK

How can you tell when a person is doing his best work? How can you tell when a person is not doing his best work? What's the difference between working as if you're working for the Lord and working as if you're working for people? If you do your best work and nobody seems to care or notice, was it a waste of your time? Why or why not?

PRACTICE

You and another person can challenge someone to practice fighting temptation. Do this by taking turns drawing the temptation cards from a bowl. Ask each other what you would do if you were tempted in that way, and answer by saying the appropriate verse.

TRY THIS

Make a tool print. Gather some tools from around your house (scissors, pancake turners, cheese grater, small wrench, screws, and so on). Pour a little water-based, washable paint over the bottoms of some paper plates, one paper plate for each color. Press a tool into one color of paint and then press the tool onto a piece of paper, making a print. Lay the tool onto some old newspaper while you work with the other tools. One by one, print with the tools to make a design. When you are finished, wash the tools off and put them back where you found them. Is there a way that you can know that you've done excellent work?

DAY 5

READ

Proverbs 31:10-31 ("A Good Wife," page 256 in the *Day By Day Kid's Bible*)

Who can find a wife who is good? She is better than riches... Her hands are ready to work... She is strong. She feels good about what she can do. She is not worried about the days that will come. She says wise things... She takes care of her family. She is not lazy. Her children stand up and say good things about her. Her husband does too... "Lots of women do good things," he says. "But you are better than all of them."

THINK AND TALK

How can people tell that this woman does excellent work? Tell about someone you know who does excellent work. Is it always easy to do excellent work? When is it hardest for you to do excellent work?

PRACTICE

Challenge someone to practice fighting temptation. You can take turns drawing the temptation cards from a bowl. Ask each other what you would do if you were tempted in that way.

TRY THIS

After dinner, wash dishes with a sink full of suds instead of in a dishwasher. Pay attention to the textures you feel: smooth plates, fluffy suds, etc. Try to do an excellent job. Is there a difference between a good job and an excellent job? If so, what's the difference?

DAY 6

READ

Exodus 35:4–36:7 ("Rich Gifts and Hard Work," page 73 in the *Day By Day Kid's Bible*)

Moses said, "I want people who are good at making things. Come and make what God wants for his worship tent." ...Moses said that God chose one man to be a special worker. "God filled him with his

Spirit. God made him good at art. He knows how to work with gold and silver. He knows how to cut and set stones. He knows how to work with wood. God has made him to be a good teacher. God made another man good at working with cloth. He can sew."

THINK AND TALK
Who makes us able to do excellent work? Are all of us good at everything we try to do? How do we know what we do well? How do we learn to do things well? Sometimes we have to practice. Is it always easy to practice? Why or why not? What are some things you have to practice doing? What keeps you practicing when you get tired of it? What tempts you to not do your best?

PRACTICE
Challenge someone to practice fighting temptation. You can take turns drawing the temptation cards from a bowl. Ask each other what you would do if you were tempted in that way.

TRY THIS
Make a "relief." Arrange heavy twine or string on a piece of cardboard to make a design. Glue it in place and let it dry. Then lay a sheet of aluminum foil over the design and begin to press it down over the string. Smooth it out and mold it right around the design. Fold the edges of the foil around to the back of the cardboard and tape them in place. How did the gold and silver workers in today's reading become excellent at what they did?

DAY 7

READ
Daniel 5.
("The Fingers That Wrote on the Wall," page 453 in the *Day By Day Kid's Bible*)
Now King Belshazzar had a great dinner for 1,000 leaders... All of a sudden the fingers of a man's hand showed up. The fingers wrote on the wall by the lamp stand. The king... was so scared, his knees shook and hit together... So all the king's magic men came in. But they couldn't read the writing... The queen heard their

voices. She came into the great hall... "Live forever, my king!" she said. "Don't be scared. There is a man in this kingdom who is wise... Your father, King Nebuchadnezzar, put him in charge of the magic men. His name is Daniel... He can tell what to do about hard problems. Call for Daniel to come."

THINK AND TALK
Why did the queen remember Daniel? Daniel did a good job with whatever he did. (You can read Daniel 6 to find out what else happened because he did excellent work.) Proverbs 22:29 says, "Do you see a man skilled in his work? He will serve before kings." How does a person get skilled in his work? Daniel served before kings, but we don't have kings, so what could this verse mean to us?

PRACTICE
Challenge someone to practice fighting temptation. You can take turns drawing the temptation cards from a bowl. Ask each other what you would do if you were tempted in that way.

TRY THIS
Make a glass band. Put water in several glasses, filling them to different levels. As you gently tap on the glasses with a plastic spoon, put them in order from low to high notes. Try to play a simple song. You can add water or pour water out of some glasses in order to get the right notes. What does practice have to do with doing excellent work?

Being Thrifty

Your sword of the Spirit for this week is:

Keep your lives free from the love of money and be content with what you have. HEBREWS 13:5

With the above sword you can fight back when you face this temptation:

You are tempted to waste your money.

DAY 1

READ

Isaiah 55 ("Trees Will Clap," page 369 in the *Day By Day Kid's Bible*)

Why work and pay money for things that don't do you any good?... Look for God while you can find him. Talk to him while he is near. People who do wrong should... turn to God.... God will forgive them for free.

THINK AND TALK

Being *thrifty* means managing your money carefully. What are some ways to manage your money carefully? What are some things people do to waste their money? Have you ever paid money for something that didn't do you any good? If so, what was it? People can become wiser by making that mistake. How? How can you tell if something you want to buy would be a waste of your money?

PRACTICE

Read the verse. Try to repeat it several times without looking. Cut a sword shape from paper or cardboard and write the verse on it. You'll want to hang it up in a place where it will remind you of the Spirit's sword from Hebrews 13:5. You can use it to fight against the temptation to waste your money.

DAY 2

READ
Ecclesiastes 5 ("Riches," page 264 in the *Day By Day Kid's Bible*)
People who love money never have enough of it. This is not good either. You may get more things. But then more people come to you. They want to help you use things up. So what good are things to the one who owns them? All that person can do is look at them... then I saw that it's good to get riches and health from God. He lets us enjoy them... They're a gift from God.

THINK AND TALK
Why do people love money? How can you tell if a person loves money? Does a person have to be poor to be thrifty? Do rich people need to be thrifty too? If so, why? Why does God give people money? (2 Corinthians 9:11 gives one reason.)

PRACTICE
Challenge a friend or family member (or yourself) to a sword-fight. One person says, "What will you do when you are tempted to waste your money?" The other person answers, "I will not waste my money because it is written, 'Keep your lives free from the love of money and be content with what you have.'"

DAY 3

READ
Luke 16:1-12 ("A Little and a Lot," page 583 in the *Day By Day Kid's Bible*)
"What happens when you can be trusted with a little? Then you can be trusted with a lot," said Jesus. "What happens when you can't be trusted with a little? Then you can't be trusted with a lot. What if people can't trust you with worldly riches? Do you think you'll be trusted with heaven's riches?"

THINK AND TALK

How do people show God that they can be trusted with a little money? How can you tell if someone can't be trusted with worldly riches? Why does God want us to be thrifty? What happens when we are not thrifty?

PRACTICE

Challenge someone to sword-fight with your sword for this week. Write on an index card: "You are tempted to waste your money." Add this temptation card to the other cards you've collected. Place them in a bowl. The first person draws a card and challenges the second person with that temptation. The second person repeats the sword of the Spirit that he can use to fight the temptation. Then it's his turn to draw a card and challenge the first person.

DAY 4

READ

James 5:1-9.

("Rotten Riches," page 766 in the *Day By Day Kid's Bible*)
Now you rich people, listen... You'll see that your riches are rotten. Moths ate up your clothes. Your gold and silver rusted away. It all shows that you held on to your riches. Look! You didn't pay the people who worked for you... The workers cried about it, and God heard them. You lived with riches all around you. You bought whatever you wanted. You made yourselves fat.

THINK AND TALK

Is it wise to buy whatever we want, even if we have the money for it? Why or why not? How does it feel when you know you've wasted your money? How does it feel to be thrifty? When is it hardest for you to be thrifty?

PRACTICE

You and another person can challenge each other to practice fighting temptation. Do this by taking turns drawing the temptation cards from a bowl. Ask each other what you would do if you were tempted in that way, and answer by saying the appropriate verse.

TRY THIS
Collect pennies and try to arrange them by date. How old is your oldest penny? How new is your newest? What are some good things you could do with your pennies?

DAY 5

READ
Proverbs 17:16; 23:4-5; 28:6, 20 ("Being Rich and Poor," page 248 in the *Day By Day Kid's Bible*)

What good is money in a fool's hand? He won't spend it to learn things. He doesn't even want to be wise.... Don't get all tired out trying to get rich. Be wise. Control yourself. Riches don't last. They seem to grow wings. They seem to fly into the sky like birds. ...Be happy to be poor and right. That's better than being rich and wrong. People in a hurry to get rich will get into trouble.

THINK AND TALK
Why would people who are in a hurry to get rich get into trouble? Why is it good to spend money to learn things? What are some other things that it's good to spend money on? What do you think Solomon meant when he wrote that riches "seem to grow wings" and "fly into the sky like birds"? Have you ever known anyone who chose to be poor and right rather than rich and wrong? If so, tell about that person.

PRACTICE
Challenge someone to practice fighting temptation. You can take turns drawing the temptation cards from a bowl. Ask each other what you would do if you were tempted in that way.

TRY THIS
Lay several different coins out on a table and place a sheet of typing paper on top of them. If you have coins from a different country, use them also. Some of them may have different shapes. Now rub over the paper with a pencil or crayon to show the designs of the coins underneath. Add wings on the coins to make a picture of the proverb that says that riches seem to grow wings and fly away like birds.

DAY 6

READ

2 Kings 20:12-20 ("Riches," page 359 in the *Day By Day Kid's Bible*)

King Hezekiah was very rich... He built places to keep his silver and gold and riches... Now the king of Babylon sent men to see Hezekiah. They took him letters and a gift... Hezekiah showed the men everything in his store houses. He showed them his silver and gold... and all his riches... Then Isaiah went to King Hezekiah... "What did they see?" asked Isaiah. "Everything," said Hezekiah... "Someday Babylon will take away all your riches," said Isaiah.

THINK AND TALK

What did Hezekiah do that was wrong? Why was it wrong? Would it be all right for you to tell a friend about how much money and how many things you have? Why or why not? If someone is rich, does that mean they are thrifty? If someone is poor, does that mean they are not thrifty? Explain. Is it always easy to be thrifty? What are some ways you can keep from wasting your money?

PRACTICE

Challenge someone to practice fighting temptation. You can take turns drawing the temptation cards from a bowl. Ask each other what you would do if you were tempted in that way.

TRY THIS

Fold a paper towel several times to make a thick padding. Place the paper towel on a plate and put a few pennies on the paper towel. Then pour vinegar onto the paper towel to make it wet. Leave it for a day and then see what has happened. This happens because of the chemical reaction when the vinegar (acetic acid) mixes with the copper that the pennies are made of. What might happen to our money if we brag about it?

DAY 7

READ

Matthew 20:1-16 ("Workers Who Fussed," page 588 in the *Day By Day Kid's Bible*)

A farmer... went to town early in the morning. He got men... to work in his field... At nine o'clock... he saw more people... So the farmer took them... The farmer got more workers at noon. He got more workers at three o'clock... At five o'clock, the farmer still found people... The farmer said, "You can work in my field." ...The farmer paid each worker for one day's work. The workers who had worked all day started fussing... "You treated them just like us. We worked all day long." ...The farmer said,..."I want to give the others what I gave you. It's my money. Can't I do what I want with it? Or are you mad because I'm being kind to them?"

THINK AND TALK

What choices did the farmer make? Why were the men who worked all day angry? Would you have been angry too? Why is it not wise to compare how rich (or poor) you are with how rich (or poor) someone else is? In the story, if the workers are the people in the world, who is the farmer? This story is not really about money. Can you figure out what the story really means? If so, tell its meaning.

PRACTICE

Challenge someone to practice fighting temptation. You can take turns drawing the temptation cards from a bowl. Ask each other what you would do if you were tempted in that way.

TRY THIS

Try standing a quarter on its edge. Now hold the quarter on its edge with the tip of one finger while you flick it with a finger on your other hand to make it start spinning. See how long it can spin. Try spinning it on different kinds of surfaces. Which surface seems to be the best? What might you do with your money after you have saved four quarters?

Showing Loyalty

Your sword of the Spirit for this week is:

Do not forsake your friend. PROVERBS 27:10

With the above sword you can fight back when you face this temptation:

You are tempted to betray a friend.

DAY 1

READ

Judges 15 ("Fighting with a Jaw Bone," page 118 in the *Day By Day Kid's Bible*)

The enemies got an army together. They camped around the land of Judah. The men from Judah wondered what was happening. "Why are you coming to fight us?" they asked. "We came to get Samson," said the enemies... So 3,000 men went from Judah to Samson's cave. "These enemies are in charge of our land," they said [to Samson]. "Don't you know that? Why are you making them angry?...We have come to take you to them," said the men. "Just promise me that you won't kill me," said Samson... They tied Samson up with two new ropes. Then they led him away.

THINK AND TALK

Being *loyal* means standing up for someone, defending the person, helping her. It means not telling the other person's secrets. Who are some people we might be expected to be loyal to? To *betray* or *forsake* someone means turning away from him, not being loyal. The 3,000 men in the story were from Samson's own country. Would you expect them to be loyal to Samson? Why or why not? What choice did they make?

305

PRACTICE

Read the verse. Try to repeat it several times without looking. Cut a sword shape from paper or cardboard and write the verse on it. You'll want to hang it up in your house where it will remind you of the Spirit's sword from Proverbs 27:10. You can use it to fight against the temptation to betray a friend.

DAY 2

READ

1 Samuel 14 ("Jonathan Climbs up a Cliff," page 134 in the *Day By Day Kid's Bible*)

One day Jonathan had an idea. He told it to a young man who was his helper. "Let's go where the enemy is," said Jonathan. Jonathan didn't tell his father he was going. So no one knew Jonathan had left... "Follow me," said Jonathan to his helper. "God will help us win."...Then Jonathan began to fight the enemies. His helper came right behind him. They killed about 20 men... The enemies didn't know what was going on... The Jews who were hiding heard about it. So they came out to fight. And God saved his people.

THINK AND TALK

What choices did Jonathan's helper have? What did he choose to do? What happened because of his choice? How did Jonathan's helper show that he was loyal? How do your friends show that they are loyal to you? How do you show that you are loyal to your friends? Who else are you loyal to? Why does God want us to be loyal? What happens when we're not?

PRACTICE

Challenge a friend or family member (or yourself) to a sword-fight. One person says, "What will you do when you are tempted to betray someone?" The other person answers, "I will be loyal because it is written, 'Do not forsake your friend.'"

DAY 3

READ

1 Chronicles 19 ("A Rude King," page 165 in the *Day By Day Kid's Bible*)

The king of Ammon died. His son became king. David thought, "I'll be kind to him. His father was always kind to me." So David sent a group of men to see the new king. They told him David was sorry that his father had died. But... the king took David's men. He shaved off half their beards. He cut their clothes in half across the middle. Then he sent them home... The leaders of Ammon began to see what they had done. They had been rude to David. So their king paid for chariots to come from other lands... They all got ready to fight David's army.

THINK AND TALK

To *betray* or *forsake* someone means to treat them as if they are not your friends. David's country and the country of Ammon had been friends. What did the king of Ammon do to betray the countries' friendship? What happened because of the king's choice? How can you tell if a person is loyal? How can you tell if a person is not loyal? Which kind of person would you rather have as a friend?

PRACTICE

Challenge someone to sword-fight with your sword for this week. Write on an index card: "You are tempted to betray someone." Add this temptation card to the other cards you've collected. Place them in a bowl. The first person draws a card and challenges the second person with that temptation. The second person repeats the sword of the Spirit that he can use to fight the temptation. Then it's his turn to draw a card and challenge the first person.

DAY 4

READ

2 Kings 2 ("A Chariot and Horses of Fire," page 294 in the *Day By Day Kid's Bible*)

"You stay here," said Elijah... "I won't leave you," said Elisha. So they went to Bethel together... Elijah told Elisha, "You stay here... " "I won't leave you," said Elisha. So they went to Jericho together.... Elijah told Elisha, "You stay here." ..."I won't leave you," said Elisha. So they walked on together... All of a sudden, horses of fire appeared. They pulled a chariot of fire. It went between Elijah and Elisha. Then a wind came, turning around and around. It took Elijah up to heaven. Elisha saw it... he picked up Elijah's coat... The prophets... were watching. "Elijah's spirit is upon Elisha now," they said.

THINK AND TALK
Being *loyal* means standing up for people–staying with your friend or your team no matter what. Who else are you loyal to? What did Elisha choose to do? What happened because of his choice? How does it feel to betray someone? How does it feel to be loyal? When is it hardest for you to be loyal?

PRACTICE
You and another person can challenge each other to practice fighting temptation. Do this by taking turns drawing the temptation cards from a bowl. Ask each other what you would do if you were tempted in that way, and answer by saying the appropriate verse.

TRY THIS
Make a fiery design using yellow and red tissue paper. Tear the tissue paper into pieces about three inches by five inches, any shape. Pour about one-eight cup of white glue into a bowl and add just enough water to make it like paint. Lay a piece of tissue paper on a piece of white paper, poster board, or cardboard. Use a paintbrush to paint the glue over the tissue, completely covering that piece of tissue. Lay another piece of tissue paper on the paper. The pieces of tissue paper can overlap. Keep adding the paper and painting glue over them until you are pleased with your design. Let it dry. Remember the horses of fire and the chariot that came between Elijah and Elisha.

DAY 5

READ
Luke 22:1-6 ("Thirty Silver Coins," page 607 in the *Day By Day Kid's Bible*)
Judas was one of Jesus' 12 special friends. But Satan took control

308

of Judas now. So Judas went to the leaders at the worship house. He told them he could show them where Jesus was. "What will you give me if I do?" he asked. The leaders counted out 30 silver coins for Judas. Judas took the money. Then he waited and watched. He looked for a time when no crowds were around.

THINK AND TALK

What choices did Judas have? What did Judas choose to do? What happened because of his choice? Why do you think Judas betrayed Jesus? Has anyone ever betrayed you? If so, how does it feel? If someone betrays you, is it all right for you to betray that person? Why or why not? Tell about someone you know who is loyal to you. Tell about a time when you were loyal to someone, or to a team, or to your country.

PRACTICE

Challenge someone to practice fighting temptation. You can take turns drawing the temptation cards from a bowl. Ask each other what you would do if you were tempted in that way.

TRY THIS

Make a coin bag by cutting a circle of fabric about ten inches across. Cut about six small holes spaced evenly around the edge of the circle. Thread a shoe string in one hole and out the next all around the circle. Tying the ends of the shoestring together will close the top of the bag. Recall the story of Judas and the 30 coins.

DAY 6

READ

John 19:38-42 ("The Grave," page 624 in the *Day By Day Kid's Bible*)

Evening came. A man named Joseph went to see Pilate. Joseph was a Jewish leader. But he was watching for God's kingdom to come. He was very brave. He asked Pilate if he could have Jesus' body... So Pilate said Joseph could take Jesus' body. Nicodemus went with Joseph. Nicodemus was the man who once came to see Jesus at night... They took Jesus' body.... Then they put it in a grave.

THINK AND TALK

Joseph and Nicodemus were leaders who knew and met with the same group of men who took Jesus to Pilate to be killed. How did they show that they were loyal to Jesus? Why did they have to be brave to do this? What happened because of their choice? Is it always easy to be loyal? Do you think it was easy for Joseph and Nicodemus to be loyal to Jesus?

PRACTICE

Challenge someone to practice fighting temptation. You can take turns drawing the temptation cards from a bowl. Ask each other what you would do if you were tempted in that way.

TRY THIS

Sit in a circle with a group of friends. Choose one person to stand in the middle of the circle and close her eyes. Everyone else holds hands. Choose a leader to start the "electric current" by squeezing the hand of the person on his right. That person squeezes the hand of the person next to him, and the squeeze (the "electricity") goes from person to person around the circle. It can change direction at any time. Tell the person in the middle when she can look. She tries to see someone squeeze someone else's hand. When she sees it, she points it out, and she gets to trade places with that person. Being loyal means supporting your friends. Sometimes holding hands shows that you support your friend. What else shows loyalty to a friend?

DAY 7

READ

Galatians 2 ("The Law and the Good News," page 658 in the *Day By Day Kid's Bible*)

Peter sometimes ate with people who were not Jewish. Then some Jews came to see Peter. Peter was afraid of what they would think. So he stopped eating with people who were not Jewish. That's not what the Good News is all about. So I talked to Peter in front of everyone.

THINK AND TALK

Jewish people would not eat with people who were not Jews. But Peter knew that God wanted people to be part of his kingdom too. So Peter had made friends with people who were not Jewish, and he ate with them. Why did he stop eating with them when some Jews came to see him? Was he being loyal to his friends who were not Jews? What are some things that might tempt us to betray or forsake someone we should be loyal to? Are there times when you should *not* be loyal? Explain.

PRACTICE

Challenge someone to practice fighting temptation. You can take turns drawing the temptation cards from a bowl. Ask each other what you would do if you were tempted in that way.

TRY THIS

On a large sheet of manila paper, trace around your foot and a friend's foot. Across the top or bottom of the paper, write, "I'll stand by you." What do we mean when we say we'll stand by someone?

Being Diligent

Your sword of the Spirit for this week is:

Lazy people are soon poor; hard workers get rich. PROVERBS 10:4

With the above sword you can fight back when you face this temptation:

You are tempted to be lazy.

DAY 1

READ

Proverbs 6:6-8; 14:23; 24:30-34; 26:14 ("Working Hard or Being Lazy," page 249 in the *Day By Day Kid's Bible*)

Look at the ant, you lazy person. Think about what the ant does. Be wise. The ant doesn't have a king to tell it what to do. But it stores up its food in the summer.... All hard work brings good things. But if all you do is talk, you'll grow poor.... I passed a lazy man's field. Weeds were everywhere. The stone wall was broken down. I thought about what I saw, and I learned something. You sleep a little. You sleep a little more. You fold your hands to rest. Then you grow poor.

THINK AND TALK

Diligence is being a hard worker. It's treating your work or study as something important, doing it as soon as you can, and staying at it until it's done. How can you tell if someone is diligent? How can you tell if they are lazy? What is your favorite thing that Solomon said in these proverbs about being lazy?

PRACTICE

Read the verse. Try to repeat it several times without looking.

313

Cut a sword shape from paper or cardboard and write the verse on it. You'll want to hang it up in your house where it will remind you of the Spirit's sword from Proverbs 10:4. You can use it to fight against the temptation to be lazy.

DAY 2

READ

2 Chronicles 24 ("Turning Away," page 315 in the *Day By Day Kid's Bible*)

Joash thought he'd fix up God's worship house. He talked to the priests about it. "Gather money... at the worship house," he said. "Use the money to fix whatever needs to be fixed." ...But the priests didn't do it right away... "Why aren't you fixing up the worship house?" asked Joash. "Stop taking money for yourselves. Give it to someone who can fix the worship house." One priest made a hole in the top of a large wooden box. He put it by the altar. A message went to all the people. It said to bring their tax money to God. So people from all over Judah brought money....Then they paid workers to fix up the worship house. The workers did good work. They worked hard. They fixed up the worship house.

THINK AND TALK

Were the priests diligent or lazy at first? What happened because of their choice? After Joash talked to them about the worship house again, what did they choose to do? Did you ever have to be asked more than once to do something? Why? Why does God want us to be diligent? What happens when we are lazy?

PRACTICE

Challenge a friend or family member (or yourself) to a sword-fight. One person says, "What will you do when you are tempted to be lazy?" The other person answers, "I will not be lazy because it is written, 'Lazy people are soon poor; hard workers get rich.'"

DAY 3

READ

2 Chronicles 26 ("Forts, Towers, and Rock-Throwing Machines,"

King Uzziah built towers in Jerusalem... He made them like forts.... King Uzziah dug wells. He had lots of cows. People worked in his fields. He loved to grow things. King Uzziah also made machines in the city. They were placed on the towers. They were used to shoot arrows and throw rocks when their enemies came.

THINK AND TALK

How can you tell that King Uzziah was a diligent king? How do you feel when you know you've been diligent in doing a job? How do you feel when you know you've been lazy? When is it hardest for you to be a diligent worker?

PRACTICE

Challenge someone to sword-fight with your sword for this week. Write on an index card: "You are tempted to be lazy." Add this temptation card to the other cards you've collected. Place them in a bowl. The first person draws a card and challenges the second person with that temptation. The second person repeats the sword of the Spirit that she can use to fight the temptation. Then it's her turn to draw a card and challenge the first person.

DAY 4

READ

Luke 12:35-48 ("The Wise Servant," page 544 in the *Day By Day Kid's Bible*)

"Be ready to help and serve," said Jesus... "Be like servants waiting for their master... It's good if the servants are ready for him." ...Peter said, "Lord, is this story just for us?" ..."It's for people who do what they say they will do," said Jesus. "That's what a wise servant does... A good servant does what his master tells him. He will be following orders when his master comes back. His master will put him in charge of everything... The master may give his servant a lot," said Jesus. "Then he will want his servant to give a lot too."

THINK AND TALK

How can a person who works in a restaurant be a hard worker and show diligence to the people who come to be served? How can a person who works in a store show diligence to the people who come to buy something? In what other kinds of jobs do the workers serve others? Tell about someone you know who is diligent. Tell about a time when you wanted to be lazy, but you chose to be a diligent, hard worker instead.

PRACTICE

You and another person can challenge each other to practice fighting temptation. Do this by taking turns drawing the temptation cards from a bowl. Ask each other what you would do if you were tempted in that way, and answer by saying the appropriate verse.

TRY THIS

Write the word *diligence* across the top of a piece of paper. Try to see how many words you can make out of the letters in this word.

DAY 5

READ

1 Thessalonians 4 ("A Quiet Life," page 669 in the *Day By Day Kid's Bible*)

Don't be like people who don't know God. Don't treat people the wrong way... God didn't plan for us to have dirty minds. He plans for us to live sinless, good lives... Try to live a quiet life. Mind your own business. Work with your hands. That way, people who don't know God will look up to you. Then you won't need other people's help.

THINK AND TALK

Paul wrote our reading for today. What did he say happens because of a person's choice to mind his own business and work with his hands? Why would lazy people need other people's help? Is it always easy to be diligent? Why or why not?

PRACTICE

Challenge someone to practice fighting temptation. You can take turns drawing the temptation cards from a bowl. Ask each other what you would do if you were tempted in that way.

TRY THIS

Make a rebus by writing the memory verse on a piece of paper. When you come to a word that can be drawn as a picture, draw it instead of writing it.

DAY 6

READ

2 Thessalonians 3 ("Lazy Busybodies," page 672 in the *Day By Day Kid's Bible*)

Stay away from God's people who are lazy. We weren't lazy when we were with you. We paid for the food we ate. We worked hard day and night. We didn't want to be any trouble to you... We told you this rule. "If a person won't work, then he shouldn't eat." We've heard that some of you are being lazy. You're not busy. Instead, you're busybodies. You just think about what other people should be doing. Stop this. Work for what you eat. Some of you are good followers of Jesus. Don't get tired of doing what's right.

THINK AND TALK

Why did Paul tell the people to stay away from God's people who are lazy? What's a busybody? (Another word for "busybody" might be *nosy*.) Is there such a thing as being too busy? How can you tell if you are really resting and getting your energy back, or if you're just being lazy?

PRACTICE

Challenge someone to practice fighting temptation. You can take turns drawing the temptation cards from a bowl. Ask each other what you would do if you were tempted in that way.

TRY THIS

With a broom, sweep under furniture that rarely gets swept under.

Lift up couch cushions and chair cushions and vacuum underneath them. Do you find anything interesting under them? Why isn't it a good idea to be lazy?

DAY 7

READ

Hebrews 6 ("Like a Ship's Anchor," page 782 in the *Day By Day Kid's Bible*)
God is fair. He won't forget your work. He won't forget your love. Keep on working hard to the very end. We don't want you to start being lazy... God made a promise to Abraham. He said, "You can be sure I will bring good things to you." ...And he got what God promised. God doesn't change. He doesn't lie... God keeps his promise. This is our hope.

THINK AND TALK

Have you ever been diligent in your work, but nobody noticed? God knows. Remember Proverbs 14:23 from the *Day By Day Kid's Bible*: "All hard work brings good things." What are some good things that happen because of diligent, hard work? What are some things that might tempt us to be lazy? What are some things you can do to help yourself be diligent?

PRACTICE

Challenge someone to practice fighting temptation. You can take turns drawing the temptation cards from a bowl. Ask each other what you would do if you were tempted in that way.

TRY THIS

Make a picture of your pet or of a friend's pet. Then glue it to the inside of a box lid to make a picture frame. Decorate the inside of the lid by drawing, coloring or painting designs around the border. Or place animal stickers around it. How can a person show diligence in taking care of a pet?

Keeping Promises

Your sword of the Spirit for this week is:

It is better to say nothing than to promise something that you don't follow through on.
ECCLESIASTES 5:5

With the above sword you can fight back when you face this temptation:

You are tempted to break a promise.

DAY 1

READ

Proverbs 3:3-4; 25:19 ("Keeping Promises," page 239 in the *Day By Day Kid's Bible*)

Keep your promises. Write them on your heart. Then God and people will speak well of you... Don't trust someone who doesn't keep his promises. That's as bad as having a hurting tooth. It's as bad as walking on a foot that you broke.

THINK AND TALK

What does it mean to promise to do something? Did anyone ever make a promise to you and then break their promise? If so, how did you feel? Another way to say "keeping your promise" is "keeping your word" or "being true to your word." How can you tell if a person is someone who keeps his promise?

PRACTICE

Read the verse. Try to repeat it several times without looking. Cut a sword shape from paper or cardboard and write the verse on it. You'll want to hang it up in your house where it will remind you of the Spirit's sword from Ecclesiastes 5:5. You can use it to fight against the temptation to break a promise.

319

DAY 2

READ

2 Corinthians 1 ("Cheer Up," page 693 in the *Day By Day Kid's Bible*)

Two times I made plans to visit you. I wanted to help you. Did I plan this without thinking? Do I plan like people of the world do? Do I say yes and no at the same time? God always keeps his promises. That's for sure. And we don't say yes and no at the same time. That's just as sure.

THINK AND TALK

Is a plan the same as a promise? Why or why not? Sometimes we have to change our plans. Tell of a time when you or your family were planning to do something but the plans had to change. Sometimes changing plans is disappointing. How can a person handle the disappointment when plans have to change? How can a person handle the disappointment when someone breaks a promise?

PRACTICE

Challenge a friend or family member (or yourself) to a sword-fight. One person says, "What will you do when you are tempted to break a promise?" The other person answers, "I will not break my promise because it is written, 'It is better to say nothing than to promise something that you don't follow through on.'"

DAY 3

READ

Malachi 2 ("Promises," page 484 in the *Day By Day Kid's Bible*)

One God made us. But we break the promise we made together with him. We do it by breaking promises to each other... God has seen you break your promises. You did not stay with your wife. But you made a promise to her when you married her. God made a husband and wife to be like one person... Why? ...It's because God wants children who care about what he says... So guard yourself. Don't break your promises.

THINK AND TALK

What kind of promise does Malachi write about in our reading for today? What happens when a husband and wife break their promise to stay with each other? Sometimes husbands and wives break their promises. Sometimes people break other kinds of promises. Will God forgive us when we break promises? Why or why not? Can we forgive other people for breaking their promises to us? Why or why not? Why do you think God wants us to keep our promises?

PRACTICE

Challenge someone to sword-fight with your sword for this week. Write on an index card: "You are tempted to break a promise." Add this temptation card to the other cards you've collected. Place them in a bowl. The first person draws a card and challenges the second person with that temptation. The second person repeats the sword of the Spirit that he can use to fight that temptation. Then it's his turn to draw a card and challenge the first person.

DAY 4

READ

Joshua 9 ("Stale Bread and Worn-Out Shoes," page 100 in the *Day By Day Kid's Bible*)

All the kings of the land got together to fight God's people. But the people of Gibeon didn't want to fight. So they played a trick on God's people. They put old, worn-out bags onto donkeys... The men put on worn-out shoes. They wore old clothes....And they went to see Joshua. They said, "We come from a land far away. We want to make a deal with you." God's people said,... "Maybe you live close to us. Then God wouldn't want us to make a deal with you." ...Some of Joshua's men took a look. They saw...the worn-out bags. They could see the worn clothes.... But they didn't ask God about it... They promised not to fight them. Three days passed. Then God's people found out that these men lived nearby... But they didn't fight. They had promised not to.

THINK AND TALK

What choices did Joshua's men make? What happened because of their choices? Psalm 15:1 is a question that David asked God: "Who may enter your presence?" And verse 4 tells one of God's answers: "Those who...keep their promises even when it hurts" (NLT). What did Joshua's men learn about making promises? Did you ever make a promise and later wish you hadn't made it? If so, tell about it. Did you keep your promise, even though it hurt?

PRACTICE

You and another person can challenge each other to practice fighting temptation. Do this by taking turns drawing the temptation cards from a bowl. Ask each other what you would do if you were tempted in that way, and answer by saying the appropriate verse.

TRY THIS

Make a book bag out of a kitchen towel. Fold the towel in half. The fold is the bottom of the bag. Sew the sides together. Then sew the ends of a wide ribbon about 10 inches long to each side of the bag to make handles. Recall the story of the people from Gibeon.

DAY 5

READ

Matthew 14:1-12. ("John in Trouble," page 555 in the *Day By Day Kid's Bible*)

John, who baptized people... had told Herod, "It's not right to marry your brother's wife." So King Herod had put John into jail... Herod knew that John was a good man. He knew that John did what was right. Herod liked to listen to John.... One day King Herod had a party. It was his birthday. All the leaders of the land came. Herodias [his wife] had a daughter who came too. She danced for the people. They all liked the way she danced. So Herod promised to give her anything she wanted... "I want John's head on a plate! Right now!" she said. This made Herod very upset. But he had promised. He didn't want to say no in front of everyone. So he sent a man to the jail. He gave the man orders to kill John. So he did.

THINK AND TALK

What choices did King Herod make? Do you think these choices were wise or unwise? What did King Herod learn about making promises? Why didn't he break or change his promise when he found out what the daughter wanted? Would it have been right to break his promise or change it? Are there times when it's right to break a promise? Why or why not?

PRACTICE

Challenge someone to practice fighting temptation. You can take turns drawing the temptation cards from the bowl. Ask each other what you would do if you were tempted in that way.

TRY THIS

Color a rainbow on a piece of paper, but use colors that start with each letter in the word *promise*. If your crayons don't have labels with names that start with some of these letters, rename some of the colors you have. For example, green can be "mint," black can be "ebony," and so on. The rainbow is a sign of God's good promise to never cover all the earth with a flood. Are all of your promises good ones?

DAY 6

READ

2 Samuel 19:9-23 ("King David Goes Back Home," page 180 in the *Day By Day Kid's Bible*)

A man came across the river to the king. He had thrown rocks at David before. But now he bowed down with his face to the ground. "Please don't be angry at me," he said. "Forget the bad things I said when you left. I know I sinned. But today I'm coming to be the first to meet you." "We should kill this man," said Joab's brother. "He said bad things about you." "You don't think like I do," said David... Then David promised the man who had thrown rocks, "You won't die."

THINK AND TALK

What choices did David have? What choice did he make?
Sometimes people say, "His word is as good as a promise." What
does that mean? Jesus said, "Simply let your 'Yes' be 'Yes,' and
your 'No,' 'No'" (Matthew 5:37). What did Jesus mean? Is there a
difference between breaking a promise and lying? If so, what's the
difference?

PRACTICE

Challenge someone to practice fighting temptation. You can take
turns drawing the temptation cards from the bowl. Ask each other
what you would do if you were tempted in that way.

TRY THIS

Sit on the floor facing a friend. You both bend your knees. Then
you sit on top of your friend's feet and your friend sits on top of your
feet. Hold each other's arms. Now rock back and forth and try to
move forward by lifting first one person and then the other as you
also stretch out your legs and then bend your knees. If you have
two more friends who do the same thing, you can have a race. Do
friends work together best when they keep their promises to one
another?

DAY 7

READ

Jeremiah 34:8-22 ("The People Change Their Minds," page 402 in
the *Day By Day Kid's Bible*)
King Zedekiah... said all the slaves could go free. So the people
said they would let their slaves go free. And they did. But later, the
people changed their minds. They took their slaves back. They
wouldn't let them go. So God spoke to Jeremiah, "I made a
promise to your families long ago," said God. "I took them out of
Egypt. I said my people could be slaves for no more than six years.
Then you would have to let them go free...." "You didn't obey me.
You didn't let your slaves go free... So I will set you free. You are
free to die in fights... free to go without food, and free to get sick."

THINK AND TALK
What choices did God's people have? What did they choose to do? Why do you think they changed their minds? Is there a difference between breaking a promise and changing your mind? If so, what's the difference? Is it always easy to keep a promise? When is it hardest for you to keep a promise? What are some things that might tempt us to break our promises?

PRACTICE
Challenge someone to practice fighting temptation. You can take turns drawing the temptation cards from the bowl. Ask each other what you would do if you were tempted in that way.

TRY THIS
Make a promise box. Decorate a shoe box with Con-Tact paper and stickers. Keep a stack of small note cards or index cards beside it. As you read your Bible, look for promises that God makes to those who love and follow him. Write each promise on a card and place it in your box. if you want to start your Bible reading at a place where there are lots of promises, try the Psalms.

Wanting to Please God

Our purpose is to please God, not people.
1 THESSALONIANS 2:4

With the above sword you can fight back when you face this temptation:

You are tempted to be a people-pleaser.

DAY 1

READ

2 Corinthians 3 ("A Letter from Jesus," page 695 in the *Day By Day Kid's Bible*)

Seeing you is like reading a letter from Jesus. This letter wasn't written with ink. It was written with God's living Spirit. God doesn't write on stone. He writes on human hearts. We can't brag, because we're not able to do anything by ourselves. Being able to do something comes from God.

THINK AND TALK

How can you tell if you are pleasing people? What does it mean for people to praise you? How do you feel when people tell you how good you are or how well you've done? Some people like it so much when others praise them that they will do almost anything to please people. They are people-pleasers. What's dangerous about being a people-pleaser? Are there some people we should want to please? If so, who would they be?

PRACTICE

Read the verse. Try to repeat it several times without looking. Cut a sword shape from paper or cardboard and write the verse on it. You'll want to hang it up in your house where it will remind you of the Spirit's sword from 1 Thessalonians 2:4. You can use it to fight against the temptation to be a people-pleaser.

DAY 2

READ

Romans 2 ("Rules That Are in the Heart," page 704 in the *Day By Day Kid's Bible*)

Being Jewish is great. But that's true only if you obey God's laws... Let's say people obey God's laws. But they aren't Jewish. Then to God, they are his people... A real Jew has the heart of a Jew. He loves God in his heart... This person wants God to cheer for him. He doesn't look for praise from people.

THINK AND TALK

When a person loves God in his heart, who is it that he wants to cheer for him? Why? How can you tell if a person is a people-pleaser? How can you tell if a person would rather please God than people? Sometimes when we please God, we end up pleasing people as well. Give an example of a time when you could please people as well as God.

PRACTICE

Challenge a friend or family member (or yourself) to a sword-fight. One person says, "What will you do when you are tempted to be a people-pleaser?" The other person answers, "I will please God because it is written, 'Our purpose is to please God, not people.'"

DAY 3

READ

Luke 12:1-12 ("From the Roof Tops," page 543 in the *Day By Day Kid's Bible*)

[Jesus] said, "Watch out! What the leaders say and do isn't right... Don't be afraid of people who can kill your body. After that, they

328

can't do anything else," said Jesus. "Tell people you know me... People might... take you to the leaders. But don't worry about what you'll say. The Holy Spirit will tell you what to say."

THINK AND TALK

The leaders Jesus was talking about were able to put people in jail and even kill people. That's what they did to Jesus. Why did Jesus tell his followers not to be afraid of them? If Jesus' followers were people-pleasers, what might they have done when the leaders didn't like what they said about Jesus? Are there people today who don't like to hear about Jesus? Jesus said we are to love everyone. How can we show love to them without being people-pleasers to them?

PRACTICE

Challenge someone to sword-fight with your sword for this week. Write on an index card: "You are tempted to be a people-pleaser." Add this temptation card to the other cards you've collected. Place them in a bowl. The first person draws a card and challenges the second person with that temptation. The second person repeats the sword of the Spirit that he can use to fight the temptation. Then it's his turn to draw a card and challenge the first person.

DAY 4

READ

John 5:16-47 ("Father and Son," page 526 in the *Day By Day Kid's Bible*)

The Jewish leaders got angry at Jesus... "It's not important that people cheer for me. But I know you," said Jesus. "I know God's love isn't in your hearts. I come to you in my Father's name. But you don't believe me. Other people come in their own names. You believe them. You want other people to cheer for you. But you don't even try to get God to cheer for you."

THINK AND TALK

Who did the leaders want to please? Why do people usually want to please other people? Who did Jesus try to please? Why? Why does God want us not to be people-pleasers? How does it feel when you know you've pleased people, but not God? How does it feel when you know you've pleased God, but not people? How does it feel when you know you've pleased God and people, too?

PRACTICE

You and another person can challenge each other to practice fighting temptation. Do this by taking turns drawing the temptation cards from the bowl. Ask each other what you would do if you were tempted in that way, and answer by saying the appropriate verse.

TRY THIS

Do something that you know will please your mom or dad. Remember that you'll be pleasing God at the same time!

DAY 5

READ

1 Samuel 15 ("Why Do I Hear Sheep?" page 136 in the *Day By Day Kid's Bible*)

Samuel went to King Saul. Samuel said, "God says to fight the enemy... But don't take anything that belongs to them." So... they marched out to fight....But Saul... kept the best sheep and cows. The army men kept everything that looked good to them... Samuel went and found Saul. King Saul said,... "I did what God said." "Then why do I hear sheep?" asked Samuel. "Why do I hear cows? ... You have turned against God. So he is turning against you."... "I have sinned," said King Saul. "I was afraid of the people. So I let them do what they wanted."

THINK AND TALK

What choices did King Saul have? What did he choose to do? Why? What happened because of the choice he made? Sometimes we please people instead of God because we are afraid of what people might do or say. Tell about someone you know who pleased God instead of trying to please people. Tell about a time when you pleased God instead of trying to please people.

PRACTICE
Challenge someone to practice fighting temptation. You can take turns drawing the temptation cards from the bowl. Ask each other what you would do if you were tempted in that way.

TRY THIS
Play "Cow" with a basketball and hoop. Take turns shooting baskets. The first person shoots the basket any way he likes. The second person must shoot the same way. If the first person misses, he takes the first letter of the word *COW*. Then the second person can shoot the ball anyway she wants. If she makes the basket, the first person must copy her shot. Whenever anyone misses, he or she gets the next letter in the word. Whoever gets all the letters first begins counting his or her next misses starting with one and going up. But the other person keeps shooting until he or she has collected all the letters of the word *COW*. Then you "bury the cows" and start over. Why did Saul let his people keep the cows?

DAY 6

READ
2 Samuel 15 ("Absalom Takes Over," page 174 in the *Day By Day Kid's Bible*)
Absalom [King David's son] would get up early every morning. He would go to the road that led to the city gate. There he'd stand. People would come into the city to see the king... Now Absalom would meet them at the gate. He'd call to these men, "Where are you from?" They would tell him.... They'd start to bow to him. But he'd shake their hand and kiss them... So all the people loved Absalom... One day a man brought a message to King David. It said, "God's people are following Absalom."...So King David left Jerusalem.

THINK AND TALK

Absalom wanted to please the people for a reason. What was it? Do you think Absalom was interested in pleasing God? Why or why not? What happened because of the choices Absalom made? Is it always easy to please God when you know that people would not be pleased? When is it hardest for you to choose to be a God-pleaser rather than a people-pleaser?

PRACTICE

Challenge someone to practice fighting temptation. You can take turns drawing the temptation cards from the bowl. Ask each other what you would do if you were tempted in that way.

TRY THIS

With a friend, shake hands in as many different ways as you can. Make up a handshake of your own and name it. Why did Absalom shake hands with the people?

DAY 7

READ

Acts 17 ("Paul Visits Many Towns," page 665 in the *Day By Day Kid's Bible*)

On three worship days, Paul told the people about God's Word... Some Jewish people were angry. They didn't want anyone to believe Paul and Silas... They shouted, "Paul and Silas made trouble all over the world. Now they've come to our city... The crowd yelled when they heard this... When it got dark, Paul and Silas left. They went to the town of Berea... But the Jews... heard where Paul was... So they went to Berea. They began to upset the crowds there. Right away, Jesus' followers sent Paul to the sea side.

THINK AND TALK

If Paul had wanted to please people, what could he have done? What did Paul choose to do? How do you feel around people-pleasers? Does being around people-pleasers tempt you to please people too? What are some things that might tempt us to be people-pleasers?

PRACTICE
Challenge someone to practice fighting temptation. You can take turns drawing the temptation cards from the bowl. Ask each other what you would do if you were tempted in that way.

TRY THIS
Think about the reading for today. Then think about how a news reporter would describe these events if this were really happening in the world now. Write a headline for it. Then write a newspaper article as if it were happening today.

Being Gentle

Your sword of the Spirit for this week is:

Be completely humble and gentle.
EPHESIANS 4:2a

With the above sword you can fight back when you face this temptation:

You are tempted to be grouchy or harsh.

DAY 1

READ

1 Timothy 5 ("Older Women and Younger Women," page 752 in the *Day By Day Kid's Bible*)

You can tell an older man what's wrong. But don't be hard on him when you do. Teach him as if he were your father. Treat younger men like brothers. Treat older women like your mother. Treat younger women like sisters. Be good and right in the way you treat them.

THINK AND TALK

Paul wrote these words to Timothy. Timothy was a young man. Sometimes young men and women are tempted to be grouchy or harsh in the way they talk and act toward older men and women. Why? Sometimes we are tempted to be grouchy or harsh toward people who are younger than we are. Why? What did Paul tell Timothy about how to act toward older people? Why? How did Paul say to act toward younger people? Why?

PRACTICE

Read the verse. Try to repeat it several times without looking. Cut a sword shape from paper or cardboard and write the verse

335

on it. You'll want to hang it up in your house where it will remind you of the Spirit's sword from Ephesians 4:2a. You can use it to fight against the temptation to be grouchy or harsh.

DAY 2

READ

1 Thessalonians 2 ("Like a Mother," page 668 in the *Day By Day Kid's Bible*)
We were brave when we told you the Good News. Many people tried to stop us... We could have made things hard on you. But we were kind. We were like a mother taking care of little children. We loved you very much. So we were happy to share God's Good News with you.

THINK AND TALK

What is a loving mother like when she takes care of her little children? In what way do you think Paul was like this when he told the Good News to people? What does it mean to be *humble*? What does it mean to be *gentle*? What does it mean to be *grouchy*? What does it mean to be *harsh*? Why does God want us to be gentle?

PRACTICE

Challenge a friend or family member (or yourself) to a sword-fight. One person says, "What will you do when you are tempted to be grouchy or harsh?" The other person answers, "I will be gentle because it is written, 'Be completely humble and gentle.'"

DAY 3

READ

Galatians 4 ("Promised Children," page 660 in the *Day By Day Kid's Bible*)
I was with you the first time because I was sick. That's when I told you the Good News. My sickness was hard on you. But you didn't treat me badly. You didn't laugh at me. Instead, you welcomed me. You treated me as if I were God's angel. You treated me as if I were Jesus.

THINK AND TALK

Paul wrote these words to God's people in Galatia. What choices did they have in the way they treated Paul? How did they choose to treat him? How did that make Paul feel? How do you feel when people are grouchy or harsh with you? How do you feel when people are kind and gentle with you?

PRACTICE

Challenge someone to sword-fight with your sword for this week. Write on an index card: "You are tempted to be grouchy or harsh." Add this temptation card to the other cards you've collected. Place them in a bowl. The first person draws a card and challenges the second person with that temptation. The second person repeats the sword of the Spirit that she can use to fight the temptation. Then it's her turn to draw a card and challenge the first person.

DAY 4

READ

Matthew 7:1-12 ("The Dust and the Log," page 535 in the *Day By Day Kid's Bible*)

"Let's say your son asks you for bread," said Jesus. "Will you give him a rock? What if he asks you for a fish? Will you give him a snake? You know how to give good gifts to your children. So, of course, your Father in heaven gives good gifts when you ask. Treat people the way you want them to treat you."

THINK AND TALK

Jesus' words, "Treat people the way you want them to treat you" are sometimes called the Golden Rule, even by people who don't believe in Jesus. Why would they call these words the Golden Rule? How do you want people to treat you? Why would Jesus want you to treat others this same way?

PRACTICE

You and another person can challenge each other to practice fighting temptation. Do this by taking turns drawing the temptation cards from a bowl. Ask each other what you would do if you were tempted in that way, and answer by saying the appropriate verse.

TRY THIS
Find at least two people and choose one to be the caller. Hold onto the sides of a large old sheet. Place a large lightweight ball in the center of the sheet and use the sheet to toss the ball up and catch it again. Try not to let the ball fall off onto the ground. The caller can control the play by calling "rough" or "gentle." When she says, "rough," the players toss the ball high and fast. When she calls, "gentle," slow down the tossing and don't toss the ball as high. It's up to the caller to try to slow the tossing down when it looks like the ball is going to fly out of control and fall onto the ground.

DAY 5

READ
Proverbs 3:27-28; 14:31; 19:17 ("Being Kind and Giving," page 249 in the *Day By Day Kid's Bible*)
Do good when you can. Let's say you have something your neighbor needs. Don't say, "Come back tomorrow, and I'll give it to you then." ...When people are kind to the poor, they lend to God. God will pay them well for what they've done... People who are mean to the poor don't care about God. But people who are kind to the poor do care about God.

THINK AND TALK
Why do you think God says it's important to be kind to the poor? How can we be kind to the poor? Sometimes when we are around poor people, we are tempted not to be humble. Why? Why should we be humble and gentle when we are around people who have less than we do?

PRACTICE
Challenge someone to practice fighting temptation. You can take turns drawing the temptation cards from the bowl. Ask each other what you would do if you were tempted in that way.

TRY THIS

Invent a code by making up a shape symbol for each letter of the alphabet. Write this code down. Then write the memory verse for this week in your code. Give someone this verse in code. Then give them the sheet of symbols and see if they can decode the verse.

DAY 6

READ

Joshua 1–2 ("Hiding on the Roof," page 95 in the *Day By Day Kid's Bible*)

Joshua sent two men across the Jordan River. He told them,... "Take a careful look at the city of Jericho." So the two Jewish men went... into the city of Jericho. They went to stay at a house there. The house belonged to a woman named Rahab... Rahab had let the men hide up on her roof... "I've been kind to you," said Rahab. "Promise you'll save my life." ...The men said, "Don't tell what we're doing. Then we'll be kind to you. We'll save you when God gives us this land."

THINK AND TALK

How did Rahab show that she was humble, gentle, and kind to the spies? How did the spies show that they were humble, gentle, and kind to Rahab? Sometimes we think of *gentle* as meaning weak. But Jesus said, "Learn from me, for I am gentle and humble in heart" (Matthew 11:29). Was Jesus weak? What does Jesus mean when he says, "I am gentle"? Gentle means not being harsh or violent. Tell about someone you know who is gentle but also strong or bold.

PRACTICE

Challenge someone to practice fighting temptation. You can take turns drawing the temptation cards from the bowl. Ask each other what you would do if you were tempted in that way.

TRY THIS

Ask friends or family to join you for a penny hunt. This is like an Easter egg hunt, except that you hide pennies instead of Easter eggs. Give each person a zipper-locking sandwich bag. Encourage all of them to be gentle as they look for pennies and put them into their bags. See who can find the most.

DAY 7

READ

Acts 27:1-3 ("Stormy Seas!" page 728 in the *Day By Day Kid's Bible*)

The time came to sail to Rome to see Caesar. Paul and some others were taken out of jail. They were given to an army captain named Julius. Some of Paul's friends went with him. They got on a ship and sailed out to sea. The next day, they landed at Sidon. Julius was kind. He let Paul go to see his friends in Sidon.

THINK AND TALK

What choices did Captain Julius have? What did he choose to do? Is it always easy to be humble and gentle? When is it hardest for you to be humble and gentle? What are some things that might tempt us to be grouchy or harsh?

PRACTICE

Challenge someone to practice fighting temptation. You can take turns drawing the temptation cards from the bowl. Ask each other what you would do if you were tempted in that way.

TRY THIS

Save five or six seeds from an apple. Fill a glass about three-fourths full with club soda. Drop the seeds into it. Watch what happens. Be patient until you see it. The seeds start to have a stormy ride. At first the seeds sink. Then bubbles gather around them and lift them to the surface of the soda where the bubbles pop or float away. Then the seeds sink back to the bottom. When you are grouchy or harsh, does your life feel like a stormy ride?

Finding Salvation

Your sword of the Spirit for this week is:

If you confess with your mouth, "Jesus is Lord," and believe in your heart that God raised him from the dead, you will be saved.

ROMANS 10:9

With the above sword you can fight back when you face this temptation:

You are tempted to think that you are not saved.

DAY 1

READ

John 8:12-59 ("The World's Light," page 572 in the *Day By Day Kid's Bible*)

Jesus talked to the people at the worship house again. "I'm the World's Light," he said. "Follow me. Then you won't live in the dark... Keep obeying me. Then you'll be my followers. You'll know the truth. The truth will set you free." "We've never been anybody's slaves," they said. "So how could we be set free?" "Anybody who sins is a slave to sin," said Jesus.... "If the Son sets you free, you really are free."

THINK AND TALK

Confess means to tell the truth about something. What is the truth that our "sword" tells us to confess? What do we need to be saved from? There are two kingdoms that we can't see in this world. One is the kingdom of light, and one is the kingdom of darkness. Who rules each kingdom? Some people think that God is harsh and judging, and that he wants to bring them trouble and punish them if they don't do what he says. Read John 3:16-21 ("A Night Visit," page 516 in the *Day By Day Kid's Bible*). God loves people. He sent Jesus to save people. People are already in trouble, because they are in the kingdom of darkness. If they will just choose the kingdom of light, God will save them from punishment. What are some ways that God already shows his love to all people? (Read Matthew 5:45.)

PRACTICE

Read the verse. Try to repeat it several times without looking. Cut a sword shape from paper or cardboard and write the verse on it. You'll want to hang it up in your house where it will remind you of the Spirit's sword from Romans 10:9. You can use it to fight against the temptation to think you are not saved.

But if you do not believe in Jesus or you have not confessed that Jesus is Lord, then thinking you are not saved is not a temptation. It is a true thought. You can be saved right now by praying to God. Tell him that you have been living in the kingdom of darkness and you have been sinning. Tell him that you want to live in his kingdom of light. Ask Jesus to be your Lord and Savior. Tell him you give your life to him now. And tell someone else that you've asked Jesus to be Lord and Savior of your life. If you think you are not saved after that, it's just a temptation. Fight it with your new "sword."

DAY 2

READ

John 12:20-36 ("A Seed," page 598 in the *Day By Day Kid's Bible*) "Right now I feel troubled," said Jesus. "What can I say? 'Father, save me from what's going to happen'? No. I came into the world because of what's going to happen... It's time to chase away Satan, the world's sinful prince. I'll be lifted up from the earth. Then I'll draw all people to me." Jesus was talking about how he would die... "People in the dark don't know where they're going. Trust in the light while it's here. Then you can be children of the light."

THINK AND TALK
Can you tell if someone is saved? If so, how? (Read John 13:35 and 1 John 2:1-17.) Why does God want us to be saved? Why does he want us to admit that we have sinned? What did Jesus mean when he said, "Trust in the light"?

PRACTICE
Challenge a friend or family member (or yourself) to a sword-fight. One person says, "What will you do when you are tempted to think you are not saved?" The other person answers, "I will know I am saved because it is written, 'If you confess with your mouth, 'Jesus is Lord,' and believe in your heart that God raised him from the dead, you will be saved.'"

DAY 3

READ
Matthew 27:11-23 ("Pilate" and "A Dream," pages 618 and 619 in the *Day By Day Kid's Bible*)
Pilate... called Jesus to him. "Are you really the King of the Jews?" he asked... "I have a kingdom," said Jesus. "But it's not from this world." ..."Then you are a king?" asked Pilate. "Yes," said Jesus. "That's why I was born. That's why I came to the world. I came to show the truth." ...So Pilate called the Jewish leaders together.... "What should I do with Jesus," asked Pilate. "Kill him!" they cried. "Why?" asked Pilate. "What has he done that's so bad?" Pilate wanted to let Jesus go.

THINK AND TALK
What was the reason Jesus gave for coming to this world? What s the truth that Jesus was talking about? How does it feel to b saved? Does being saved mean that now you can sin all you wa and God won't blame you for it? If we sin, even though we d mean to, are we out of God's kingdom, and do we have to be s again? (Read Romans 7 and 8, "Doing What I Don't Want and "More than Winners," in the *Day By Day Kid's Bible*.)

343

PRACTICE

Challenge someone to sword-fight with your sword for this week. Write on an index card: "You are tempted to think that you are not saved." Add this temptation card to the other cards you've collected. Place them in a bowl. The first person draws a card and challenges the second person with that temptation. The second person repeats the sword of the Spirit that he can use to fight the temptation. Then it's his turn to draw a card and challenge the first person.

DAY 4

READ

Isaiah 59:2; Romans 3 ("Like a Spider's Web" and "Even If Every Person Lies," pages 371 and 704 in the *Day By Day Kid's Bible*)
It's your sins that keep you from God [said Isaiah]....Everyone sins. No one is good enough for God's greatness... God showed how fair he is. Somebody has to get in trouble for what people have done wrong. So God sent Jesus to die on the cross for our sin. That pays for our sin. It also makes us clean from sin. If we believe in Jesus, it's just as if we'd never sinned.

THINK AND TALK

God is perfect. What he does is always right. Nothing sinful or bad can live with him. That's a problem for us. Why? Since Adam and Eve sinned, no human being has ever lived without sinning or making wrong choices. That means we can't live in God's perfect kingdom now or after we die. Who is the only one who does what's right all the time? God. So he came to earth in the form of a man, Jesus. He was perfect. But he chose to get in trouble for our sins. He chose to be blamed for our sins. So he got the punishment we deserved. Since our sins have been punished, what does that do for us? If we believe and accept this gift, it makes us sinless! That's Good News! Why did God do this for us? Is there any sin he does not forgive through Jesus' death?

PRACTICE

You and another person can challenge each other to practice

fighting temptation. Do this by taking turns drawing the temptation cards from a bowl. Ask each other what you would do if you were tempted in that way, and answer by saying the appropriate verse.

TRY THIS

Collect some dirty, dark pennies. Put them into a bowl. Mix one teaspoon of salt with one tablespoon of water. First drip a drop of salt mixture onto the pennies. Then drip a drop of vinegar onto them. Keep changing from one to the other: first a drop of salt mixture, then a drop of vinegar. Let the pennies soak for about five minutes. Then wipe each of them off with a moist paper towel. When we sin, we feel dirty inside, in our hearts. That feeling is called guilt. How can we get rid of our guilt and make our hearts "clean" again?

DAY 5

READ

Hebrews 9 ("Better Gifts," page 784 in the *Day By Day Kid's Bible*) The first promise between God and people had rules for worship. There was a worship house here on earth... Only the high priest went into the Most Holy Place... He always took a gift with him. It was animal blood. He gave this gift to pay for his sins. The gift also paid for the sins of other people... No one but the high priest could go in... Then Jesus came. He became our high priest... Jesus went into the real Most Holy Place in heaven just one time. He went for all people. He went with his own blood. He got people's sins taken away forever. Animal blood made people sinless for a while. But then Jesus died for us. Jesus never sinned. So his blood makes us sinless forever.

THINK AND TALK

Why do you think animal blood paid for sins? Could it be that God was trying to show us how serious sin is? Romans 6:23 tells us that if we live in sin, we earn death. But God offers us a gift: life forever. How would it feel to know that your sins were *not* forgiven and that someday you'd be punished for all of them? The only way that could happen is if you chose not to come into God's kingdo of light. Then you'd stay in the kingdom of darkness, because there are only two kingdoms. You are in one or the other. How does it feel to know that God has given you a way out of the kingdom of darkness? How does it feel to know that Jesus has taken away *all* of your sins so that you are now sinless and perfect?

PRACTICE

Challenge someone to practice fighting temptation. You can take turns drawing the temptation cards from the bowl. Ask each other what you would do if you were tempted in that way.

TRY THIS

Lay some clean popsicle sticks or craft sticks side by side. With a sharp marker or pen, write the memory verse across the sticks as if the sticks were a sheet of paper. You can even design a border around the edge of the sticks using colored markers. This makes a puzzle. Mix up the sticks and then try to put the puzzle back together again. Store the sticks in a zipper-locking sandwich bag.

DAY 6

READ

Romans 6 ("Into the Water," page 706 in the *Day By Day Kid's Bible*)

Being baptized is like going into the grave with Jesus. We go into the water. Then we come out again. We can live a new life. It's just like Jesus did when he came back to life again. We were dipped in water. So we shared Jesus' "grave." Our old self died with him. Now sin is gone from us. Sin doesn't conrol Jesus. When he died, the power of sin died. He is alive now, living for God. You're like that too. You're dead to the power of sin. Now you live for God. So don't let sin control you.

THINK AND TALK

What is baptism? Why is it like Jesus' death? What does your baptism tell God and everyone else? After you have asked Jesus to be your Lord, does that mean you will never do or say anything wrong again? After you have been baptized, does that mean you will never sin again? What does it mean? It means sin no longer *controls* you. Who controls you? What do you do if you are tempted and you sin? You admit that you sinned. You thank God for forgiving you when Jesus died. And you ask God to help you grow stronger and wiser and make the right choice next time.

PRACTICE
Challenge someone to practice fighting temptation. You can take turns drawing the temptation cards from the bowl. Ask each other what you would do if you were tempted in that way.

TRY THIS
Cut a sponge into a cross shape. Spread some water-based washable paint onto a paper plate. Dampen the sponge and press it onto the paint on the plate. Then press it onto a piece of paper to make a cross-print painting. If you want, you can write the Scripture for this week beneath the cross print on the paper.

DAY 7

READ
Romans 5 ("At the Right Time," page 706 in the *Day By Day Kid's Bible*)
We could not save ourselves. We had no power. But at the right time, Jesus came. He died for people who sin. Sometimes a person will die for another good person. But we were sinners. Jesus died for us anyway. That shows just how much God loves us... What's more, we'll be saved from God's anger! We were God's enemies. But now he lets us be his children, because Jesus died. His life saves us... We can have life forever. It's all because of Jesus our Lord.

THINK AND TALK
Paul wrote these words. What does he mean when he says, "We were God's enemies"? Sometimes we hear a story about someone who dies to save someone else. Can you think of a story like that? What's the difference between that and Jesus' death for us? Why do you think some people do not believe this Good News? If you

know some people who don't believe in Jesus, what can you pray for them? How can you help them?

PRACTICE
Challenge someone to practice fighting temptation. You can take turns drawing the temptation cards from the bowl. Ask each other what you would do if you were tempted in that way.

TRY THIS
Make a poster that announces the good news. In big block letters write, "JESUS IS LORD!" Decorate your poster.

A Note for You:

All through this book, you've been learning how to fight temptation. But you could memorize Scriptures all day long and still give in to temptation unless you have the help of Jesus, who lives inside all believers through his Holy Spirit. Jesus' Spirit grows love, joy, peace, patience, kindness, goodness, faithfulness, gentleness, and self-control within you. He gives you the power to say no to sin. So if you have not asked Jesus to be your Lord and Savior, please do it now. If you need help, read again the Day 1 "Think and Talk" and "Practice" sections from this last week on Finding Salvation. You will still have temptations, but at least you will have help to fight them. God will forgive you for your sins. And best of all, you will be able to know God, talk with him, and live with him—not only now, but after this life here on earth. You'll live in God's perfect, peaceful kingdom forever.

God bless you! Enjoy your new life!

357

James 2 / *Week 25*
James 3 / *Week 33*
James 4 / *Week 38*
James 5:1-9 / *Week 46*

1 Peter 1 / *Week 32*
1 Peter 2 / *Week 25*
1 Peter 3 / *Week 42*
1 Peter 4 / *Week 37*
1 Peter 5 / *Week 27*

1 John 2 / *Week 37*
1 John 3 / *Week 37*

Hi Friends,

I began memorizing Scriptures when I was young. But I did it just because the Sunday school teacher said to. I had no idea why I was memorizing Bible verses. And I forgot much of what I memorized because I didn't use the verses in my life.

It wasn't until I had children of my own that I understood how important it is to memorize Scriptures. In fact, I wondered then why I hadn't seen it before.

Jesus knew the Scriptures, and he used them to fight back when he was tempted. If Jesus fought temptation that way, I needed to fight temptation that way. And I wanted my own sons to know Scripture so they could fight temptation, too. That's why I made up a game that we called "Sword Fighting." We learned a new Scripture, a "sword of the Spirit," each week, and we practiced fighting temptations by saying the Scriptures.

I hope you are learning to sword-fight by playing the same game I played with my sons. It's not only important and useful, it's fun as well!

By God's grace, to his glory,

Karyn Henley

- Read the whole Bible story in 1 year, 7 minutes a day!
- Designed for kids 7 to 10 • Chronological • Time line inside
- Go to **www.karynhenley.com** and click on "How is it different?"
- Free downloadable sample pages at "FREE Downloads"

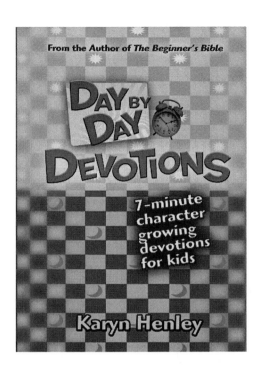

Day by Day Devotions contains a full year's worth of age-appropriate teaching for kids ages 6-10 (listeners ages 4 and up). Each week focuses on a single topic like "Talking with God," "You Can Do It!," or "Putting God First." Every day's devotion includes a different selected passage from the **Day by Day Kid's Bible** along with a kid-friendly reading and prayer.

Each week's topic includes several activity ideas to help kids anchor the truths they've learned with hands-on fun things to make or do!

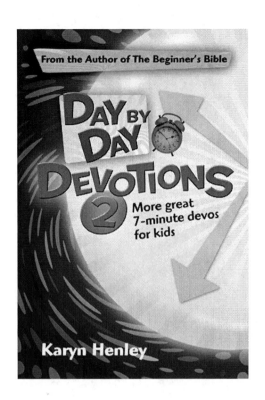